SCIENCE AND EDUCATION
IN THE
SEVENTEENTH CENTURY

The Webster – Ward Debate

History of Science Library

Editor: MICHAEL A. HOSKIN
Lecturer in the History of Science, Cambridge University

History of Science Library: Primary Sources

SCIENCE AND EDUCATION IN THE SEVENTEENTH CENTURY

THE WEBSTER - WARD DEBATE

ALLEN G. DEBUS

Professor of the History of Science,
University of Chicago

MACDONALD : LONDON
AND
AMERICAN ELSEVIER INC. : NEW YORK

First published 1970
Sole distributors for the United States and Dependencies
American Elsevier Publishing Company, Inc.
52 Vanderbilt Avenue
New York N.Y. 10017

Sole distributors for the British Isles and Commonwealth
Macdonald & Co. (Publishers) Ltd
49–50 Poland Street
London W1A 2LG

All remaining areas
Elsevier Publishing Company
P.O. Box 211
Jan van Galenstraat 335
Amsterdam
The Netherlands

Library of Congress Catalog Card Number 76–114270
Standard Book Numbers
British SBN 356 03329 5
American SBN 444 19659 5

Printed in Great Britain by
Unwin Brothers Limited
The Gresham Press, Old Woking, Surrey
A member of the Staples Printing Group

Contents

Chapter One

Introduction

FEW would dispute that the changes which occurred in man's concept
of nature in the sixteenth and the seventeenth centuries merit the
title 'Scientific Revolution'. The dramatic nature of these changes has
led historians to emphasize the clash between the adherents of the old
and the new, and working within this tradition Richard F. Jones aptly
titled his best known work *Ancients and Moderns*. On the surface this
approach seems justified. The magnitude of the Newtonian achieve-
ment has led us to its sources, and historians of science have been
arrested not only by the work of Galileo in which we find the familiar
dichotomy expressed in the Simplicio-Salviati dialogue, but also by a
host of other titles and texts which point to a contemporary awareness
of this conflict.[1]

And yet, we need not go much beyond the texts of Galileo to see
a far more complex picture arise. In recent years research on other
seventeenth century debates – and I am thinking primarily of investigations on the seventeenth century reaction to Robert Fludd's exposition
of the macrocosm and the microcosm – have helped to give us a more
balanced understanding of the period.[2] Another important debate was
that engendered by the publication of John Webster's *Academiarum
Examen* in 1654. This work was clearly connected with Fludd's statements on the inadequacy of the higher learning of his day. Webster's
plan for the reform of the English universities on the basis of a new
understanding of nature evoked replies from John Wilkins, Seth Ward
and Thomas Hall in a conflict which might appear to be a classic case
of the confrontation of 'ancients' and 'moderns'.[3] Yet, a quick glance
at recent literature relating to this debate clearly points out the difficulty
of trying to define just what was modern in the middle decades of the
seventeenth century. Readers who are dependent on secondary sources

may well wonder just what John Webster actually proposed in his short book. Thirty years ago R. F. Jones wrote that

> Webster's treatise is the most important expression of the new scientific outlook between Bacon and the Restoration. It is clear, practical in most of its suggestions, and comprehensive . . . his words reveal understanding of the inductive method and complete consciousness of its importance and efficacy. He is scientifically minded. . . . His attitude towards the ancients, his characterization of, and attack on, the old science and philosophy left little for the defenders of the Royal Society to say. Finally, the spirit which turns from the past to face the future, which insists on the freedom of investigation and thought, and which burns with reforming zeal, in short, the spirit of seventeenth-century science is his in good measure.[4]

Jones clearly viewed Webster as a 'modern', but if we turn to the more recent publications of Phyllis Allen and Mark H. Curtis we might think that an entirely different set of texts had been used. Phyllis Allen stated that

> John Webster launched a violent attack on university methods. . . . After deriding Aristotle, Webster eulogized the subjects of *magic* and chemistry! Such a curious mixture of science and superstition laid his attack wide open to the ridicule of his contemporaries in the universities, and Seth Ward lost no time in replying to it by means of his *Vindiciae Academiarum* (1654), in which he pointed out that conditions had changed since Webster had been in a university.[5]

For Mark Curtis, Webster was an 'ignorant critic' who had 'fantastic hopes to turn judicial astronomy, magic, and the arcana of hieroglyphics and emblems to the betterment of mankind'.[6] On the one hand, then, Jones viewed Webster as a Baconian and a 'modern' while on the other hand Allen and Curtis saw him only as an incompetent Puritan reformer unable to offer more than destructive criticism, a man who was rightly refuted by the 'moderns' Ward and Wilkins.[7]

If, then, we are to think in terms of 'ancients' and 'moderns', we must conclude that these terms are not well defined. And if we are to properly assess John Webster's proposed reforms and the replies of his opponents we must do this on the basis of a broader understanding than that commonly implied by the use of these categories. Indeed, the roots of the Webster-Ward debate are buried in the history of the late Middle Ages and the Renaissance. The study of this background will help to clarify not only the basis of the educational crisis of the seventeenth century, but also some of the major issues of the Scientific Revolution.

REFERENCES

1. In addition to Richard F. Jones, *Ancients and Moderns. A Study of the Rise of the Scientific Movement in Seventeenth Century England* (St. Louis: Washington University Press, 1961; first ed., 1936), see H. Rigault, 'Histoire de la querelle des Anciens et des Modernes' in his *Oeuvres complètes*, **1** (Paris, 1859), H. Gillot, *La Querelle des anciens et des modernes en France* (Paris, 1914) and O. Diede, *Der Streit der Alten und Modernen in der englischen Literaturgeschichte des XVI und XVII Jahrhunders* (thesis Greifswald, 1912).

2. On the Fluddean debates see Robert Lenoble, *Mersenne ou la naissance du mécanisme* (Paris, 1943); Wolfgang Pauli, 'The Influence of Archetypal Ideas on the Scientific Theories of Kepler', in C. G. Jung and W. Pauli, *The Interpretation of Nature and the Psyche*, trans. Priscilla Silz (New York, 1955); Allen G. Debus, *The English Paracelsians* (London: Oldbourne Press, 1965), pp. 105–27; Allen G. Debus, 'Robert Fludd and the Circulation of the Blood', *Journal of the History of Medicine and Allied Sciences*, **16** (1961), 374–93; Allen G. Debus, 'Robert Fludd and the Use of Gilbert's *De Magnete* in the Weapon-Salve Controversy', *Journal of the History of Medicine and Allied Sciences*, **19** (1964), 389–417; Allen G. Debus, 'Harvey and Fludd: The Irrational Factor in the Rational Science of the Seventeenth Century', *Journal of the History of Biology* (in press); C. H. Josten, 'Truth's Golden Harrow. An Unpublished Alchemical Treatise of Robert Fludd in the Bodleian Library', *Ambix*, **3** (1949), 91–150; C. H. Josten, 'Robert Fludd's "Philosophical Key" and his Alchemical Experiment on Wheat', *Ambix*, **11** (1963), 1–23. Additional information of importance on Fludd will be found in P. J. Ammann, 'The Musical Theory and Philosophy of Robert Fludd', *Journal of the Warburg and Courtauld Institutes*, **30** (1967), 198–227; D. P. Walker, 'Kepler's Celestial Music', *Journal of the Warburg and Courtauld Institutes*, **30** (1967), 228–50. The Paracelsian Debates are discussed with considerable understanding by W. P. D. Wightman, *Science and the Renaissance. An Introduction to the Study of the Emergence of the Sciences in the Sixteenth Century* (2 vols.), (Edinburgh/London, Oliver and Boyd, 1962), **1**, pp. 237–63. Additional information on the conflict over the Paracelsian concepts will be found in Walter Pagel's *Paracelsus. An Introduction to Philosophical Medicine in the Era of the*

3

Renaissance (New York/Basel, 1958). The mid-seventeenth century English conflict over the validity of the chemical medicine has been discussed by Sir Henry Thomas, 'The Society of Chymical Physitians: An Echo of the Great Plague of London – 1665', in *Science, Medicine and History*, ed. E. A. Underwood (2 vols., London, 1953), **2**, pp. 56–71; P. M. Rattansi, 'Paracelsus and the Puritan Revolution', *Ambix*, **11** (1963), 23–32; P. M. Rattansi, 'The Helmontian-Galenist Controversy in Restoration England', *Ambix*, **12** (1964), 1–23; C. Webster, 'The English Medical Reformers of the Puritan Revolution: A Background to the "Society of Chymical Physitians" ', *Ambix*, **14** (1967), 16–41.

3. John Webster, *Academiarum Examen, or the Examination of Academies. Wherein is discussed and examined the Matter, Method and Customes of Academick and Scholastick Learning, and the insufficiency thereof discovered and laid open; As also some Expedients proposed for the Reforming of Schools, and the perfecting and promoting of all kind of Science. Offered to the judgements of all those that love the proficiencie of Arts and Sciences, and the advancement of learning* (London: Giles Calvert, 1654); (Set)H War(D), *Vindiciae Academiarum containing, Some briefe Animadversions upon Mr. Websters Book, Stiled The Examination of Academies. Together with an Appendix concerning what M. Hobbs, and M. Dell have published on this Argument* (Oxford: Leonard Lichfield Printer to the University for Thomas Robinson, 1654) [with an introduction by (Joh)N (Wilkin)S]; Thomas Hall, *Vindiciae Literarum, The Schools Guarded: Or the Excellency and Usefulnesse of Humane Learning in Subordination to Divinity, and preparation to the Ministry . . . Whereunto is added An Examination of John Websters delusive Examen of Academies* (London: W. H. for Nathaniel Webb and William Grantham, 1655).

4. R. F. Jones, *op. cit.*, pp. 108–9.

5. Phyllis Allen, 'Scientific Studies in the English Universities of the Seventeenth Century', *Journal of the History of Ideas*, **10** (1949), 219–53 (237).

6. Mark H. Curtis, *Oxford and Cambridge in Transition 1558–1642* (Oxford: Clarendon Press, 1959), p. 232.

7. In addition to the views of Jones, Allen and Curtis on this debate we may refer also to Rattansi's 'Paracelsus and the Puritan Revolution', 27–29, which sympathetically presents the works of Webster, Ward and Wilkin in the intellectual context of the period.

Chapter Two

The Historical Roots of the Educational Problem

GARIN has described two dominant themes in Renaissance scholarship. The first of these was centred on medical and philosophical problems; this was essentially a scholastic self-criticism within the Aristotelian-Galenic tradition. The second he characterizes as predominantly 'rhetorical and philological' or basically 'humanist' in nature. Both themes affected the sciences and the educational system that John Webster reacted against in 1654.[1]

Scholastic self-criticism was nothing new. We now know that not all of the universities of the sixteenth century were as reactionary as they are sometimes described. John Herman Randall, Jr., in his 'Development of Scientific Method in the School of Padua', links the fourteenth century critical re-evaluation of Aristotelian philosophy at Oxford and Paris with the northern Italian schools in the fifteenth and sixteenth centuries.[2] This tradition, Randall emphasizes, should be interpreted not as a shift from Aristotle to Plato, but rather, as a living self-critical Aristotelianism.[3] Kristeller goes farther to argue that as far as Italy is concerned, 'Aristotelian scholasticism . . . is fundamentally a phenomenon of the Renaissance period whose roots can be traced in a continuous development to the very latest phase of the Middle Ages'.[4] Indeed, he continues,

> if we pass from the humanist scholars to the professional philosophers and scientists, it appears that the most advanced work of Aristotle's logic, the *Posterior Analytics*, received greater attention in the sixteenth century than before, and that at the same time an increased study of Aristotle's biological writings accompanied the contemporary progress in botany, zoology, and natural history.[5]

5

Thus, in this Aristotelian tradition a bridge is formed with major figures of the seventeenth century – men such as Harvey, Fabricius and Galileo. There is no better example than Harvey who, as an Aristotelian, sought out the method of the *Posterior Analytics* and the *Physics* – works which called for a dual role of experiment and reason.[6]

However, the significance of Padua should not blind us to the fact that many other universities were extremely conservative and that their prime function was generally thought to be the preservation of the learning of the past rather than the quest for new knowledge through research.[7] This is surely in keeping with the spirit of the literary Renaissance through which scholars were encouraged to seek out the lost treasures of antiquity rather than make new discoveries of their own. An excellent example of this may be taken from the field of medicine. Thomas Linacre (1460–1524), chief among the founders of the College of Physicians in London (1518), had obtained his M.D. degree at Padua (*c.* 1492) and there he had diligently sought previously unknown Greek texts of the ancient medical authorities. These he published with his own translations.[8] Linacre, with many of his colleagues who were founders of the College, excelled in this typically Renaissance form of research. In England both the Elizabethan Statutes for Cambridge (1570) and the Laudian Code for Oxford (1636) maintained the authority of the ancients,[9] and this spirit also was carried over to professional societies. When Dr. John Geynes had the temerity in 1559 to suggest that Galen was not infallible, he was forced to sign a recantation before being received back into the company of the Royal College of Physicians.[10] It was surely acceptable – even commendable – for the humanist to criticize the vulgar annotations and emendations foisted on the works of the ancients by the Arabs and the Scholastic philosophers, but for many the original and pure texts seemed like an impregnable fortress of truth not to be added to or altered in any way.

Garin's second theme, Renaissance humanism, affected the sciences and education by placing a new emphasis on the moral character of man rather than the study of philosophy, theology and the sciences which remained of prime interest to the university scholar. The desire to mould a youth's personality placed a new interest on elementary education and for many humanists the problems of the universities receded into a dim background. An excellent example may be found in the famous humanist school of Vittorino da Feltre (1378–1446) at

Mantua.[11] Here the student was urged to excel at games and military exercises so that he might strengthen his body. In the classroom he studied not philosophy and science, but rhetoric, music, geography – above all, history, from which he might find examples of moral principle and political action.

This was an educational setting far removed from that of the Italian universities. If, on the one hand, the humanist expressed a love of nature, on the other, he reacted sharply against the Aristotelian-Galenist atmosphere of the schools.[12] The result of this may be seen in Renaissance tracts on education. Matteo Palmieri (1406–1476) considered the study of natural philosophy to be far less important than that of moral philosophy. While it is laudable, he wrote, to investigate the secrets of nature, 'we hold them still of the minutest interest in the supreme task of solving the problem how to live'.[13] Erasmus (1466–1536) was not far removed from Palmieri when he suggested that the student might learn most of what he needed to know about nature by the diligent study of sound classical authors. As for mathematics, this was of relatively little importance for the educated man.[14]

Few humanist educators are better known than Juan Luis Vives (1492–1540).[15] Arguing in his *De Tradendis Disciplinis* (1531) that man could best reach a knowledge of God through the study of His works, he stated that the medical student should learn through observation all the powers and essences of mineral substances while the educated man should know all the phenomena of nature. But if Vives on occasion spoke of the senses as the key to true understanding, he was also quite willing to point to Aristotle as the major single source of scientific truth. Like Erasmus, he believed that the humanist student need devote little time to arithmetic and algebra. Indeed, mathematical abstractions tend to 'withdraw the mind from the practical concerns of life, and render it less fit to fuse concrete and mundane realities'.[16] Nor need the student really concern himself with research into causes and principles. This sort of abstract contemplation would only lead to metaphysical subtleties. These were surely of interest to those at the universities, but they would hardly prepare a man for the practical affairs of life or lead to a wholesome intellectual development.

One cannot avoid being impressed by a growing sense of disillusionment found in so many authors of the sixteenth century. To be sure some notable universities maintained a critical appreciation of the classical texts they used, but most of them did not. And if some authors might suggest new academies as a novel approach to educational needs, others sought reform within the established system. Few exhibit the discontent of this period better than Peter Ramus (1515–1572). It was with a sense of despair that he recalled his own academic training:

> After having devoted three years and six months to scholastic philosophy, according to the rules of our university: after having read, discussed, and meditated on the various treatises of the *Organon* (for of all the books of Aristotle those especially which treated of dialectic were read and re-read during the course of three years); even after, I say, having put in all that time, reckoning up the years completely occupied by the study of the scholastic arts, I sought to learn to what end I could, as a consequence, apply the knowledge I had acquired with so much toil and fatigue. I soon perceived that all this dialectic had not rendered me more learned in history and the knowledge of antiquity, nor more skilful in eloquence, nor a better poet, nor wiser in anything. Ah, what a stupefaction, what a grief! How did I accuse my deficiencies! How did I deplore the misfortune of my destiny, the barrenness of a mind that after so much labour could not gather or even perceive the fruits of that wisdom which was alleged to be found so abundantly in the dialectic of Aristotle![17]

Turning first to the very basis of the scholastic system Ramus proposed a new system of logic. And, as he continued in his criticism, he proceeded to reject the natural science and physics of Aristotle while he called instead for new observations which were to be tested and arranged methodically.[18]

The recognition of a need for a new approach to nature becomes ever more apparent in the texts of the sixteenth century. Rabelais (*c.* 1495–1553) argued that the student should addict himself studiously to learning the facts of nature

> so that there be no sea, river or lake of which thou knowest not the fish; so that all the birds of the air, and all the plants and fruits of the forest, all the flowers of the soil, all the metals hid in the bowels of the earth, all the gems of the East and the South, none shall be foreign to thee. Most carefully pursue the writings of physicians, Greek, Arab, Latin, dispising not even the Talmudists and Cabalists; and by frequent searching gain perfect knowledge of the microcosm, man.[19]

The nature philosophers of the sixteenth century show the influence of the neo-Platonic and Hermetic revival of Marsilio Ficino (1433-1499) and his disciples.[20] Here was to be found a Christianized Platonism that stressed the importance of man in the universe. This vitalist interpretation of the universe was founded on the interrelation of the macrocosm and the microcosm and its acceptance implied that the study of God's Creation might be a valid approach to an understanding of our Creator. It was hoped by many that in these texts there might be found an answer to the 'irreligious' Aristotelianism of the schools. With Telesio, Campanella, Patrizi and Bruno one finds a militant rejection of the classical authors and their medieval commentators in vogue at the universities along with a conscious search for a new scientific method.[21] Telesio launched a strong attack on scholasticism, not within the existing university framework, but apart from it in his Academy at Cosenza. In his *De rerum natura* he stressed fresh observations as the basic ingredient for the necessary new interpretation of nature. His disciple, Campanella, took a similar approach in the pages of his first book, the *Philosophia sensibus demonstrata*. With Francesco Patrizi and Giordano Bruno we find other neo-Platonic and Hermetic attempts to seek out an understanding of the universe. With these men there is a special emphasis on mystical themes which are common to most neo-Platonic authors.

It is characteristic of the Italian nature philosophers that they stressed the need for a new observational science to replace the sterile writings of the ancients. This is a theme which continues in the new century. In his work on the magnet William Gilbert (1544-1603) stated that his natural philosophy 'is almost a new thing, unheard of before. . . . Therefore we do not at all quote the ancients and the Greeks as our supporters.'[22] And the Aristotelian, William Harvey (1578-1657), before discussing the circulation of the blood, stated that 'I profess both to learn and to teach anatomy, not from books but from dissections; not from the positions of philosophers but from the fabric of nature'.[23] Similarly we find an ever increasing number of witnesses who reacted against the barrenness of their own educational experience. No account is more famous than that of Descartes (1596-1650) who tells us that after completing the entire course of study at one of the most celebrated Schools of Europe, 'I found myself embarrassed with so many doubts and errors that it seemed to me that the effort to instruct myself had no effect other than the increasing of my own ignorance'.[24] Perhaps, he adds, the whole body of the sciences need not be reformed, 'but as regards all the opinions which up to this time I had embraced, I thought I could not do better than endeavour once and for all to sweep them away, so that they might later be replaced . . .'.[25]

If we turn to Francis Bacon (1561–1626), we find in the midst of his search for a new scientific method a critical re-appraisal of the university system. After complaining of the low salaries allotted to university teachers, and after questioning the wisdom of concentrating students on specific professions rather than the arts and sciences, he goes on:

> Again, in the customs and institutions of schools, academies, colleges and similar bodies destined for the abode of learned men and the cultivation of learning, everything is found adverse to the progress of science. For the lectures and exercises these are so ordered, that to think or speculate on anything out of the common way can hardly occur to any man. And if one or two have the boldness to use any liberty of judgment, they must undertake the task all by themselves, they can have no advantage from the company of others. And if they can endure this also, they will find their industry and largeness of mind no slight hindrance to their fortune. For the studies of men in these places are confined and as it were imprisoned in the writings of certain authors, from whom, if any man dissent he is straightway arraigned as a turbulent person and an innovator. . . . [The] arts and sciences should be like mines, where the noise of new works and further advances is heard on every side. But though the matter be so according to right reason, it is not so acted on in practice; and the points above mentioned in the administration and government of learning put a severe restraint upon the advancement of the sciences.[26]

In his utopian *New Atlantis* Bacon went on to describe 'Solomon's House' with its provision for workshops, scientific instruments and laboratories – all of the requirements for the proper collection of scientific data according to Bacon's scheme for a new science. This was to become a major source of inspiration for the founders of the Royal Society of London.

In short, even though recent research has pointed out the importance of Padua and other Italian universities in keeping alive the critical spirit of inquiry found at Oxford and Paris in the fourteenth century, one does not have to go far beyond these Peninsular universities to see that they did not represent the norm for the period. Nor did the humanist educational schemes help much. On the whole they were aimed at the proper training of youths, and in their rejection of scholasticism their authors turned primarily to the long neglected literary classics of antiquity for moral guidance. While they might speak of nature and of the importance of sense perception, the Renaissance humanists generally were less concerned with the actual study of natural phenomena than they were with the search for a different sort of classical literature than that studied by their more traditional colleagues. It is little wonder then, when we look at Ramus, Telesio, Gilbert, Harvey, Descartes and Bacon – all of whom have been referred to as founders of modern scientific method, we sense a disillusionment with the formal training of the period with its emphasis on the infallible truths of antiquity. And no matter what differences there might be between them in their own views on scientific method, they were agreed that in the future more attention must be paid to fresh observation and experiments.

REFERENCES

1. Eugenio Garin, *L'Educazione in Europa (1400–1600) Problemi e Programmi* (Bari: Editori Laterza, 1957), p. 31. The sixteenth-century scholar was much concerned with problems of method and studies have been devoted to this. Important among them are Neill W. Gilbert, *Renaissance Concepts of Method* (New York, 1960); W. J. Ong, *Ramus: Method and the Decay of Dialogue* (Cambridge, Mass., 1958); and W. S. Howell, *Logic and Rhetoric in England, 1500–1700* (Princeton, 1956). No attempt will be made here to discuss this topic in detail. The references in these works may serve as a guide to the reader who wishes to pursue this theme further.

2. John Herman Randall, Jr., 'The Development of Scientific Method in the School of Padua', *Journal of the History of Ideas*, **I** (1940), 177–206.

3. John Herman Randall, Jr., 'Scientific Method in the School of Padua', in *Roots of Scientific Thought. A Cultural Perspective*, edited by Philip P. Wiener and Aaron Noland (New York: Basic Books, 1957), pp. 139–146 (145).

4. Paul Oskar Kristeller, *Renaissance Thought. The Classic, Scholastic and Humanist Strains* (New York: Harper and Row, Harper Torchbooks, 1961), p. 36.

5. *Ibid.*, p. 40.

6. The case of Harvey is described in detail by Walter Pagel, *William*

Harvey's Biological Ideas. Selected Aspects and Historical Background (Basel/ New York: S. Karger, 1967), pp. 28–47. On method the reader is also referred to the pertinent sections in Wightman, *Science and the Renaissance*. See also Wightman's views as expounded in his paper 'Myth and Method in Seventeenth-century Biological Thought', *Journal of the History of Biology*, **2** (1969), 321–336. No attempt will be made in the present paper to assess the role played by Aristotelian thought on science in the sixteenth and seventeenth centuries.

7. See Allen, 'Scientific Studies', 219–53; William T. Costello, S.J., *The Scholastic Curriculum at Early Seventeenth-Century Cambridge* (Cambridge, Mass.: Harvard U.P., 1958), p. 9; Curtis, *Oxford and Cambridge in Transition*, p. 227.

8. William Munk, M.D., F.S.A., *The Roll of the Royal College of Physicians of London* . . . (2nd ed., 3 vols., London: Published by the College, 1878), **I**, pp. 12–21.

9. Allen, 'Scientific Studies', 219.

10. W. S. C. Copeman, *Doctors and Disease in Tudor Times* (London, 1960), p. 36.

11. William Harrison Woodward, *Studies in Education during the Age of the Renaissance 1400–1600* (Cambridge: University Press, 1906), pp. 10–23. On Vittorino da Feltre see William Harrison Woodward, *Vittorino da Feltre, and Other Humanist Educators. Essays and Versions* (Cambridge, 1905). A useful survey will be found in William Boyd, *The History of Western Education* (7th edition, London: Adam and Charles Black, 1964), pp. 159–82. Paul Monroe has prepared an important translation and a valuable commentary in his *Thomas Platter and the Educational Renaissance of the Sixteenth Century* (New York: D. Appleton and Co., 1904). The English scene has been discussed by Kenneth Charlton, *Education in Renaissance England* (London: Routledge and Kegan Paul, 1965). Important also are Foster Watson's *The Beginnings of the Teaching of Modern Subjects in England* (London, 1909) and *The English Grammar Schools to 1660: their Curriculum and Practice* (London, 1908). There is a considerable literature on Roger Ascham: see Lawrence V. Ryan, *Roger Ascham* (Stanford, Calif., 1963). Ascham's important *The Scholemaster* (*1570*) has recently been reprinted (Menston, 1967). An early Tudor work (first published in 1517) has also recently been made available in translation, Richard Pace, *De Fructu qui ex Doctrina Percipitur* (*The Benefit of a Liberal Education*), ed. Frank Manley and Richard S. Sylvester (New York: F. Ungar for The Renaissance Society of America, 1967).

12. Both themes may be seen early in the Renaissance in the writings of Petrarch (1304–1374) who attacked the learning of the scholastics and turned instead for inspiration to classical antiquity and nature. Although

he was willing to grant that the original Aristotle far surpassed the works of his more recent followers, he still turned with far more enthusiasm to Plato, the 'Prince of Philosophers'. For him the knowledge of God was to be the main goal of philosophy and he found little difficulty in branding the studies of the scholastics as basically irreligious. With a special interest in the nature of man and his character, Petrarch and his followers turned to Cicero, Virgil, Seneca and Homer rather than the philosophical texts in vogue at the universities.

13. Woodward, *Studies in Education*, p. 76.

14. *Ibid.*, p. 123. See also William Harrison Woodward, *Desiderius Erasmus Concerning the Aim and Method of Education* (Cambridge, 1904).

15. Juan Luis Vives, *On Education. A Translation of the De Tradendis Disciplinis*, introduction by Foster Watson (Cambridge: University Press, 1913; first published in 1531); J. L. Vives, *Ludovicus Vives and the Renaissance Education of Women*, ed. by F. Watson (London, 1912); J. L. Vives, *Tudor Schoolboy Life. Dialogues translated for the First Time into English with an introduction by F. Watson* (London, 1908).

16. W. H. Harrison, *Studies in Education*, p. 203.

17. Frank Pierrepont Graves, *Peter Ramus and the Educational Reformation of the Sixteenth Century* (New York: Macmillan, 1912), pp. 23–4. Important for the study of Ramus is Ong's *Ramus: Method and the Decay of Dialogue* (cited above, note 1) and R. Hooykaas, *Humanisme, science et reforme: P. de la Ramée, 1515–72* (Leyden, 1958). The latter work compares Ramus and Paracelsus.

18. F. P. Graves, *Ramus*, p. 169.

19. Rabelais, *Les Oeuvres*, edited by Ch. Marty-Laveaux (6 vols., Paris: Lemerre, 1870–1903), **I**, p. 256.

20. See P. O. Kristeller, *The Philosophy of Marsilio Ficino* (New York, 1943); R. Klibansky, *The Continuity of the Platonic Tradition during the Middle Ages: Outlines of a Corpus Platonicum Medii Aevi* (London: Warburg Institute, 1939); D. P. Walker, *Spiritual and Demonic Magic from Ficino to Campanella* (London: Warburg Institute, 1958); Frances A. Yates, *Giordano Bruno and the Hermetic Tradition* (Chicago: Univ. of Chicago Press, 1964); Walter Pagel, *Das Medzinische Weltbild des Paracelsus: seine Zusammenhänge Neuplatonismus und Gnosis* (Wiesbaden, 1962); Charles B. Schmitt, *Gianfrancesco Pico della Mirandola (1469–1533) and his Critique of Aristotle* (The Hague: Martinus Nijhoff, 1967).

21. P. O. Kristeller, *Eight Philosophers of the Italian Renaissance* (Stanford: Stanford U.P., 1964), pp. 39–138, *passim*.

22. William Gilbert, *On the Loadstone and Magnetic Bodies, and on The Great Magnet the Earth*, trans. P. Fleury, Mottelay (London: Bernard Quaritch, 1893), p. 1.

23. William Harvey, *The Works of William Harvey, M.D.*, trans., and with a life by Robert Willis, M.D. (London: Sydenham Society, 1847), p. 7.

24. R. Descartes, *Discours de la Méthode*, Introduction and notes by Etienne Gilson (Paris: J. Vrin, 1964), p. 49.

25. *Ibid.*, p. 62.

26. *The Philosophical Works of Francis Bacon . . . Reprinted from the Texts and Translations*, notes and prefaces of Ellis and Spedding, ed. with an Introduction by John M. Robertson (London: Routledge and Sons; New York: Dutton, 1905), p. 286 from the *Novum Organum*. See also *On the Advancement of Learning*, p. 76.

Chapter Three

The Paracelsians and Educational Reform

IF we shift our attention to the sixteenth century iatrochemists, Paracelsians and alchemists, we find the same emphasis on new observations as a basis for a new science. In addition we find that they shared the same distrust of the traditional learning at the universities. Their solution was to be a chemically oriented universe in which medicine and chemistry were for all practical purposes equated. Only on these new truths could a proper reform of education be founded.

The chemists' views on the need for an observational-experimental science and on the inadequacy of the established educational system can be quickly documented. First, the observational basis of the new science. Writing in 1538, Paracelsus (1493–1541) stated 'I do not here write out of speculation, and theorie, but practically out of the light of Nature, and experience, lest I should burden you and make you weary with many words'.[1] The Paracelsian chemical physician is a man who is not afraid to work with his own hands. He is a pious man who praises God in his work and who lays aside all those vanities of his Galenist competitor and instead finds his delight in a knowledge of the fire while he learns the degrees of the science of alchemy.[2] The Paracelsian physician to the King of Denmark, Peter Severinus (1542–1602), wrote in 1571 that honest students of nature should sell their possessions and burn their books. With the proceeds they must buy sturdy clothes and set out to examine and observe everything with their own eyes. Above all, they should purchase coal, 'build furnaces, watch and operate with the fire without wearying. In this way and no other you will arrive at a knowledge of things and their properties.'[3] And R. Bostocke (fl. c. 1585) who effectively introduced

15

Paracelsian thought to England in 1585 compared the traditional scholar who quoted Galen and Aristotle alone as the procedure for obtaining the doctorate with the new chemical physicians who try 'all things by fire whereby the vertue, nature, and propertie of each thing appeareth to the palpable and visible experience . . .'.[4] Bostocke goes on: 'He that listeth to leane to Bookes, let him learne of those Bookes which *Paracelsus* hath most Godly and learnedly expressed in his *Labyrinth*. In comparison of which al other Aucthorities in those matters are small or none.'[5] If we follow Bostocke's advice and turn to the *Labyrinthus Medicorum* of Paracelsus (1538) we find no written books discussed at all. Instead we are told to seek out God through nature. We must turn to the book of the heavens, the book of the elements, the book of man, the book of alchemy and the book of medicine. In effect, published books are nothing for science and knowledge must be based on experience and observation. 'Scientia enim est experientia.'[6]

Secondly, let me turn to the chemist's view of the state of formal education in their day. As Descartes and Bacon were appalled by the universities, so too were these chemical philosophers. The teaching of Paracelsus at the University of Basel in 1527 had been an unhappy experience notable largely for his conflict with the students and professors alike as well as his insistence on lecturing in Swiss-German and his burning of the *Canon* of Avicenna. The Paracelsian disillusionment with the schools is reflected throughout the sixteenth and the seventeenth centuries. Bostocke complained that although Paracelsian chemistry can be shown by experience to be true, its followers were in a desperate state since no one would give them a fair trial.

> . . . in the scholes nothing may be received nor allowed that savoureth not of *Aristotle*, *Gallen*, *Avicen*, and other Ethnikes, whereby the young beginners are either not acquainted with this doctrine, or els it is brought into hatred with them. And abrode likewise the Galenists be so armed and defended by the protection, priviledges and authorities of Princes, that nothing may bee received that agreeth not with their pleasures and doctrine . . . .[7]

Or we may compare Descartes' account of his education with that of van Helmont (1579–1644) who was surely the most influential seventeenth century iatrochemist:

At the age of seventeen I had finished my course in philosophy, and it was then that I noticed that nobody was admitted to the examination who was not masked in his gown and hood, as if the robes warrant scholarship. The professors made a laughing stock of the academic youth that was to be introduced to the arts and learning, and I could not help wondering at a sort of delirium in the behaviour of the professors, nay of everybody as much as the simplicity of the credulous youth. I retired into a deliberation in order to judge myself how much I was of a philosopher and had attained truth and science. I found myself inflated with letters and, as it were, naked as after partaking of the illicit apple—except for a proficiency in artificial wrangling. Then it dawned on me that I knew nothing and that what I knew was worthless. I did astronomy, logic and algebra for pleasure, as the other subjects nauseated me, and also the *Elements* of Euclid, which became particularly congenial to me since they contained the truth. . . . But I learned only vain eccentricities and a new revolution of the celestial bodies, and what seemed hardly worth the time and labours I had spent. . . . Having completed my course I refused the title of Master of Arts since I knew nothing substantial, nothing true; unwilling to have myself made an archfool by the professors declaring me a Master of the Seven Arts, I who was not even a disciple yet. Seeking truth and science, though not their outward appearance, I withdrew from the University.[8]

There seemed no question that a new experimental science was needed and that the universities of the day were not providing this. But before discussing the reforms of the chemists, we must take up the question of what these men meant by chemistry and what they sought as their goal.[9] Above all, living in an intensely religious age they sought a true understanding of their Creator. Because of this, Aristotle and Galen could be – and were – severely attacked. Aristotle had been a heathen whose work had been condemned repeatedly in Church Councils, yet his works still formed the basis of philosophical thought at the universities. And for the Paracelsians, for whom medicine was a godly science second only to theology – and here witness *Ecclesiasticus* chapter 38 where the priestly office of the physician is described, and where medicine is referred to as a divine rather than a mundane science – for these men Galen was pictured primarily as a persecutor of Christians who had totally debased the study of man by his own slavish addiction to the Aristotelian corpus. In contrast, the work of Paracelsus in medicine was compared with that of Copernicus in astronomy and with that of Luther, Melanchthon, Zwingli and Calvin in theology. It is hardly surprising then that we should find these men continually referring to the two-book theory of knowledge. Man may obtain truth both through the Holy Scriptures or some mystical religious experience and also through his diligent study of nature, God's book of Creation. Following the Hermetic tradition special emphasis was placed on the first chapter of *Genesis.* Here was a divine account of the formation of the world – an indisputable account. However, interpretations were not out of order, and for the Paracelsians the Creation was seen essentially as a divine *chemical* separation in which special emphasis was placed on the elements from which all other substances derive. Whether the particular author centred his discussion around the ancient Aristotelian elements or the newer Paracelsian principles, or even if he set up an independent system of his own, he was able to think of the element system as a basis for all created substances as well as a cosmological system. Indeed, the significance placed on this Biblical account goes far to explain why there exists such a voluminous literature relating to element theory in the Renaissance, and why attacks on the Paracelsian principles should have been considered essential by opponents of the iatro-chemists.[10]

Chemistry then had a divine significance. Since the Creation might be understood as a chemical process, it was thought that nature must continue to operate in chemical terms. Chemistry was the key to nature – all Created nature. Both earthly and heavenly phenomena were thought of as chemical processes and interpreted in this fashion. The scholar should go out to observe nature and collect specimens for study. These samples were then to be subjected to chemical analysis – that is, decomposition by heat. Aristotelians and Paracelsians alike believed that heat would reduce a substance to its elements. Chemistry then seemed to be a basic method of getting to fundamentals in nature.

However, there was more to the system than this. Most of these men were convinced of the truth of the macrocosm-microcosm relationship. The universe was conceived to be relatively small with all of its parts interconnected. In particular, man was seen as a small copy of the great world. The true physician will study all nature as he learns of man. Oswald Croll (1580–1609) concentrated on this 'divine Analogy of this visible World and Man' in his influential *Basilica Chymica* of 1609. He affirmed that

Heaven and Earth are Mans parents, out of which Man last of all was created; he that knowes the parents, and can Anotomize them, hath attained the true knowledge of their child man, the most perfect creature in all his properties; because all things of the whole Universe meet in him as in the Centre, and the Anatomy of him in his Nature is the Anatomy of the whole world . . . .[11]

And while the ordinary philosopher might identify relationships between heaven and earth through outward signs, the chemical philosopher could learn far more through the use of his art and his analyses which might bring forth the hidden secrets of earthly bodies – and through analogy teach of the heavens. In the literature we find tables of correspondences between macrocosmic and microcosmic events. Robert Fludd (1574–1637) gives a chemical description of the circulation of the blood which parallels the circular motion of the Sun in the great world.[12] Similarly Joseph Quercetanus (c. 1544–1609) related man to the great world about him. This is seen clearly in his discussion of respiratory diseases (characterized by the formation of phlegm at the nose and a high bodily temperature) in terms of an internal bodily distillation. Here his position reflected both the Aristotelian explanation of catarrh and also the persistent search for chemical analogies among the Paracelsians. But beyond this, he argued that these diseases were similar to the formation of clouds and rain so that if we investigate the microcosmic phenomena we may also hope to learn of macrocosmic truths such as the source of winds, sleet and snow.[13] Glauber (1603/1604–1668/1670), one of the greatest of the practical chemists of the mid-seventeenth century, was quite willing to assert that since it had now been proved that the blood circulates in the body, we could hardly argue about the truth of such circulations in the macrocosm.[14] These examples from Croll, Fludd, Duchesne and Glauber help to explain the difficulties encountered in reading sixteenth and seventeenth century texts of this *genre*. Because of the widespread acceptance of the macrocosm-microcosm analogy and the belief that chemistry was the key to nature, one finds a host of subjects discussed which seem to have little meaning for the twentieth century chemist.

In short, these men spoke of the need for new observations and 'experientia' no less than did authors whom we today honour as founders of the new science of the seventeenth century. Similarly they rejected the formal university training of the period in no uncertain terms. On these grounds they may be classed as 'moderns'. On the other hand, this science had incorporated in it an archaic world view which fundamentally separates it from man's approach to nature today. It is hardly surprising that Paracelsian thought should have had a natural appeal for physicians interested in a new science. It stressed medicine as the apex of natural philosophy, it bolstered its claims with the testimony of the Bible in an age when theology claimed the attention of every man, and it urged the merits of observation.

Evidence of the popularity of the chemical–Paracelsian approach to nature may be found in the ever-increasing number of books published on these topics in the seventeenth century. Even more convincing is the alarm we note in the works of men we might class as sounder scientists. We find Father Marin Mersenne (1588–1648) disturbed about the new works of the chemists and seriously discussing the question whether alchemy should be considered an exact science.[15] We find Pierre Gassendi preparing a careful refutation of the works of Robert Fludd.[16] And we find Kepler (1571–1630) engaged in a verbal duel with Fludd also – a debate which lasted for years.[17] As for the chemists themselves, we sense a spirit of success. Oswald Croll felt certain that Paracelsus's dream of overturning the ancient doctrines of the schools was imminent if not yet quite achieved. He pointed out that the courts of Europe did not lack competent Paracelsians, and he attributed their success to the truth of their chemical hypotheses, to the inherent progress of medical knowledge, and to the elegant simplicity of the macrocosm–microcosm analogy.[18]

With the apparent success of their system, the problem of educational reform became much more important for the chemical philosophers. It is a topic referred to in many works – far more than can be discussed here. Let us choose only a few examples. The least promising of them all might appear to be the Fama Fraternitas and the Confessio (1614, 1615). These are the texts which launched the Rosicrucian movement which to many may seem to represent the very essence of modern occultism. Reading these tracts in the framework of early seventeenth century thought, however, an appreciably different picture emerges. The Fama Fraternitatis in effect represents a call for a new learning.[19] Scholars today, the author complained, still pore over the atrophied learning taught in the schools – Aristotle, Galen and Porphyry – while instead they should be seeking a more perfect knowledge of the 'Son Jesus Christ and Nature'.[20] All truly learned men agree that the basis of natural philosophy is medicine and that this is a godly art.[21] The true secrets of medicine – and thus all science – had been learned by the founder of their order, Christian Rosenkreuz, and he had set them down in the secret books which are studied by the brethren of the order.[22] But great truths are to be found among those who are not members at all. In Germany today there are many learned magicians, physicians and philosophers – and such a one was the great Theophrastus Paracelsus whose works are concealed within the hidden vault of the Rosicrucians next to the books of Christian Rosenkreuz.[23] This was indeed a neo-Paracelsian and an alchemical movement – and a missionary one at that. How much might be accomplished if the truly learned scholars of Europe united for the benefit of mankind? But, the author continues, where are we to find them? Surely they are not at the universities. They must declare themselves and join the Brotherhood in this reformation of learning. Accordingly one reads a plea in the *Fama Fraternitatis* addressed to all the learned scholars of Europe to examine their art 'and to declare their minds, either *Communicatio consilio* or *singulatim* by Print'.[24] Both the *Fama* and the *Confessio* were to be published simultaneously in five languages so that no one could excuse himself and say that he had not seen the message – and while the Brothers refused at this time to give out their names or announce their meetings, they were willing to assure those who answered their call that their works would not go unnoticed.[25]

The *Fama* was actually published in four languages in nine editions between 1614 and 1617 – and an English translation appeared in 1652.[26] Indeed, the response to this appeal must have been beyond the wildest dreams of the promoters. In the course of less than ten years several hundred books and tracts appeared debating the merits of this secret group, while major cities – such as Paris in 1623[27] – were visited by men who announced themselves as members of the Brotherhood and promised to show all of their secrets to those who wished to be initiated. In an account written in 1619 we read:

What a confusion among men followed the report of this thing, what a conflict among the learned, what an unrest and commotion of imposters and swindlers, it is needless to say. There is just this one thing which we would like to add, that there were some who in this blind

21

> terror wished to have their old, and out-of-date, and falsified affairs
> entirely retained and defended with force. Some hastened to surrender
> the strength of their opinions; and after they had made accusation
> against the severest yoke of their servitude, hastened to reach out after
> freedom.[28]

In the rash of utopian schemes of this era we find the *Christianopolis*
(1619) of Johann Valentin Andreae (1587–1654), the man who may
have been the author of the *Fama*. While this work is little known today
it bears striking similarities to the *New Atlantis* of Bacon which was
written shortly after, and its importance for seventeenth century
science seems even greater than this.[29] Andreae's close association with
Comenius who was in turn the friend of Samuel Hartlib (d. *c.* 1670),
John Dury (1596–1680) and William Petty (1623–1687) connects him
with the background which culminated in the foundation of the
Royal Society of London.[30]

In the *Christianopolis* Andreae deplores the decay of learning and
religion and suggests that a proper community be formed – open to
all of good intent and character.[31] We need not discuss this model in
detail. We need only note that here again we see a reaction against
tradition in the spirit of the contemporary chemical philosophers. The
citizens of *Christianopolis*, for instance, have a large library, but they
use it little, and concentrate only on the most thorough books. The
meaning is clear:

> The highest authority among them is that of sacred literature, that is,
> of the Divine Book; and this is the prize which they recognize as
> concealed by divine gift to men and of inexhaustible mysteries; almost
> everything else they consider of comparatively little value . . . .[32]

The scholars here prefer to get their knowledge directly from the
Book of Nature. A study of nature brings about a greater understanding
of our Creator for 'a close examination of the earth will bring about
a proper appreciation of the heavens, and when the value of the
heavens has been found, there will be a contempt of the earth'.[33]

Accordingly we are more than justified in looking at the centre for
such studies, the laboratory. As we might expect, it is a chemistry
laboratory fitted out with the most complete equipment and it is here
that 'the properties of metals, minerals, and vegetables, and even the
life of animals are examined, purified, increased, and united, for the

use of the human race and in the interests of health'.[34] More important, however, is the fact that it is here that 'the sky and the earth are married together', and it is here that the 'divine mysteries impressed upon the land are discovered'.[35] These are clearly references to the macrocosm-microcosm analogy and the doctrine of signatures.

The importance of chemistry for Andreae becomes even more evident when one compares it with his treatment of other sciences. In the hall of physics we do not find basic studies of motion. Instead one views natural history scenes painted on the walls – views of the sky, the planets, animals and plants. The visitor may examine rare gems and minerals, poisons and antidotes and all sorts of things beneficial and injurious to the several organs of man's body.[36] Here the study of mathematics rises above vulgar arithmetic and geometry to the mystical numerical harmonies of the heavens – a subject known to the Pythagoreans of old.[37] The relation of heaven and earth is everywhere stressed, and for this reason astrology is raised to its proper place. Andreae states that

> he who does not know the value of astrology in human affairs, or who foolishly denies it, I would wish that he would have to dig in the earth, cultivate and work the fields, for as long a time as possible, in unfavourable weather.[38]

The implication is clear. A new learning is required, and if it cannot be accommodated to the current university system, a separate academy or college must be founded. Andreae's proposals could have been seconded by any of the chemical philosophers.

We have yet to examine any schemes for educational reform proposed by the chemists themselves. Let me confine my remarks to two contemporaries, Robert Fludd and Jean Baptiste van Helmont. These men represent two extremes within the same camp. We must take up Fludd first since his views are not too far removed from the Hermetic approach of the *Christianopolis* and the *Fama Fraternitatis*. Indeed, Fludd is one of those who answered the plea to the learned community of Europe printed in this Rosicrucian text. Fludd was a knight, a man of substance who had been educated at Oxford and then had spent years touring the educational centres on the continent.[39] After his return home he was admitted as a fellow of the Royal College of Physicians (1609) where he became the friend of William Harvey and Mark Ridley (1560–1624). Yet, this man was far from being a 'modern'. Fludd wrote with sincerity about the mystical alchemical Creation, and he considered kabbalistic analysis to be a proper method in the scholar's search for divine secrets. His publications were controversial in tone and widely discussed.

When the *Fama Fraternitatis* appeared Fludd had as yet put nothing into print. However, as a Hermeticist of long standing he was attracted by its message, and when another noted chemist, Andreas Libavius (*c.* 1540–1616), attacked the Rosicrucians, Fludd rapidly penned a reply in which he made a plea for a new learning.[40] Nowhere did he feel that there was more useless knowledge being spewed forth than at the universities. These were strongholds of the classical scholars who felt that truth could only be found in the writings of the ancients. One could only shudder at their reliance on Aristotle in philosophy and Galen in medicine, for in the ancient world none set forth doctrines more opposed to Christianity than they. Aristotle and Galen had been heathens, and their followers were no better. The universities must be reformed so that the divine light of Christian teachings could flourish. In a chapter on natural philosophy, medicine and alchemy, Fludd tells us that although innumerable authors have written on natural philosophy, they have presented to us only a shade of truth.[41] They fill whole volumes with definitions, descriptions and divisions, and they drone on about the four causes. They lecture on motion, the continuum, the contiguum – of termini, loci, of space, vacua, time and number. This for them is the basis of physics. They go forth then to generation, corruption and descriptive accounts of the heavens and the universe.[42] 'But, good God, how superficial this all is.'[43] It is impossible for anyone to attain the highest knowledge of natural philosophy without a thorough training in the occult sciences.[44]

One must turn first to medicine, the most perfect science of all. There should not be understood by this word a simple description of diseases and the workings of the human body. Rather, it is the very basis on which natural philosophy must rest.[45] Our knowledge of the microcosm will teach us of the great world, and this, in turn, will lead us to our Creator. Similarly, the more we learn of the universe, the more we shall be rewarded with a perfect knowledge of ourselves. Obviously the medical schools must change their emphasis.

The art of alchemy from which we might expect so much in reality aids us little. Alchemists like Andreas Libavius do not call for a reform, but rather describe calcination, separation, conjunction, putrefaction, and all the other operations by which men are deceived and persuaded to part with their money. Although Fludd was well aware of the importance of chemistry in the preparation of the new medicines, here he was concerned with a higher goal.[46] True chemical authors, he continued, are of a different sort than Libavius for they write of occult secrets.[47] The science is a system of nature – not a refuge for gold-makers.

Real wisdom may be found in the writings of the natural magicians, men who are in truth mathematicians.[48] But if Fludd was distressed about the state of natural philosophy, medicine and alchemy in his day, he felt even more strongly about mathematics.[49] The texts of arithmetic were filled with definitions, principles and discussions of theoretical operations. We learn of addition, subtraction, multiplication, division, golden numbers, fractions, square roots and the extraction of cubes.[50] But of the old wisdom and doctrines of the Pythagoreans the Arithmeticians pay little heed. These men of old were silent about the arcane arithmetic, and like mystical alchemists they hid their profound mysteries from the vulgar crowd.[51]

And, Fludd continues, if we go beyond arithmetic to other mathematical studies, we find the same superficiality. Those who are really profound in these arts are considered impious and magicians.[52] Indeed, we can learn more from the silent wisdom of the Pythagoreans than we can from the useless books of the philosophers. The disciples of Pythagoras reached a certainty of belief in God through their profound study of numbers and their ratios. In the same way, we may learn of the unity of God in trinity – and more, of the very construction of the world.[53]

We need not continue much farther. For Fludd, music really deals with the joining of the elements, the proportions of light and weight in the stars, and their influence on the terrestrial world – in short, it relates primarily to the celestial harmony.[54] Geometry really concerns other hidden secrets. Surely the greater geometer of all time was Archimedes, and Fludd turns no less resolutely than the mechanical philosophers to Archimedes as a guide to a new science. Why? – because of his wondrous machines.[55] In effect, Archimedes is to be considered as the archetype of the perfect natural magician.

Fludd represents an extreme case of the mystical alchemist who sought hidden secrets in the writings of the sages of old. When pressed to do so he could debate over the problems of experimental method as a modern, but experiment for him always was to be subservient to the revealed truths of religion, and Holy Writ would always carry greater weight than laboratory results. It is significant that his whole scheme was chemically oriented, and that for him only reforms of the most drastic sort could save the university system.

No greater contrast to Fludd could be found among the chemical philosophers than Jean Baptiste van Helmont, a man who was appalled by the mystical approach of Fludd and who deplored the use of the macrocosm-microcosm analogy in nature. He writes that

> The name of Microcosm or little World is Poetical, heathenish, and metaphorical, but not natural, or true. It is likewise a Phantastical, hypochondriacal and mad thing, to have brought all the properties, and species of the universe into man, and the art of healing.[56]

We have already noted his disillusionment with his training at school. Yet, in his reaction to this, he had immersed himself in the Hermetic and Paracelsian texts as the only major alternative. Consequently, even though he later rejected elements of Paracelsism, here too we find many of the same currents of thought. No less than Paracelsus or Fludd, van Helmont insists that man may safely rely on *Genesis* as a basis for physical truth. When he rejects the Aristotelian four elements it is just for this reason – they are not mentioned in the Creation account.[57] He could write almost in rapture

> I praise my bountiful God, who hath called me into the Art of the fire, out of the dregs of other professions. For truly chymistry, hath its principles not gotten by discourses, but those which are known by nature and evident by the fire: and it prepares the understanding to pierce the secrets of nature, and causeth a further searching out in nature, than all other Sciences being put together: and it pierceth even unto the utmost depths of real truth . . . .[58]

Van Helmont's disillusionment with the teachings of the schools and their emphasis on Galen and Aristotle may be traced at least in part to his views on mathematics. As a student he had laboured over logic and the principles of Euclid which seemed to contain truth, but when he sought theorems and axioms in medicine, he found this quest quite hopeless.[59] Medicine is a divine rather than an ordinary science because Scripture teaches us that the Lord created physicians.[60] Rational, mathematically-inspired investigations may aid us in the study of physics, but not in the chief goal of natural philosophy, medicine, for to 'understand and favour these things from the spring or first cause is granted to none without the special favour of Christ the Lord'.[61] Neither the cosmic mathematics of the mystical alchemists nor the logical-mathematical method of the Galenist may help us here.

And if we turn to the mathematical physics of the Aristotelians we will do no better than before. The teachings of Aristotle dominate our own schools and turn the minds of our scholars into erroneous paths. Yet, if we examine his writings we shall unmask him. It is true that Aristotle had a most persuasive manner in arranging rules and maxims. In a later – and more lazy – age students willingly accepted these as a guide to truth while they prostrated themselves to him almost in worship.[62] But the evidence shows, van Helmont adds, that Aristotle surely had little ability as a scientific observer. Therefore he relied heavily on mathematics in preparing his vast system simply because he was 'far more skilful in this, than Nature'. And since this man had subdued nature under the rules of mathematics, our scholars are now cursed with an improper approach to science.[63]

Thoroughly sickened by the logical-mathematical methods of the schools, van Helmont could only hope – as did so many of his generation – for a new learning based upon a total reform. In his early work on the magnetic cure of wounds we see van Helmont's acceptance of natural magic as 'the most profound inbred knowledge of things'[64] and if he was to reject the most occult aspects of Paracelsian thought, we still find his emphasis on experiment and chemistry in his scheme for educational reform. No longer should young men waste their youth on Aristotelian thought – a term which for van Helmont could almost be equated with mathematical thought. In a seven year programme they may devote three years to arithmetic, mathematical science, the *Elements* of Euclid, and geography (which is to include the study of seas, rivers, springs, mountains and minerals). In addition – in this three year period – they are to study the properties and customs of nations, waters, plants, living creatures, and the ring and astrolabe. Only then, van Helmont continues

. . . let them come to the Study of Nature, let them learn to know and seperate the first Beginnings of Bodies. I say, by working, to have

27

known their fixedness, volatility, or swiftness, with their seperation, life, death, interchangeable course, defects, alteration, weakness, corruption, transplanting, solution, coagulation or co-thickening, resolving. Let the History of extractions, dividings, conjoynings, ripenesses, promotions, hinderances, consequences, lastly, of losse and profit, be added. Let them also be taught, the Beginnings of Seeds, Ferments, Spirits, and Tinctures, with every flowing, digesting, changing, motion, and disturbance of things to be altered.

And all those things, not indeed by a naked description of discourse, but by handicraft demonstration of the fire. For truly nature measureth her works by distilling, moystening, drying, calcining, resolving, plainly by the same meanes, whereby glasses do accomplish those same operations. And so the Artificer, by changing the operations of nature, obtains the properties and knowledge of the same. For however natural a wit, and sharpness of judgement the Philosopher may have, yet he is never admitted to the Root, or radical knowledge of natural things, without the fire. And so everyone is deluded with a thousand thoughts or doubts, the which he unfoldeth not to himself, but by the help of the fire. Therefore I confess, nothing doth more fully bring a man that is greedy of knowing, to the knowledge of all things knowable, than the fire. Therefore a young man at length, returning out of these Schooles, truly it is a wonder to see, how much he shall ascend above the Phylosophers of the University, and the vain reasoning of the Schooles.[65]

This is the Helmontian-iatrochemical programme for a reform in education. Students are to spend the bulk of their time learning the true facts of nature through observation and chemical operations with the fire.

In many ways the Renaissance chemical philosophers were typical of their period. Seemingly unaware that their own views were often imbedded in the concepts of antiquity, they lashed out at the traditionalism of the universities. At the same time they agreed with others that the desired new understanding of nature must be based on fresh observational evidence. Yet, their background gave a special orientation to their concept of the universe. Their cosmology was a chemical cosmology and their 'experiments' were generally chemical analyses by fire. As for their hope of educational reform there seemed to be two avenues of approach. Some were willing to dismiss the universities as useless in their more enlightened age and hope rather to set up in their stead separate associations for scholars seeking a new understanding of nature. Other chemists still hoped for radical reform within the existing institutions. These might well argue that reform was possible. Had not Paracelsus lectured at Basel and had not Bostocke called only for a fair hearing for the chemical philosophy at the universities? Yet, granted this, there is little question that van Helmont's educational system would have been a difficult one to have integrated into the existing system. It is basically this problem – specifically applied to the English universities – that faced John Webster and his opponents in 1654.

REFERENCES

1. Paracelsus, *Of the Nature of Things* in Michael Sendivogius, *A New Light of Alchymy* (London: A. Clark for Tho. Williams, 1674), sig. L8 recto. For the original text, see Paracelsus, *Opera Bücher und Schrifften* (2 vols., Strassburg: L. Zetzner, 1616), **1**, p. 881.
2. *Ibid.*, pp. 252–3.
3. Petrus Severinus, *Idea Medicinae* (3rd ed., Hagae Comitis, 1660), p. 39.
4. R. Bostocke, Esq., *The difference betwene the auncient Physicke . . . and the latter Phisicke* (London, Robert Walley, 1585), sig. Dv verso.
5. *Ibid.*, sig. Dvi recto.
6. Paracelsus, *Labyrinthus Medicorum* in *Opera Omnia* (3 vols., Geneva: Joan Antonii and Samuel De Tournes, 1658), **1**, pp. 264–88 (275).
7. Bostocke, *The difference . . .*, sig. Fiii recto.
8. Walter Pagel's translation may be found in his 'The Reaction to Aristotle in Seventeenth-Century Biological Thought' in *Science, Medicine and History. Essays on the Evolution of Scientific Thought and Medical Practice written in honour of Charles Singer* (2 vols., London/New York/Toronto: Oxford U.P., 1953), **1**, pp. 489–509 (491–2). A seventeenth-century translation will be found in John Baptista van Helmont, *Oriatrike or Physick Refined*, trans. J. Chandler (London: Lodowick Loyd, 1662), pp. 11–12. For the Latin, see *Opera Omnia* (Frankfurt, 1682), p. 16.
9. The following account is based primarily on the present author's 'Renaissance Chemistry and the Work of Robert Fludd' in *Alchemy and Chemistry in the Seventeenth Century* (Los Angeles: William Andrews Clark Memorial Library, 1966), pp. 3–29. This essay was printed in slightly revised form in *Ambix*, **14** (1967), 42–59. See also Debus, *The English Paracelsians*.
10. See Allen G. Debus, 'Fire Analysis and the Elements in the Sixteenth and Seventeenth Centuries', *Annals of Science*, **23** (1967), 127–47.
11. Osw. Crollius, *Discovering the Great and Deep Mysteries of Nature* in

Philosophy Reformed and Improved, trans. H. Pinnell (London, 1657), p. 24. For the Latin, see Crollius, *Basilica Chymica* (Frankfurt: Gottfried Tampach, c. 1623), p. 14.

12. Debus, 'Robert Fludd and the Circulation of the Blood', 374–93.

13. Joseph Du Chesne Quercetanus, *Traicte de la Matière, Preparation et excellente vertue de Médicine balsamique des Anciens Philosophes* (Paris, 1626 —first Latin edition, 1603), p. 183.

14. J. R. Glauber, *Works*, trans. Christopher Packe (London, 1689), pp. 248 f.

15. P. Marin Mersenne, *La Vérité des Sciences Contre Les Sceptiques ou Pyrrhoniens* (Paris, 1625). This is discussed by Lenoble, *Mersenne ou la naissance du mécanisme*.

16. Pierre Gassendi, *Epistolica exercitatio in qua principia philosophiae Roberti Fluddi, medici, reteguntur, et ad recentes illius libros adversus R. P. F. Marinum Mersennum . . . respondetur* (Paris, 1630).

17. The Kepler-Fludd debate has been described in part by Wolfgang Pauli in 'The Influence of Archetypal Ideas on the Scientific Theories of Kepler'. See above, chapter 1, note 2.

18. Crollius, *Discovering the Great and Deep Mysteries of Nature*, pp. 142–7.

19. Frances A. Yates discusses the Rosicrucian movement and early modern science in her 'The Hermetic Tradition in Renaissance Science' in *Art, Science and History in the Renaissance*, edited by Charles S. Singleton (Baltimore, 1968), pp. 255–74.

20. *The Fame and Confession of the Fraternity of R:C: Commonly, of the Rosie Cross. With a Praeface annexed thereto, and a short Declaration of their Physicall Work*, by Eugenius Philalethes (Thomas Vaughan) (London: J. M. for Giles Calvert, 1652), pp. 1–2.

21. *Ibid.*, p. 36.

22. *Ibid.*, p. 5.

23. *Ibid.*, p. 10.

24. *Ibid.*, p. 31.

25. *Ibid.*

26. A listing – and discussion – of the early Rosicrucian texts will be found in F. Leigh Gardner, *A Catalogue Raisonné of Works on the Occult Sciences, vol. 1. Rosicrucian Books*, intro. Dr. William Wynn Westcott (2nd ed., privately printed, 1923). Here on pages 4–6, 21 (items 23–29, 144) will be found a discussion and description of the first editions of the *Fama Fraternitatis* and the *Confessio* (1614–1615). Other early editions are listed in Johann Valentin Andreae, *Christianopolis. An Ideal State of the Seventeenth Century*, trans. with an historical introduction by Felix Emil Held (New York: Oxford U.P., 1916), p. 11.

27. Gabriel Naudé, *Instruction à la France sur la Verité de l'Histoire des Frères de la Roze-Croix* (Paris: Francois Iulliot, 1623). See also James V. Rice,

Gabriel Naudé 1600–1653 (Baltimore: Johns Hopkins Press, 1939), pp. 47–72.

28. Andreae, *Christianopolis*, pp. 137–8.

29. *Ibid.*, pp. 53 ff.

30. The influence of the *Christianopolis* has been touched on briefly by W. H. G. Armytage, 'The Early Utopists and Science in England', *Annals of Science*, xii (1956), 247–54. Held has discussed the relation of the *Christianopolis* to the founding of the Royal Society in his edition of the text (cited above, note 39), pp. 100–25. Considerable attention is paid to this work by Margery Purver, *The Royal Society: Concept and Creation* (London: Routledge and Kegan Paul, 1967); this should be read alongside the essay review by Charles Webster, 'The Origins of the Royal Society', *History of Science*, **6** (1967), 106–27. See also G. H. Turnbull *Hartlib, Dury and Comenius. Gleanings from Hartlib's Papers*, (Liverpool: University of Liverpool Press, 1947), and H. R. Trevor-Roper, 'Three Foreigners and the Philosophy of the English Revolution', *Encounter*, **14** (1960), 3–20.

31. Andreae, *Christianopolis*, p. 29.

32. *Ibid.*, p. 191.

33. *Ibid.*, p. 187.

34. *Ibid.*, pp. 196–7.

35. *Ibid.*

36. *Ibid.*, p. 200.

37. *Ibid.*, pp. 221–3.

38. *Ibid.*, p. 228.

39. In addition to the works cited in note 9, see J. B. Craven, *Doctor Robert Fludd* (Kirkwall, 1902) and Josten, 'Truth's Golden Harrow'.

40. Robert Fludd, *Apologia Compendiaris Fraternitatem de Rosea Cruce Suspicionis et Infamiae Maculis Aspersam, Veritatis quasi Fluctibus abluens et abstergens* (Leiden, 1616). This short pamphlet was greatly enlarged the following year as the *Tractatus Apologeticus Integritatem Societatis De Rosea Cruce defendens* (Lugduni Batavorum, 1617). This is the edition which will be cited here. A German translation of this text appeared as *Schutzschrift für die Aechtheit der Rosenkreutzergesellschaft . . . übersetzt von Ada Mah Booz* (Leipzig: Adam Friedrich Böhme, 1782).

41. *Tractatus Apologeticus*, p. 91.

42. *Ibid.*, pp. 91–3.

43. *Ibid.*, p. 93.

44. *Ibid.*

45. *Ibid.*, p. 89.

46. *Ibid.*, pp. 100–01. At the same time it is interesting to see Fludd constantly giving mechanical examples to illustrate his cosmological concepts.

47. *Ibid.*, p. 101.

48. *Ibid.*, p. 23.

49. *Ibid.*, p. 103.

50. *Ibid.*

51. *Ibid.*, p. 105.

52. *Ibid.*

53. *Ibid.*, p. 107. Fludd would have rejoiced in the publication in the same year of a book on mystical geometry by Fortunatus, *Decas Elementorum Mysticae Geometrae Quibus Praecipua Divinitatus Arcana Explicantur* (Padua: Peter Paul Tozzi, 1617). I am indebted to Walter Pagel for this reference.

54. *Tractatus Apologeticus*, p. 109.

55. *Ibid.*, p. 114.

56. van Helmont, *Oriatrike*, p. 323; *Opera Omnia*, p. 310.

57. *Oriatrike*, p. 48; *Opera Omnia*, p. 51.

58. *Oriatrike*, p. 462; *Opera Omnia*, p. 441.

59. *Oriatrike*, p. 13; *Opera Omnia*, p. 17.

60. *Oriatrike*, p. 4; *Opera Omnia*, p. 9.

61. *Oriatrike*, p. 4; *Opera Omnia*, p. 9.

62. *Oriatrike*, p. 33; *Opera Omnia*, p. 36.

63. *Oriatrike*, p. 33; *Opera Omnia*, p. 38.

64. *Oriatrike*, p. 784; *Opera Omnia*, p. 725.

65. *Oriatrike*, p. 45; *Opera Omnia*, pp. 47–48.

Chapter Four

John Webster, Seth Ward, and the English Universities

THE search for a new learning based on chemistry and the occult sciences reached its peak in the middle decades of the seventeenth century. England in the Civil War period was particularly susceptible to such speculations. Indicative of the increased interest is the case of an astrological work written in 1608 which was withheld from the printer until 1650. In the preface we are told that men need no longer be afraid to set forth such views. They are now received favourably by a large segment of the scholarly public and they are well defended by the members of the learned London Society of Astrologers.[1] Paracelsian and Helmontian chemistry shared in the growing interest in all schemes for a new science. In the decade of the 1650s more Paracelsian and mystical chemical works were translated than in the entire century before 1650. At the same time, and with good reason, there was also a greater interest in the Rosicrucian movement. John Heydon (fl. 1667) gave his books such titles as *A New Method of Rosie Crucian Physicke* (1658) and *The Rosie Crucian Infallible Axiomata* (1660) while Eugenius Philalethes (Thomas Vaughan) (1622–1666) prepared a lengthy introduction to a translation of *The Fame and Confession of R: C:* (1652). The connection was quite clear for George Hakewill (1578–1649) in his survey of scholarship. He praised the '*Chimiques, Hermetiques*, or Paracelsians (and a branch of them as I conceive is the order Roseae Crucis)'.[2]

The frustration of the chemists is shown by their attempt to break the control over physicians exerted by the Royal College. This they hoped to do by forming rival societies of chemical physicians. And if

33

the schools were not open to their teachings, let a public test be made to prove the truth of their assertions. Listen to van Helmont:

> Oh ye Schooles. . . . Let us take out of the hospitals, out of the Camps, or from elsewhere, 200, or 500 poor People, that have Fevers, Pleurisies, etc. Let us divide them into halfes, let us cast lots, that one halfe of them may fall to my share, and the other to yours; . . . we shall see how many Funerals both of us shall have: *But* let the reward of the contention or wager, be 300 Florens, deposited on both sides: Here your business is decided.[3]

This challenge was repeated continuously by the chemical physicans of the Commonwealth and the early Restoration.[4]

In England this call for reform was closely connected with utopian schemes. Early in the century (*c.* 1605), Joseph Hall (1574–1656) wrote his *Mundus Alter et Idem* which described mythical new found lands in the southern hemisphere.[5] In 'Fooliana' a university exists which is composed of a college of Skeptikes and a college of Gewgawiasters. The provost of the latter is none other than Paracelsus who has invented a 'Supermonicall' language for the fellows 'who give themselves wholly to the invention of novelties, in games, buildings, garments, and governments'.[6] Hall's conservative approach to Paracelsian thought and innovation is not unusual for the period, but how different it is from the search for reform only a few decades later. Francis Bacon's *New Atlantis* and his attitude toward the universities has already been mentioned. Samuel Gott (1614–1671) discussed life in 'Nova Solyma' (1648).[7] Here he questioned the validity of the pursuance of knowledge for its own sake and suggested that the study of the chemistry of nature should be made not for personal fame, but for the glory of God.

Samuel Hartlib dedicated to Parliament his tract on the ideal kingdom of Macaria (1641). Here we read of a 'college of experience' where scholars develop medicines for the benefit of mankind. These men are so honoured that they are rewarded by the populace.[8] When it is suggested that this is contrary to traditional medical practice, the narrator points out the divine nature of medicine:

> In Macaria the parson of every parish is a good physician, and doth execute both functions; to wit, *cura animarum*, & *cura corporum*; and they think it as absurd for a divine to be without the skill of physick,

as it is to put new wine into old bottles; and the physicians, being true naturalists, may as well become good divines, as the divines do become good physicians.[9]

Hartlib was deeply convinced of the need of an experimental college and he was closely connected with the 'Invisible College' of London which began meeting in the mid-1640s. Furthermore, we find the young Robert Boyle (1627–1691) corresponding with Hartlib on the various utopian texts. In a letter dated 8 April 1647 Boyle specifically suggested that Campanella's *Civitas Solis* and Andreae's *Christianopolis* be translated for the benefit of English readers.[10]

It was Hartlib also who had turned to the great Czech educational reformer, John Amos Comenius (1592–1670), for aid. Comenius had prepared a great reform of learning, his encyclopedic 'pansophia', in which universal knowledge was to be gathered. He surely admired the work of Francis Bacon, but Bacon's work seemed deficient since his method aimed only at uncovering the secrets of nature.[11] Similarly the works of Jungius (1587–1657) were lauded, while

If any be uncertain if all things can be placed before the senses in this way, even things spiritual and things absent (things in heaven, or in hell, or beyond the sea), let him remember that all things have been harmoniously arranged by God in such a manner that the higher in the scale of existence can be represented by the lower, the absent by the present, and the invisible by the visible. This can be seen in the *Macromicrocosmus* of Robert Flutt, in which the origin of winds, of rain, and of thunder is described in such a way that the reader can visualize it. Nor is there any doubt that even greater concreteness and ease of demonstration than is here displayed might be attained.[12]

Yet, in preference to all other authorities, Comenius referred to Andreae 'who in his golden writings has laid bare the diseases not only of the Church and the state, but also of the Schools, and has pointed out the remedies . . .'.[13]

The views of Comenius bear a marked similarity to the works of the chemical philosophers mentioned earlier. The heretical works of the Aristotelians are to be discarded and instead the new philosophy is to turn to the two-book concept of knowledge.[14] The truth of the Mosaic account of the Creation is not questioned and the importance of the evidence of the senses in the study of nature is continually emphasized.[15] All this coupled with his plans for a universal reform made him a scholar of great interest to Hartlib who arranged for his visit to England in 1641.[16] His hopes for the establishment of a Baconian Universal College failed to materialize at a time when the government faced collapse. The outbreak of the Civil War in 1642 resulted in the departure of Comenius for Sweden.

Nevertheless, the departure of Comenius in no way diminished the call for reform. Rather, his brief stay in England would appear to have catalysed the reformers to greater efforts. In the decade from 1642 to 1652 one finds a host of tracts dedicated to the educational problem. Within their pages one senses an awareness of the need for a new science – and if it might be argued that some real changes were already underway at the universities, few of their authors indicated this. Most of them wrote of universities dominated by a rigid Aristotelianism unwilling to bend to the new views of nature. And yet, it seemed to them that they had good reason to write as they did. How could the new chemical philosophy or the mechanical philosophy be appreciated if the Sedleian lecturer of Natural Philosophy at Oxford was confined to discussing

> Aristotle's *Physics*, or the books concerning the heavens and the world, or concerning meteoric bodies, or the small Natural Phenomena of the same author, or the books which treat of the soul, and also those on generation and corruption.[17]

At Cambridge the lecturer in medicine was admonished to 'read Hippocrates and Galen' and he was not permitted officially to lecture on recent authors.[18] Medical students did not perform dissections themselves and the situation seemed so bleak that John Caius permitted his medical students to study abroad. Those that did so incorporated at Oxford or Cambridge on their return.[19] So prevalent was this procedure that in the period from 1559 to 1642 37% of the members of the Royal College of Physicians received their medical education abroad.[20]

The situation at the universities remained a galling thorn for the chemists. There seemed little reason for optimism in a system which adhered rigidly to the writings of the ancients and took no notice of the wondrous inventions of the moderns. In his *Art of Distillation* (1650), John French (1616–1657) spoke of alchemy 'which is more noble than all the other six Arts and Sciences . . .'.

This is that true natural philosophy which most accurately anatomizeth Nature and natural things, and ocularly demonstrates the principles and operations of them: that empty natural philosophy which is read in the universities, is scarce the meanest hand-maid to this Queen of Arts. It is a pity there is such great encouragement for many empty, and unprofitable Arts, and none for this; and such like ingenuities, which if promoted would render an University far more flourishing, than the former. I once read or heard, of a famous University beyond Sea, that was faln into decay, through what cause I know not: but there was a general counsel held by the learned, how to restore it to its primitive glory: The *Medium* at last agreed upon, was the promoting of Alchymie, and encouraging the Artists themselves: But I never expect to see such rational actings in this nation till shadows vanish, substances flourish, and truth prevail . . . .[21]

French may have almost given up hope for such rational behaviour in England, but not others. In an inflammatory work we find Noah Biggs (fl. *c.* 1650) – called a 'Psittacum Helmontii' by an opponent – demanding chemistry as the proper model science for students at the universities (1651),[22] while John Hall (1627–1656), addressing *An Humble Motion to the Parliament of England Concerning the Advancement of Learning: and Reformation of the Universities* (1649), asked: 'Where have we any thing to do with Chimistry, which hath snatcht the keyes of Nature from the other Sects of Philosophy, by her multiplied real experiences?'[23]

JOHN WEBSTER AND THE *Academiarum Examen*

These pleas for a reform of higher education came into direct conflict with the proponents of the mechanical philosophy. This may be seen in the debate between John Webster and Seth Ward in 1654. John Webster (1610–1682) represents the reforming chemists of the era, men who passionately sought a new science and a reformed educational system which would develop it. For them the works of Fludd, Helmont and the Paracelsians seemed to offer a Christian answer to the stale learning taught at the universities. Webster is a typical example of this school.[24] Attracted early to the study of both nature and religion, he had studied chemistry (*c.* 1632) under the Hungarian alchemist John Hunyades (1576–1650),[25] and had been ordained as a minister shortly afterwards. With his Puritan sympathies he had served both as surgeon

37

and chaplain with the Parliamentary army during the Civil War. By 1648 his reaction against the established Church had forced him to become a nonconformist, and in later years he supported himself as a 'practitioner in Physick and Chirurgery'. Although most of his writings are on religious topics, his important *Metallographia* (1671) and his *Displaying of Supposed Witchcraft* (1677) are of considerable interest to the intellectual historian and the historian of science.

It was Webster's concern with the educational training of the minister that inspired him to write both *The Saints Guide* and the *Academiarum Examen* in 1653. In *The Saints Guide* he decried the teaching of the schools that taught worldly wisdom through books and disputations. This was of no use in any true understanding of the Gospel truths. For this we need God's Spirit through the grace of the Holy Ghost.[26] Webster returned to the same subject a few months later in the *Academiarum Examen*. Again it was the problem of the training of the ministry that first attracted his attention. The insufficiency of the Universities was clear – surely the student should study God's own Creation rather than the books of ancient authors who knew nothing of God's revelation.

Webster's chemical approach is evident throughout his attack on the universities. In a typical Paracelsian fashion he attacked Aristotle as a heathen and argued that his work could not really be made the basis of Christian education. He went on to detail further failings in the university curricula in a method that clearly parallels Fludd's *Tractatus Apologeticus* of 1617. The emphasis of the universities on deductive logic was detestable – especially since van Helmont had pointed out glaring errors in the use of this subject and Bacon had rightly shifted the attention of scholars to inductive logic.[27] Similarly, Aristotelian physics was to be condemned because of its concentration on the study of moving bodies.

> Is there no further end nor consideration in Physicks but onely to search, discuss, understand, and dispute of a natural moveable body, with all the affections, accidents and circumstances thereto belonging?

If this is so, then *'our Philosophy is made Philologie, from which we teach to dispute, not to live'*.[28]

Little more could be said for the mathematical sciences, where Webster found the important work of John Napier (1550–1617),

Henry Briggs (1561–1630) and William Oughtred (1575–1660) ignored and geometry decayed to valueless verbal disputes. Music had become little more than the singing of songs and the playing of instruments while Ptolemaic astronomy was still taught even though the truth of the Copernian system was well known.[29] But above all, the Aristotelian approach emphasized mathematics in an incorrect fashion as the basic guide to truth in nature. This is no small error

> for though the Mathematics be exceedingly helpful to Natural *Philosophy*, yet is confusion of terms very hurtful; for if a mathematical point or superficies be urged in a Physicall argument it will conclude nothing, but only obfuscate, and disorder the intellect.[30]

We need a new science which is based less on logic and mathematical abstractions and more on reality determined through observations and experiments. Deductive logic might be safely discarded and we must develop inductive reasoning.[31] In mathematics we must advance beyond arithmetic and geometry to the harmonies which exist between the great and the small worlds. In astronomy the

> learning of *Copernicus, Ticho Brahe, Galilaeus, Ballialdus,* and such like, might be introduced, and the rotten and ruinous Fabrick of *Aristotle* and *Ptolomy* rejected and laid aside.[32]

Aristotle's observations on minerals might well be retained, but the whole of his natural philosophy and his astronomy – and the accumulated commentaries on them – must be eradicated.[33]

For Webster even the conventional study of grammar and language was of little value although recent developments gave hope of a breakthrough toward a universal or natural language.[34] The symbols of the chemists and the new mathematical notations indicated the possibility of such a written language which might be understood by all. But the emblems and hieroglyphics of the alchemists and the occult philosophers offered far more hope, and one could scarcely deny the existence of a natural language stamped by the Creator on his Creation through divine signatures and hidden virtues. In the celestial regions we must learn to read the signs of the stars while in man and in earthly substances we must also seek the hidden signs.

> Many do superficially and by way of Analogy . . . acknowledge the Macrocosm to be the great unsealed book of God, and every creature

39

as a Capital letter or character, and all put together make up that one
work or sentence of his immense wisdom, glory and power; but alas!
who spells them aright, or conjoyns them so together that they may
perfectly read all that is therein contained? Alas! we all study, and read
too much upon the dead paper idols and creaturely invented letters,
but do not, nor cannot read the legible characters that are onely written
and impressed by the finger of the Almighty. . . .[35]

Indeed, it was to the credit of Jacob Boehme (1575–1624) and the
Rosicrucians that they have sought to decipher this language of nature.[36]

Surely, Webster continued, the whole of scholastic philosophy and
teaching was grounded on little of value. If we are to emphasize the
ancients why should we specifically single out Aristotle? Other revered
authors of antiquity such as Cicero and Quintilian preferred the much
sounder works of Plato.[37] The history of the Aristotelian books after
the death of the philosopher might make one wonder just how many
of them had actually been written by him – they might all be
apocryphal.[38] Even Aristotle admitted – in his letters to Alexander –
that his style of writing was obscure and difficult to understand.[39] This
is borne out in the *Physics* where his position is not properly defined
and also in his confusion over the doctrine of the matter of the heavens.[40]
The great van Helmont found no fewer than thirteen errors in Aristotle's definition of nature.[41]

In our search for a replacement for Aristotle Webster suggested
that we might turn with profit to the philosophy of Plato as methodized
by Ficino and also to

> That of *Democritus*, cleared, and in some measure demonstrated, by
> *Renatus des Cartes*, *Regius*, *Phocylides*, *Holwarda*, and some others; That
> of *Epicurus*, illustrated by *Petrus Gassendus*; That of *Philolaus*, *Empedocles*,
> and *Parmenides*, resuscitated by *Telesius*, *Campanella*, and some besides;
> and that excellent *Magnetical Philosophy* found out by Doctor Gilbert;
> That of *Hermes*, revived by the *Paracelsian* School, may be brought into
> examination and practice, that whatsoever in any of them, or others of
> what sort soever, may be found agreeable to truth and demonstration,
> may be imbraced, and received . . . .[42]

Indeed, demonstrations, observations and experiments are

> the only certain means, and instruments to discover, and anatomize
> nature's occult and central operations; which are found out by laborious

tryals, manual operations, assiduous observations, and the like, and not by poring continually upon a few paper Idols, and unexperienced authors.[43]

The essential key must be chemistry which teaches the unfolding of nature's secrets through the use of manual operations. Helmont is noted for his statement that no philosopher is admitted to the root of science without a knowledge of the fire.[44] Surely one year of work in a chemical laboratory will prove more beneficial than centuries of disputes over the texts of Aristotle.[45]

Yet, for Webster this is simply the method and basis of natural magic 'whereby the wonderful works of the Creator are discovered, and innumerable benefits produced to the poor Creatures'.[46] The subject of magic is, as Giovanni Pico della Mirandola (1463–1494) noted, 'to marry the world . . . that thereby nature may act out her hidden and latent power'.[47] There is nothing diabolical about this subject. Rather, it is the proper sphere of the greatest philosophers and physicians.

It is quite evident, then, why Webster believed that, from among modern authors, the universities should turn to the writings of Francis Bacon and Robert Fludd in a search for the basis of a new philosophy.

On the surface we are entitled to call Webster a Baconian. We find Bacon quoted more frequently than any other modern author, and the *Academiarum Examen* is keynoted by a quotation from the *Novum Organum* on the title page.[48] Furthermore, in his dedication Webster exhorted Major-General John Lambert (1619–1683) to reform the universities for the 'advancement of learning',[49] while he offered four 'rules' in his rejection of ancient authority which clearly reflect the influence of Bacon's four 'Idols'.[50] But it was of more interest to Webster that Bacon had defined magic as that 'which leadeth cognition of occult forms into wonderful works, and by conjoyning actives to passives, doth manifest the grand secrets of nature'.[51] In addition, Bacon had shown the significance of induction and the importance of observation and experiment as the basis of a new science.

It cannot be expected that *Physical* Science will arrive at any wished perfection, unless the way and means, so judiciously laid down by our learned Countryman the Lord *Bacon*, be observed, and introduced into exact practice. And therefore I shall humbly desire, and earnestly presse, that his way and method may be imbraced, and set up for a rule

41

and pattern: that no *Axioms* may be received but what are evidently proved and made good by diligent observation, and luciferous experiments; that such may be recorded in a general history of natural things, that so every age and generation, proceeding in the same way, and upon the same principles, may dayly go on with the work, to the building up of a well-grounded and lasting Fabrick, which indeed is the only true way for the instauration and advance of learning and knowledge.[52]

Webster was a Baconian because Bacon sought to replace the Aristotelianism of the schools with an observational-experimental natural philosophy or natural magic.

Nor, for Webster, need this conflict with the work of Robert Fludd. His critique of traditional learning was closely modelled on Fludd's *Tractatus Apologeticus*, and he emphasized that as true Christians we must seek a knowledge of nature

that is grounded upon sensible, rational, experimental, and Scripture principles: and such a compleat piece in the most particulars of all human learning (though many vainly and falsely imagine there is no such perfect work to be found) is the elaborate writings of that profoundly learned man Dr. *Fludd*, than which for all the particulars before mentioned (notwithstanding the ignorance and envy of all opposers) the world never had a more rare, experimental and perfect piece.[53]

This is a theme which Webster returned to years later in his work on witchcraft when he spoke of the initial resistance to Harvey's doctrine of the circulation of the blood and compared this lack of appreciation with the reaction to the work of his colleague.

Our Countryman Dr. *Fludd*, a man acquainted with all kinds of learning and one of the most Christian Philosophers which ever writ, yet wanted not those snarling Animals, such as *Marsennius, Lanovius, Foster,* and *Gassendus,* as also our *Casaubon* (as mad as any) to accuse him vainly and falsely of Diabolical Magick, from which the strength of his own Pen and Arguments did discharge him without possibility of replies.[54]

John Webster emerges neither as an 'ancient' nor as a 'modern'. Instead, he represents the chemical philosophers of the mid-seventeenth century – scholars who properly belong in neither camp. Natural magic was to be the goal of their new philosophy and this was defined as the search for a true understanding of the secrets of nature through observation and experiment. The macrocosm-microcosm analogy was implicit in Webster's work and it is readily understandable how Robert Fludd could be one of his idols. Yet, it is equally understandable how he could point to Francis Bacon – the natural magician – as a guide. John Webster was later to write that the secret effects of nature were being brought to light by the

> continued discoveries of those learned and indefatigable persons that are of the Royal Society, which do plainly evince that hitherto we have been ignorant of almost all the true causes of things, and therefore through blindness have usually attributed those things to the operation of Cacodemons that were truely wrought by nature . . . .[55]

And yet this duality was not unique to Webster. How similar his statements are to those of his contemporary, Elias Ashmole (1617–1692), who sought the secrets of alchemy and astrology while welcoming the creation of the 'Baconian' Royal Society of London.[56]

THE *Vindiciae Academiarum* OF JOHN WILKINS AND SETH WARD

The *Academiarum Examen* brought an immediate reaction from the Oxford proponents of the new philosophy. This was a period when Oxford was rapidly becoming a centre for the new science. Here there were gathered Robert Boyle, Thomas Willis (1621–1765), Jonathan Goddard (1617–1675), and John Wallis (1616–1703). As a group they were to form the nucleus of the 'Philosophical Society of Oxford', and this, in turn, was a forerunner of the Royal Society of London. Among them were Seth Ward (1617–1689) and John Wilkins (1614–1672), both distinguished members of this community. Wilkins had been the Warden of Wadham College since 1648 and Ward had been the Savilian Professor of Astronomy since 1649. Wilkins was already widely known for his defence of the Copernican system (1640), for his *Discovery of a World in the Moone* (1638), and his popular *Mathematical Magick* (1648). Ward had as yet published little of his research. In 1653 he had written a treatise questioning the astronomical system of Ismael Bullialdus (1605–1694), and he was currently engaged in the preparation of his *Astronomia Geometrica*, a work which appeared in 1656 in which he defended the orbital system of Kepler.

43

For both Wilkins and Ward the recent publications on educational reform were a matter of concern and it was to these that they turned in their *Vindiciae Academiarum* (1654). In his *Leviathan* (1651), Thomas Hobbes (1588–1679) had sketched a picture of the universities that – Ward charged – conformed more to the turn of the century than to the true state of affairs.[57] Recent research tends to uphold Ward's statement. Curtis, pointing to the fact that the conservative statutes of Oxford and Cambridge were not rigidly enforced and also to the growth of the tutorial system which made possible the study of recent texts, has emphasized that the actual state of science was not as bleak as it has commonly been pictured.[58]

But if Hobbes had presented an inaccurate view of the universities, William Dell (d. 1664), the Master of Gonville and Caius College, Cambridge, had written an even more disturbing work. Dell had suggested that new universities should be established in the growing urban centres, and further, that young students should work part time so that they might learn a trade while they pursued their regular course of study.[59] Such a plan was far from acceptable to Seth Ward who stated that

> I am much assured, there is not a Learned man in all the world who hath not found by experience, that skill in any Faculty . . . is not to be attained, without a timely beginning, a constancy and assiduity in study, especially while they are young . . . .[60]

But if the writings of Hobbes and Dell were dangerous, there is no question that Wilkins and Ward considered the tract of John Webster to be the most alarming of them all. Wilkins, in his introduction to Ward's detailed reply, accused him not only of ignorance of the arts and sciences he hoped to advance, but also of an almost total lack of information of the current state of the universities.[61] Logic served as an excellent example of Webster's misunderstanding. Surely, Wilkins wrote, logic is essential for any sound reasoning. But Webster had complained that the theology of the universities had become a 'confused Chaos' through the application of 'strict *Logicall Method*'.[62] How could logical order possible result in chaos? For Wilkins the points made by Webster were plagiarized from Bacon and van Helmont and beyond his comprehension.[63] In addition, if he had visited the universities in recent years he would have seen that induction as well as syllogism was being taught.

44

Webster's views on the study of grammar and languages seemed even more dangerous. Seth Ward, noting Webster's plea for the study of hieroglyphic emblems and cryptographs, replied that these forms 'were invented for *concealment* of things' in contrast to grammar and languages which serve for their explanation.[64] The new mathematical symbolism of Vieta, Harriott, Oughtred and Descartes had been invented to avoid confusion over the understanding of words. This should not be confused with the emblems and symbols of the alchemists.[65]

The question of a true universal language was something quite different – it was a subject which both Wilkins and Ward had studied in detail. Ward was willing to agree that enough symbols might be found so that the result would be a universal language 'wherein all Natives might communicate together, just as they do in number and in species'.[66] Yet, although this is a possibility, in reality it would be necessary to have an almost infinite number of characters at one's command and because of this the scheme may be dismissed as impractical. Sarcastically Ward added that his arguments might be easier for Webster to understand if he presented them in an alchemical style. 'The Paradisicall Protoplast', he suggested

> being Characteristically bound to the Ideal Matrix of Magicall contrition, by the Symphoniacall inspeaking *Aleph tenebrosum*, and limited by *Shem hamphorash* to the centrall Idees, in-blowne by the ten numerations of *Belimah*, which are ten and not nine, ten and not eleaven; consequently being altogether absorpt in decyphering the signatures of Ensoph, beyond the sagacity of either a Peritrochiall, or an Isoperimetricall expansion. The lynges of the featiferous elocution, being disposed only to introversion, was destitute at that time of all Peristalticall effluxion, which silenced the Otacousticall tone of the outflying word, and suppressed it in singultient irructations. But where the formes are thus enveloped in a reluctancy to *Pamphoniacall* Symbols, and the *Phantasmaticall* effluviums checked by the tergiversation of the *Epiglottis*, from its due subserviency to that concord and harmony which ought to have been betwixt lapsed man and his fellow strings, each diatesseron being failed of its diapente necessary to make up a Diapason no perfect tone could follow. And consequently this Language of nature must needs be impossible.

Perhaps, Ward added, 'this demonstration may to some seeme somewhat obscure, but I am very sure that if Mr. *Webster* doth understand what he hath transcribed upon this subject it must have to him (to use his own phrase) an *evidentall perspicuity*.[67]

As Savilian Professor of Astronomy Ward had a special interest in John Webster's suggestions for the reform of the mathematical sciences. Ward admitted that like Webster he had often complained 'against the neglect of Mathematics in our method of study',[68] but nevertheless he was appalled by what he had read in the *Academiarum Examen*. To have suggested that the universities had ignored the work of Napier, Briggs and Oughtred was patently false. Oughtred had been a Fellow of King's College at Cambridge while Briggs had been Professor of Geometry at Gresham College.[69] Webster's assertion that arithmetic and geometry have been neglected certainly was not true, while the phenomena of optics were now being studied by competent scholars and at long last removed from the realm of magic.[70] Webster's plea for a more profound study of music as a key to the nature of universal harmonies was quite lost on Ward who commented that our instruments have 'been lately out of tune, and our harpes hanged up, but if such men as he should please to come among us, and put us to an examen, without doubt we should then have a fit of Mirth &c.'[71]

'But of all things', Ward continued, 'the *Astronomy* Schooles he is most offended at, as maintaining with Rigour the *Ptolemaick System*'. This is hardly the case, for in reality

> The Method here observed in our Schooles is, first to exhibit the *Phenomena*, and shew the way of their observation, then to give an account of the various Hypotheses, how those Phenomena have been salved . . . .[72]

While it is true that the Ptolemaic system ranks as one of the major systems which have 'salved the *Phenomena*' of planetary motion, the Copernican system is taught at Oxford 'as it was left by him, or as improved by *Kepler, Bullialdus*, our own Professor and others of the Elliptical way'.[73] Indeed, while the teaching of the mathematical sciences may not yet have reached perfection at Oxford, these subjects are taught – and taught well – by those who know their importance. How different this is from Webster's plea that music should be made a major key for the mathematical interpretation of the heavens, and that astrology should be considered a worthy goal for true mathematicians. The latter is a subject fit only for those educated in the 'Academy of *Bethlem*', and is based not upon observation and experiment, but the Aristotelian system which Webster professes to abhor.[74]

Ward saw very little new in Webster's attack on Aristotle. A comparison of the *Examination* with the work of Gassendi and van Helmont showed that he had closely followed these sources without satisfactorily citing them.[75] This man had charged that in the schools natural magic was prosecuted, that chemistry was neglected, that medicine had declined, that anatomy was sterile, that surgery was defective, and that the professors remained ignorant of celestial signatures, the three principles, and the magnetic and atomic philosophies.[76] But, Ward countered, if we have little respect for the magic of Agrippa, Porta and Wecker, it is because of their deceit rather than their use of the word 'magic'.

> The discoveries of the Symphonies of nature, and the rules of applying agent and materiall causes to produce effects is the true naturall Magic, and the generall humane ends of all Phylosophicall enquiries; but M. *Webster* knew not this . . . .[77]

As for his chemistry, it is not neglected at Oxford. Rather, there has been

> a conjunction of both the Purses and endeavours of severall persons towards discoveries of that kind, such as may serve either to the discovery of light or profit, either to Naturall Philosophy or Physick. But Mr. *Webster* expects we should tell him, that we have found the *Elixir.* (surely we are wiser then to say so) . . . .[78]

One need say little more. Medicine is now firmly based upon experiment and observation.[79] This has resulted in great new discoveries. Similarly the magnetic and atomic philosophies are not neglected.[80] Indeed, a whole school could be furnished with the scientific instruments which are used at Oxford.[81]

And what may be said of Webster's two main remedies for the reformation of learning? It is true that he has stated '*that my L. Bacons way may be embraced. That Axioms be evidently proved by observations, and no other be admitted &c.*'[82] Here Webster and Ward are in agreement as the latter admits.

> It cannot be denied but this is the way, and the only way to perfect Naturall Philosophy and Medicine; so that whosoever intend the one

or the other, are to take that course, and I have not neglected occasionally to tell the World, that this way is pursued amongst us.[83]

It might seem that Webster has cleared away the shades of the astrologers and the Rosicrucians and perhaps if he had stopped at this point he would have merited some praise. Unfortunately he did not. Rather, he followed directly with the statement

> That some Physicall Learning may be brought into the Schooles, that is grounded upon sensible, Rationall, Experimentall, and Scripture Principles, and such an Author is Dr. Fludd; then which for all the particulars, the World never had a more perfect piece.[84]

For Seth Ward this is too much.

> How little trust there is in villainous man! he that even now was for the way of strict and accurate induction, is fallen into the mysticall way of the Cabala, and numbers formall; there are not two waies in the whole World more opposite, then those of the L. Verulam and D. Fludd, the one founded upon experiment, the other upon mysticall Ideal reasons; even now he was for him, now he is for this, and all this in the twinkling of an eye, O the celerity of the change and motion of the Wind.[85]

Webster had suggested further that the works of Descartes should be studied by scholars at the universities. Yet, surely these must be empty words. Seth Ward was convinced that Webster had no greater understanding of Descartes than he had of Bacon.[86] And as for his plea that there should be a deeper examination of the philosophies of Plato, Democritus, Epicurus, Philolaus, Hermes and Gilbert, Ward could only reply that 'if De Fluctibus be so perfect, what need we go any farther?'[87]

Webster might best be dismissed as an impertinent pamphleteer.[88] To be sure, he called for a new philosophy, but he did not really understand the Authors he had recommended. Webster's evaluation of Bacon and Descartes was surely wrong, and even his condemnation of Aristotle seemed unjustified. And if Webster would make natural philosophy the basis of educational reform, his was a dream which could not be fulfilled. Ward pointed out that the nobility and the gentry sent their sons on to the Inns of Court while not one student in a hundred desired to proceed in natural philosophy.[89] For this very reason the universities can never be oriented in this direction.

THOMAS HALL's *Whip for Webster*

The exchange between John Webster on the one hand and Seth Ward and John Wilkins on the other clearly has unexpected overtones for the twentieth century observer. It was the 'occultist' Webster who called for observation and experiment as a basis for educational reform while those who defended the existing system were the 'moderns' – the 'mechanical philosophers'. Against this background it is illuminating to note that an unyielding Aristotelian, Thomas Hall (1610–1665), thought his views were closely in accord with those of Wilkins and Ward rather than John Webster.

Thomas Hall was an Oxford graduate (1629) and although at first he was a conformist, he later became a Presbyterian, a move which resulted in his ejection from his living after the passage of the Uniformity Act (1662). He was the author of many books and tracts, but the one of special interest to us is his *Vindiciae Literarum* (1654) to which is appended his *Histrio-Mastix. A Whip for Webster (as 'tis conceived) the Quondam Player* (1654).[90] From the title it seems obvious that Hall assumed that the author of the *Academiarum Examen* was none other than the Jacobean playwright of the same name.[91]

In his *Vindiciae Literarum* Thomas Hall spoke at length of the need for maintaining the established course of study for the training of ministers. Surely, he argued, Godly learning was not obtained from divine revelation alone. Was not Moses learned in the wisdom of the Egyptians? – and had not Solomon excelled the Egyptians in his knowledge of their secrets?[92] To be sure some fields could be improperly applied by their practitioners – no better example existed than those mathematicians who used their art to cast horoscopes[93] – but one need not condemn whole areas of knowledge because of the misdeeds of a few men.

Hall had barely completed his lengthy defence of the traditional educational system when he chanced upon a copy of the *Academiarum Examen* and the reply to it by Wilkins and Ward. Webster's denial of the value of 'humane learning' stirred him to anger, but the work of Wilkins and Ward seemed so complete that Hall was sorely tempted to give up his own defence of the established logic and philosophy.

49

Only after receiving a learned essay favouring Aristotelian logic did he decide to proceed.[94]

Writing in a state of emotional fury, Hall called Webster a 'Herculean-Leveller, . . . a dissembling Fryer . . . , a professed friend to Judicial Astrology and Astrologers, . . . [and] A great stickler for the fire and Furnace of Chymestry, for Magick and Physiognomy &c.'[95] Here is a man who speaks of the proper training of ministers and who should have defended the languages, the arts and the sciences. Surely he should have recognized that true philosophy and reason can only be an aid to religion.[96] As for the true philosophy there could be no question or argument from honest men. Aristotle was the 'Prince of Philosophers', not a blind pagan who wrote by diabolical instinct as Webster suggested.[97] But even if we were to discard these divine works of antiquity, with what should we replace them? Webster amazingly suggests magic,

> that noble, and almost divine science (as he cals it) of naturall Magick. This key (if you will believe him) will better unlock natures Cabinet, then syllogismes; yet he complaines, that this is neglected by the Schooles, yea hated and abhorred, and the very name seems nauseous and execrable to them.[98]

Further, Webster commends the study of judicial astrology even though in Scripture its practitioners 'are oft joyned with Witches, wizards, and Sorcerers . . .'.[99] Indeed, this ignorant man commends

> not only *Lilly* and *Booker*, but also Fryers *Bacon* [*sic mulus mulum*, it becomes one Fryer to claw another] and *Paracelsus*, a Libertine, a Drunkard, a man of little learning, and lesse Latine; he was not only skilled in naturall Magick, . . . but is charged also to converse constantly with Familiars, and to have the Devill for his Purse-bearer; yet this is one of Mr. *Websters* society.[100]

Hall complained further of Webster's praise of physiognomy and of his attack on professional physicians and more specifically on Galen, 'the Father of Physitians'.[101] No less detestable is his

> extolling of Chymistry, and preferring it before *Aristotelian Philosophy*, and advising schollars to leave their Libraries, and fall to Laboratories, putting their hands to the coales and Furnace . . . this is Mr. *Websters* short cut, a quick way to bring men to the Devill, or the Devill to them.[102]

In short, according to Hall, John Webster is 'against learning, against *Aristotle*, against Magistracie, against Ministrie, against Physitians, and against all that is truly good . . . .'.[103] And in place of Aristotle and true learning he would have us turn to mathematics, optics, geometry, geography, astrology, arithmetic, physiognomy, magic, pyrotechny, dactylogy, stenography, architecture, 'and to the soul ravishing study of Salt, Sulphure and Mercury [a medicine for a Horse]'.[104] He concludes with a blast at Giles Calvert who printed the *Academiarum Examen*[105] and then proceeds to append an anonymous defence of Aristotelian logic in which it is pointed out one more time that Webster and his fellow astrologers are enemies of the study of logic.[106]

The work of Hall clearly shows the approach of those who desired no change in the educational system. Aristotle, Galen, and indeed, all of the traditional authors were to be praised while no reform in the educational system could be looked on with favour. It is little wonder that Webster's plan to replace the ancients with a new curriculum based on natural magic, chemistry and astrology was anathema to him. Not only were these subjects useless, they were fundamentally diabolical in origin. Far more pleasing to this Aristotelian were the words of John Wilkins and Seth Ward in favour of the universities. These were men who seemed to be allies in this struggle against a new philosophy based on observation and experiment – scholars who would aid in this great crusade to save the Universities for 'humane learning'.

REFERENCES

1. Sir Christopher Heydon, *An Astrological Discourse, Manifestly proving The Powerful Influence of Planets and Fixed Stars upon Elementary Bodies, In Justification of the verity of Astrology, Together with an Astrological Judgement Upon the great Conjunction of Saturn and Jupiter 1603* (London: John Macock, for Nathaniel Brooke, 1650). See the note by William Lilly and the prefatory 'To the Reader' by Nicholas Fisk.

2. George Hakewill, *An Apologie or Declaration of the Power and Providence of God in the Government of the World* (3rd ed., Oxford: William Turner, 1635), p. 276.

3. van Helmont, *Oriatrike*, p. 526; *Opera Omnia*, p. 500. On the proposed English society of chemical physicians see the works by Thomas, Rattansi and Webster referred to in the introduction, note 2.

4. George Starkey, *Natures Explication and Helmont's Vindication* (London,

1651); see the 'Epistle Dedicatory'. On Tonstall's challenge, see Robert Wittie's remarks in his *Scarborough Spagirical Anatomiser dissected* (1672). This work is abstracted in Thomas Short, M.D., *The Natural, Experimental, and Medicinal History of the Mineral Waters of Derbyshire, Lincolnshire, and Yorkshire* (London, 1734), pp. 143–8. Wittie himself was similarly challenged. See F. N. L. Poynter, 'A Seventeenth-Century Medical Controversy: Robert Wittie versus William Simpson', *Science, Medicine and History. Essays on the Evolution of Scientific Thought and Medical Practice written in honour of Charles Singer* (2 vols., London/ New York/Toronto: Oxford U.P., 1953), **2**, pp. 72–81.

5. Joseph Hall's *Mundus Alter et Idem* (*c.* 1605) has recently been discussed by Nell Eurich in her *Science in Utopia. A Mighty Design* (Cambridge, Mass.: Harvard U.P., 1967), pp. 82–3.

6. Joseph Hall, *The Discovery of a New World* (*Mundus Alter et Idem*) *c. 1605*, ed. by Huntington Brown with a foreword by Richard E. Byrd (Cambridge, Mass.: Harvard U.P., 1937), p. 87.

7. See Eurich, *Science in Utopia*, pp. 83–6 and (Samuel Gott), *Nova Solyma The Ideal City: or Jerusalem Regained. An anonymous romance written in the time of Charles I. Now first drawn from obscurity, and attributed to the illustrious John Milton*, introduction, translation, essays and a bibliography by the Rev. Walter Bayley (2 vols., London: John Murray, 1900). It should be noted that this translation is not entirely complete.

8. Samuel Hartlib, *A Description of the Famous Kingdom of Macaria: shewing the excellent Government, wherein the Inhabitants live in great Prosperity, Health, and Happiness; the King obeyed, the Nobles honoured, and all good men respected; Vice punished, and Virtue rewarded. An Example to other Nations: In a Dialogue between a Scholar and a Traveller printed 1641* in *The Harleian Miscellany: A Collection of Scarce, Curious, and Entertaining Pamphlets and Tracts, as well in Manuscript as in Print. Selected from the Library of Edward Harley, Second Earl of Oxford* (vol. **1**, London: John White, John Murray and John Harding, 1808), pp. 580–5 (582).

9. *Ibid.*

10. Thomas Birch, *The Life of the honourable Robert Boyle* in Robert Boyle, *The Works of the Honourable Robert Boyle* (5 vols., London: A. Millar, 1744), **1**, pp. 22–3.

11. John Amos Comenius, *A Reformation of Schooles . . .* , trans. Samuel Hartlib (London: Michael Sparke, 1642), p. 35.

12. John Amos Comenius, *The Great Didactic*, translated and with an introduction by M. W. Keatinge (London: Adam and Charles Black, 1896), p. 339.

13. *Ibid.*, p. 159.

14. *Ibid.*, p. 26. Keatinge emphasizes the influence of Bacon and Campanella

on Comenius, while August Nebe prepared a monograph on *Vives, Alsted, Comenius in ihrem Verhältnis zu einande* (Elberfeld, 1891). There is little doubt that Comenius was well read in the literature on educational reform and the utopian tracts of the sixteenth and early seventeenth centuries.

15. Comenius, *Great Didactic*, pp. 27, 337.

16. Eurich, *Science in Utopia*, p. 148.

17. Phyllis Allen, 'Scientific Studies', 227.

18. Phyllis Allen, 'Medical Education in 17th Century England', 119.

19. Mark H. Curtis, *Oxford and Cambridge in Transition*, p. 154.

20. *Ibid.*

21. John French, *The Art of Distillation* (4th ed., London: T. Williams, 1667), sig. A3 recto. From the dedication to Tobias Garband dated London, Nov. 25, 1650.

22. Noah Biggs, Chymiatrophilos, *Mataeotechnia Medicinae Praxews. The Vanity of the Craft of Physicke. . . . With an humble Motion for the Reformation of the Universities, And the whole Landscape of Physick, and discovering the Terra Incognita of Chymistrie* (London, 1651), sig. b1 recto. Biggs was attacked by William Johnson in his preface to Leonard Phioravant's *Three Exact Pieces* (London, 1652), p. 1.

23. J(ohn) H(all), *An Humble Motion To the PARLIAMENT of ENGLAND Concerning The ADVANCEMENT of Learning and Reformation of the Universities* (London: John Walker, 1649), p. 27.

24. See the article on John Webster by Bertha Potter in the Dictionary of National Biography.

25. The work of Hunyades has been discussed by F. Sherwood Taylor and C. H. Josten in 'Johannes Banfi Hunyades 1576–1650', *Ambix*, 5 (1953), 44–52, and 'Johannes Banfi Hunyades. A Supplementary Note', Ambix, 5 (1956), 115. Here (p. 52) it is suggested that Hunyades arrived in London sometime between 1623 and 1633.

26. John Webster, *The Saints Guide, or Christ the Rule and Ruler of Saints. Manifested by way of Positions, Consectaries, and Queries . . .* (London: Giles Calvert, 1654), pp. 1–2. Regarding the mid-century dispute over educational reform; R. F. Jones has written in his 'The Humanistic Defence of Learning in the Mid-Seventeenth Century' that 'the central issue, though frequently lost sight of, was the employment of learning and reason in the preparation of a preacher and interpretation of the Gospel' [in *Reason and the Imagination: Studies in the History of Ideas, 1600–1800*; ed. J. A. Mazzeo (New York: Columbia U.P./London: Routledge and Kegan Paul, 1962), pp. 71–92 (73)].

27. *Academiarum Examen*, pp. 32–40.

28. *Ibid.*, p. 18.

29. *Ibid.*, pp. 40–9.
30. *Ibid.*, p. 68.
31. *Ibid.*, p. 102.
32. *Ibid.*, p. 103.
33. *Ibid.*, p. 104.
34. *Ibid.*, pp. 18–32.
35. *Ibid.*, p. 28.
36. *Ibid.*, p. 26.
37. *Ibid.*, pp. 56–57.
38. *Ibid.*, pp. 60–2.
39. *Ibid.*, p. 63.
40. *Ibid.*, pp. 64–5.
41. *Ibid.*, p. 65.
42. *Ibid.*, p. 106.
43. *Ibid.*, p. 68.
44. *Ibid.*, p. 71.
45. *Ibid.*
46. *Ibid.*, p. 69.
47. *Ibid.*, p. 70.
48. This is the attack on the universities cited above in chapter 2, footnote 26.
49. *Academiarum Examen*, sig. A2 verso.
50. Webster, *Displaying of Supposed Witchcraft*, pp. 13–17.
51. *Academiarum Examen*, p. 69. Here Webster is quoting Bacon's discussion of magic in the *De Augmentis Scientiarum* (Book 3, chapter 5).
52. *Academiarum Examen*, p. 105.
53. *Ibid.*
54. Webster, *Displaying of Supposed Witchcraft*, p. 9.
55. *Ibid.*, p. 268.
56. For an appreciation of Ashmole's place in seventeenth century science see the present author's introduction to Elias Ashmole's *Theatrum Chemicum Britannicum* (New York/London: Johnson Reprint Corp., The Sources of Science, No. 39, 1967), pp. ix–xlix.
57. Ward, *Vindiciae Academiarum*, pp. 58–9.
58. Curtis, *Oxford and Cambridge in Transition*, pp. 227–60.
59. Ward, *Vindiciae Academiarum*, pp. 64–5.
60. *Ibid.*
61. *Ibid.*, p. 1.
62. *Ibid.*, p. 5.
63. *Ibid.*, pp. 5, 23.
64. *Ibid.*, p. 18.
65. *Ibid.*, p. 19.
66. *Ibid.*, p. 21.

67. *Ibid.*, pp. 22–3.
68. *Ibid.*, p. 27.
69. *Ibid.*, p. 28.
70. *Ibid.*, pp. 28–9.
71. *Ibid.*, p. 29.
72. *Ibid.*, p. 30.
73. *Ibid.*, p. 29.
74. *Ibid.*, p. 31.
75. *Ibid.*, pp. 32–3.
76. *Ibid.*, p. 34.
77. *Ibid.*
78. *Ibid.*, p. 35.
79. *Ibid.*
80. *Ibid.*, p. 36.
81. *Ibid.*
82. *Ibid.*, p. 46.
83. *Ibid.*, p. 49.
84. *Ibid.*, p. 46.
85. *Ibid.*
86. *Ibid.*
87. *Ibid.*
88. *Ibid.*, p. 49.
89. *Ibid.*, p. 50.
90. See the short biography of Hall by Alexander Gordon in the *Dictionary of National Biography*. Gordon lists eighteen works by Hall printed between 1651–1661. Although John Wilkins signed the preface 'N.S.' and Seth Ward signed the main text 'H.D.', Thomas Hall correctly identified the authors of the *Vindiciae Academiarum* in his 'To the Reader' which is dated September 4, 1654. Hall, *Histrio-Mastix. A Whip for Webster* . . . , sign o2 verso.
91. *Ibid.*, title page (sig. o1 recto). This is also made clear in the anonymous work against Webster's logic appended to Hall's *Histrio-Mastix*. 'This Mr. *Webster* (as I suppose) is that Poet, whose Glory was once to be the Author of Stage-plaies.' *Ibid.*, p. 217.
92. Hall, *Vindiciae Literarum*, p. 11.
93. *Ibid.*, p. 53.
94. Hall, *Histrio-Mastix. A Whip for Webster*, sig. o2 verso.
95. *Ibid.*, p. 198.
96. *Ibid.*, pp. 199 ff.
97. Hall, *Histrio-Mastix. A Whip for Webster*, pp. 203–4.
98. *Ibid.*, p. 204.
99. *Ibid.*, p. 205.

100. *Ibid.*, p. 209. I am indebted to Dr. P. M. Rattansi for pointing out to me that this passage is quoted by Hall – without identification – from Thomas Fuller's short and uncomplimentary life of Paracelsus in *The Holy State* (2nd ed., Cambridge: John Williams, 1648), p. 53. This work appeared first in 1642.

101. Hall, *Histrio-Mastix. A Whip for Webster*, pp. 209–10.

102. *Ibid.*

103. *Ibid.*, p. 214.

104. *Ibid.*

105. *Ibid.*, p. 215. Calvert was known for publishing texts of this sort. See above chapter 3, note 20.

106. *Ibid.*, p. 238, in the *Examen Examinis. An Examination of Mr. Websters Illogicall Logick, and Reasoning even against Reason* (pp. 217–39).

Chapter Five

Conclusion

IT WOULD be erroneous to think that the tracts of Webster, Hall and Wilkins and Ward represent the total spectrum of thought on educational reform published in mid-seventeenth century England. They are only three of many works published at that time touching on a multitude of educational problems.[1] Furthermore, these three works failed to generate a great number of replies, a fact which helps to explain their rarity today. Nevertheless, they are of considerable importance to us for our understanding of the main currents affecting the growth of science in the crucial middle decades of the seventeenth century. As we have seen, the attitudes of these authors are rooted in the educational legacy they inherited from earlier centuries. In the seventeenth century many universities continued to maintain a hard line in upholding the authority of the ancients as the basis for instruction. Thomas Hall's work is an inelegant, but satisfactory example of this approach. It is no less true that the medieval tradition of self-criticism continued to exist within the Aristotelian-Galenic tradition. For some this tradition made the existing university framework a suitable place for reform. While there is no question that John Wilkins and Seth Ward may be classed as 'mechanical philosophers', it is interesting here to see them defending Aristotle, the value of logic and the importance of the universities as centres for the propagation of the new philosophy.[2] In opposition to these views one finds in the works of the sixteenth and seventeenth century nature philosophers an ever increasing feeling of despair. These men authored an ever growing number of tracts suggesting that the existing institutions must either be thoroughly renovated so that the new science might be taught properly or that new institutions or academies must be founded for this purpose. Clearly Paracelsus and the chemical

57

philosophers (and here we can include John Webster) belong to this tradition.

When reading the *Academiarum Examen*, the *Vindiciae Academiarum*, and the *Whip for Webster*, the twentieth century reader may well tend to sympathize with the views of Seth Ward and John Wilkins. They were correct in respect to the future development of science no less than they were in their insistence that there had already been a change in the teaching of the sciences at Oxford. The *Vindiciae Academiarum* reads like a learned and righteous blast against an inept occultist. It is clear that they stand on our side of the scientific watershed of the seventeenth century.

Yet, it would be ahistorical to condemn Webster on these grounds alone. He, like Wilkins and Ward, called for a new science that was to be based on induction from new observations and experiments. And for Webster as well as the members of the Oxford group Francis Bacon was a worthy prophet of the new philosophy.

It is clear that both the Helmontian chemical philosophers and the Oxford scientists sought a new approach to nature. And if we must speak of a 'revolution' in science, then surely in some respects the more revolutionary of the two were the chemical philosophers. It was not Webster, but Ward who became the defender of Aristotle. Thomas Hall, in his defence of traditional education, thought that Wilkins and Ward basically supported his point of view. Certainly Ward had stated that Aristotle's books were 'the best of any Philosophick writings', and he surely deserved 'the honours that ought to be given to one of the greatest wits, and most useful that ever the world enjoyed'.[3]

Webster, like other contemporary chemists, was so convinced of the sole necessity of the observational technique that for him a mathematical investigation of natural phenomena could only be related to traditional geometry and syllogistic logic – in short, to the basis of the Aristotelian philosophy. Scientific salvation might best be found in the non-mathematical and thoroughly observational laboratory techniques of the chemists. And surely, for Webster, this was how Bacon's method might most fruitfully be put into practice. Here was a man who spoke of the renovation of the sciences through induction, but who, like the chemists, appeared to have grave reservations about the validity of a purely mathematical interpretation of nature based on the study of motion.[4] On this point Webster seemed to hit so close to the mark that Ward was forced to admit that 'it was a misfortune to the world, that my Lord *Bacon* was not skilled in Mathematicks, which made him jealous of their Assistance in Naturall Enquiries . . .'.[5]

Yet, it was less Webster's interpretation of Bacon as a natural magician than it was his addiction to Rosicrucian and Hermetic mysteries that shows the deep cleavage between these opponents. For Webster the investigation of nature was to be a deeply religious experience whereby man learned of his Creator. This was the true natural magic that was best exemplified in the goals of the Rosicrucians and the 'experimental' writings of Robert Fludd. The mystical symbolism of the alchemists and the Kabbalists were for Webster a road to truth that could not be denied. He believed – as did most Paracelsians – that the truth of the macrocosm-microcosm analogy is self-evident and that it is a fundamental guide to the study of nature. For the mechanist, Seth Ward, such an image was unnecessary and fallacious.

Both Webster and Ward spoke of observation and experiment as an essential basis for the new science, but the former insisted that the greatest scholars must proceed beyond these data to more significant cosmic relationships. This difference between the two is clearly seen in their views on the then recent discovery of the circulation of the blood. In his discussion of recent advances in anatomy Webster wrote that this field 'seems to be growing, and arising towards a *Zenith* of perfection; especially since our never-sufficiently honoured Countryman Doctor *Harvey* discovered that wonderful secret of the Bloods circulary motion'. Yet, this is but vulgar anatomy and it has contributed little to the curing of disease. Above all, this type of study is

> defective as to that vive and *Mystical Anatomy* that discovers the true *Schematism* of that invisible *Archeus* or *spiritus mechanicus*, that is the true opifex, and dispositor of all the salutary, and morbifick lineaments, both in the seminal *guttula*, the tender *Embrio*, and the formed Creature, of which *Paracelsus*, *Helmont*, and our learned Countryman Dr. *Fludd*, have written most excellently.[6]

In short, Harvey's work is splendid and justly renowned, but here, too, Robert Fludd's works represent a sounder foundation for a new Christian interpretation of the universe. His mystical anatomy of the blood gives us a far more profound understanding of the subject than the more superficial anatomical work of Harvey.

Ward's reaction to this is predictable. The new experimental basis of medicine, he wrote, has surely resulted in the discovery of important anatomical and physiological observations – especially the circulation of the blood. But these discoveries are affecting medical practice and it is for this reason that the Royal College of Physicians of London 'is the glory of this Nation, and indeed of Europe, for their Learning and felicity, in the cures of desperate Ulcers and diseases, even of the Cancer . . .'.[7] But Webster prefers the mystical anatomy of Paracelsus and Fludd, and

> As for his *Postulatum* of discovering the signatures of the Invisible *Archeus* by Anatomy, it is one of his *Rosycrucian Rodomantados*; would he have us by dissection surprize the *anima mundi*, & shew him the impressions of a thing invisible? Yet the Schematismes of nature in matters of sensible bulk, have been observed amongst us, and collections made of them in our inquiries, and when the microscope shall be brought to the highest (whether it is apace arriving) we shall be able either to give the seminall figures of things, which regulates them in their production and growth, or evince them to lye in quantities insensible, and so to be in truth invisible.[8]

It seems obvious that for Webster observation and experiment should lead us to cosmic truths. But these truths Seth Ward rejects as the groundless dreams of mystics – men who pose the greatest threat to the birth of a new philosophy of nature.

I began by referring to the seemingly inconsistent accounts of the Webster-Ward debate given by Jones, Allen and Curtis. The apparent problem is really one which may be resolved through paying greater attention to contemporary intellectual currents and definitions. Surely Jones was right to call Webster a Baconian. He was wrong, however, in assuming that Webster, Ward and Wilkins all interpreted Bacon in the same fashion. Allen was correct in stating that Webster eulogized magic and chemistry. But she failed – in a fashion similar to Thomas Hall – to recognize that the natural magic referred to by Webster was meant to be that of Francis Bacon – surely not the superstition she called it. Similarly she misinterpreted Webster's 'chemistry' which was the chemistry of the macrocosm and the microcosm rather than the science we know. And finally, Mark Curtis's dismissal of Webster as an 'ignorant critic' is correct only if we insist on judging the texts of the seventeenth century on the basis of the truths of the twentieth century.

A more careful reading of these works in the context of the period shows that they simply cannot be forced into the familiar 'Ancient-Modern' pattern. Perhaps Thomas Hall may be called an 'Ancient', but no simple labels will suffice for the others. John Webster, Seth Ward, and John Wilkins all rejected rigid adherence to traditional scholasticism and they agreed on the need for a new science based on observation and experiment. Bacon was the hero of Ward and Wilkins no less than John Webster. In a sense then all three might be called 'moderns'. Yet their views were far from compatible when it came to problems connected with the acceptance or the rejection of the mystical Hermetic philosophy of nature. If they all eulogized Bacon, they surely found no such common ground in the writings of Robert Fludd!

The conflict between these opponents is not unimportant. The issues which they debated are points which – on a larger scale – reflect a fundamental conflict which we must understand if we are to properly interpret the course of the Scientific Revolution. Here we see in microcosm the indecisive nature of the period. We may perhaps be permitted to dismiss Thomas Hall's intemperate Aristotelianism rather curtly – as Robert Boyle dismissed the Aristotelians in the *Sceptical Chymist* (1661) because of their limited experimental knowledge and their tendency to utilize 'Experiments rather to illustrate than to demonstrate their Doctrines'.[9] We cannot allow ourselves the same privilege with Webster, Ward and Wilkins. The attack of the latter two on Webster may sound convincing to us, but how convincing was it in 1654? Only a few years earlier Comenius had commented on the indecisive nature of scientific evidence:

> . . . the common fate of all learning is this, that whosoever delivers it, others will take the pains to demolish it, or at least to lay it bare. *Plato's* philosophy seemed most elegant, and divine: but the Peripateticks accused it of too much vaine speculation. And *Aristotle* thought his *Philosophy* compleat, and trimme enough: but Christian Philosophers have found it neither agreeing with the holy Scriptures, nor answerable enough to the Truth of things. Astronomers for many ages carried away the bell with their Spheres, Eccentricks, and Epicycles, but *Copernicus* explodes them all. *Copernicus* himselfe framed a new and plausible Astronomy out of his Optick grounds, but such as will no way be admitted by the unmovable principle of naturall Truth. *Gilbertus* being carried away with the speculation of the Loadstone,

61

would out of it have deduced all Philosophy: but to the manifest injury of natural principles. *Campanella* triumphs almost in the principles of the ancient Philosopher *Parmenides*, which he had reassumed to himselfe in his naturall Philosophy, but is quite confounded by one Optick glasse of *Galilaeus Galilei*. And why should we reckon any more?[10]

Indeed, why? There was no certainty yet seen by Samuel Hartlib as he translated these words of Comenius in 1642 – and there was still no certainty twenty years later. By 1665 the Paracelso-Helmontians – shocked by what they considered the unyielding conservatism of the Royal College of Physicians – applied to the King in Council for founding a new medical college of chemical physicians. Writing in that year Marchamont Nedham (1620–1678) complained of the entrenched physicians who had stayed the advance of medicine through their refusal to permit the study of chemistry. The chemists therefore might not have fine degrees and titles, but this was not their fault. '. . . *it is not a Gown, or Degrees taken in Universities, which constitute the Physician, but a solid Knowledge of Nature, grounded upon sound Reason, and mature Judgement, improved by Practise and Experience.*'[11] Again we find the chemists to be the ones who asserted that their work was grounded on true observations and experiments. They proved their point at a fearful cost by their willingness to remain in London to treat the sick during the Plague year. Indeed it is little wonder that when Henry Stubbe (1632–1676) rose in defence of antiquity in 1670 he attacked the Helmontians and the members of the Royal Society together.[12]

Henry Stubbe's inability to distinguish between the chemical philosophers and the mechanical philosophers in 1670 is perhaps no less disturbing to the twentieth century mind than Thomas Hall's belief that John Wilkins and Seth Ward upheld his point of view in 1654. However, both cases point to the inherent difficulty in judging the views of sixteenth and seventeenth century authors in overly simplistic terms. Before the general acceptance of the Newtonian system there was little certainty to rely on – there were simply rival systems as Comenius had aptly stated. There was still room in the third quarter of the seventeenth century for serious disagreement over the choice of the new science which nearly all agreed must supersede the Peripatetic philosophy of the past.[13] As we read the texts of the debate of 1654 perhaps the most important point to be gained is that we should devote less attention in the future to the study of the wide-spread disenchantment with Scholastic philosophy than the more significant debate between the 'experimental' Paracelsian Hermeticists and the 'experimental' mechanical philosophers. When this has been done a new dimension will have been added to our view of the rise of modern science.

REFERENCES

1. The controversy is discussed in breadth – without a special emphasis on science – in James Bass Mullinger, M.A., *The University of Cambridge* (vol. **3**, Cambridge: University Press, 1911), pp. 426–83. Here the Webster-Ward-Hall exchange is treated on pages 457–70. In addition to Mullinger's references the reader will wish to consult Falconer Madan's *Oxford Books. A Bibliography of Printed Works Relating to the University and City of Oxford or Printed or Published There* (3 vols., the first titled *Early Oxford Press '1648 to 1640'*, 1895, 1912, 1931). Madan lists his references chronologically. The works relating to educational reform printed in 1653 and 1654 will be found in volume **3**, pp. 23–4, 37. Although Webster's work was not discussed widely in contemporary books, the *Academiarum Examen* was not totally ignored. An example may be found in Edward Leigh's *A Treatise of Religion and Learning, and of Religious and Learned Men* . . . (London: A. M. for Charles Adams, 1656), p. 33, where the author attacked Webster for his views on languages. Similarly, Anthony à Wood was well aware of the conflict at the time. Referring to nine tracts written since 1653, he noted in his diary (December, 1659) that 'some there were that endeavoured to make a reformation of the Universities not as to manners, but discipline; not as to a settlement and well-ordering of their lands, but to the taking of them away . . .' Andrew Clark, M.A., *The Life and Times of Anthony Wood, Antiquary, of Oxford, 1632–1695* . . . (2 vols., Oxford: Clarendon Press, 1891, 1892), **I**, p. 294. First on Wood's list was Webster's *Academiarum Examen*. It is worth noting that a paper on the general problem of science and educational reform during the Puritan Revolution is to be presented by Charles Webster to the conference on curriculum reform which is to be held in London in December, 1969.
2. It is interesting to note Bacon being quoted by some in defence of the educational system. See George Williamson, 'Richard Whitlock, Learning's Apologist (1936)', in *Seventeenth Century Contexts* (London: Faber and Faber, 1960) pp. 178–201.
3. Ward, *Vindiciae Academiarum*, p. 46.

4. On this subject see Debus, 'Mathematics and Nature in the Chemical Texts of the Renaissance', *Ambix*, **15** (1968), 1–28.

5. Ward, *Vindiciae Academiarum*, p. 25.

6. Webster, *Academiarum Examen*, p. 74.

7. Ward, *Vindiciae Academiarum*, p. 35.

8. *Ibid.*

9. Robert Boyle, *The Sceptical Chymist or Chymico-Physical Doubts and Paradoxes, Touching the Spagyrists' Principles Commonly call'd Hypostatical: As they are wont to be Propos'd and Defended by the Generality of Alchymists. Whereunto is Premis'd Part of Another Discourse relating to the same Subject* (London: J. Cadwell for J. Crooke, 1661: Dawson reprint, London, 1965, sig. A 5 recto, p. 20.

10. Comenius, *Reformation of Schooles*, p. 16.

11. Marchamont Nedham, *Medela Medicinae. A Plea For the Free Profession and a Renovation of the Art of Physick Out of the Noblest and most Authentick Writers* (London: Richard Lownds, 1665), p. 253. Here Nedham was quoting the King's Chemist, Nicholas Lefévre in his *Compleat Body of Chimistry* (London, 1664), p. 108.

12. Rattansi, 'The Helmontian-Galenist Controversy', pp. 21–2.

13. The point is made clear also in a letter to Margaret, Duchess of Newcastle, from Joseph Glanvill dated 13 October 1667. Here he states that

> . . . we have yet no certain Theory of Nature: And in good earnest, Madam, all that we can hope for, as yet, is but the History of things as they are, but to say how they are, to raise general *Axioms*, and to make *Hypotheses*, must, I think, be the happy priviledge of succeeding Ages, when they shall have gained a larger account of the *Phoenomena*, which yet are too scant and defective to raise theories upon: so that to be ingenious and confer freely, we have yet no such thing as Natural Philosophy; Natural History is all we can pretend to; and that too, as yet, is but in its Rudiments, the advance of it your *Grace* knows is the design and business of the *Royal Society;* from whom we may reasonably at last expect better grounds for general Doctrines, than any the World hath been acquainted with; but this, Madam, is an excursion.

Letters and Poems In Honour of the Incomparable Princess, Margaret, Dutchess of Newcastle (London: Thomas Newcombe, 1676), pp. 123–7.

Acknowledgements

THE research for this essay was completed during the tenure of a Guggenheim fellowship in 1966–1967 and with a research grant from the National Institutes of Health (LM 00046). The present manuscript has benefited greatly from the careful reading and many suggestions of Dr. M A. Hoskin and Dr. P. M. Rattansi. The author also wishes to express his gratitude to the Master and the Fellows of Churchill College for their interest in and encouragement of his research during the academic year 1966–1967 and again in the Summer months of 1969 when he was in residence there as an Overseas Fellow. The present essay incorporates material from a lecture titled 'The Chemical Dream of the Renaissance' given at Churchill College, Cambridge on June 2, 1967. It also draws on a paper titled 'The New Philosophy and the Problem of Educational Reform' presented at Brussels on October 22, 1968, before an International Colloquium on 'L'Univers à la Renaissance: Microcosme et Macrocosme'.

A.G.D.

The co-operation of the British Museum in the reproduction of the three tracts is gratefully acknowledged.

Academiarum Examen,   14

OR THE

EXAMINATION

OF

ACADEMIES.

Wherein is difcuffed and examined the
Matter, Method and Cuftomes of Academick
and Scholaftick Learning, and the infufficiency thereof difcovered and laid open;

As alfo fome *Expedients propofed for the*
Reforming of Schools, and the perfecting
and promoting of all kind of Science.

Offered to the judgements of all thofe that love the
proficiencie of Arts and Sciences, and the advancement of LEARNING.

By *Jo. Webster.*

---

*In moribus et inftitutis Academiarum, Collegiorum, et fimilium con-
ventuum, qua ad doctorum hominum fedes, & operas mutuas deftinata
funt, omnia progreffui fcientiarum in ulterius adverfa inveniri.* Franc.
Bacon.de Verulamio lib. de cogitat. & vif. pag. mihi 14.

LONDON, Detomb 19: 1653

Printed for *Giles Calvert*, and are to be fold at the fign of
the *Black-fpread-Eagle* at the Weft-end of *Pauls*, MDCLIV.

To the Right Honourable Major General
LAMBERT.

I Prefent not thefe rude lines, thereby to beg protection; for if they be not able to ftand of themfelves, I defire they fhould not be fupported by others; but onely becaufe fome years agoe a fhort draught of them was brought to your hands, and your Honour was then pleafed to judge it worthy of your view and confideration, which makes me bold to mind you of what then I intimated unto you, which was and is thus much, That feeing divine Providence hath made you (with the reft of thofe faithfull and gallant men of the Army) fignally inftrumental, both in redeeming the Englifh Liberty, almoft drowned in the deluge of Tyranny and felf intereft, and alfo unmanacling the fimple and pure truth of the Gofpel, from the chains and fetters of cold and dead Formality, and of reftrictive and compulfary Power, two of the greateft bleffings our Nation ever yet enjoyed, I hope the fame Providence will alfo direct you to be affiftant to continue the fame, againft all the bitternefs and cruelty of thofe, who, having obtained liberty for themfelves, care not though others be bound up and perfecuted, And moreover guide

A 2 you

69

you to set to your hand and endeavour for the pur-
ging and reforming of Academies, and the ad-
vancement of Learning, *which hitherto hath*
been little promoted or look'd into. And I am
the more imboldned in this confidence, having ex-
perimental knowledge and trial, not onely of your
Honours Abilities that way, but also of your sin-
cere affection and unparalleld love to Learning,
and to all those that are lovers and promoters ther-
of; which have been the principal motives to
incite me to tender this rude Essay, and these few
unpolish'd lines to your profound and mature
judgement, which, besides the good will of the Au-
thor, have little in them worthy your deliberate
consideration : Yet I suppose, if rightly weighed
and examined, there will appear something in them
of necessary consequence for the promoting of Lear-
ning, or at least to stir up some more able wits to
make a scrutiny into these things that are here
controverted, which is the greatest aim of my flag-
ging desires. But lest while I speak for truth and
Learning, *I may speak my self in stead thereof,*
which is natures epidemical disease, and in not glo-
rying may seem to glory, I only leave them to your
Honours censure, and my self

October 21.   Your Honours devoted servant,
    1653.   *Jo. Webster.*

TO

To all that truly love the Advancement of Learning in the Universities of Cambridge and Oxford, or elsewhere.

GENTLEMEN,

Hough my *stoical* and rigid humor might rather have induced me to have practifed that fevere Maxim, That men in publifhing their writings fhould neither make ufe of fear nor care, as having that fufficient teftimony in their own breafts of the finceiity of their intentions, and the perfpicuity, certainty and utility of thofe things they divulge, that they need not fear their pains fhall want protection, nor care for or fear the cenfures of men; Yet knowing I have to deal with Creatures more humane, civil, debonayre and ingenuous than the many-headed multitude, out of tendernefs to give any jnft fcandall or offence, and out of care to give all candid and free fpirits the ultimate content that lies in my power, I will give fome few reafons of this my prefent undertaking, efpecially confidering that he who goes about to cenfure and refute the opinions of others, cannot but ftand in need of an Apology for himfelf.

Some, I make no doubt, will at the firft fight of this artlefs *Rapfody*, look upon me as fome
Goth

Goth or *Vandal* , *Hunne* or *Scythian* , coming
like a torrent from the *Boreal* and barren mountains of cold ſtupidity and dark ignorance, vio-
lently labouring to bring a deluge or inundati-
on upon all the pleaſant Gardens of Arts and
Sciences, and to make an univerſal Conqueſt of
all the flouriſhing Kingdomes of antient and
long-eſteemed Literature, thereby to erect the
Monarchy of feral brutiſhneſs and ſavage *Barba-
riſm.* Well, whatſoever they may or can think
or ſay of me, I am ſure they cannot more experimentally and *Apodictically Anatomize* mine *I-
diocraſie* than my ſelf, nor be better acquainted
with my weakneſs, neſcience, ignorance & errors
than I am my ſelf, and I have truly more to ſay
againſt my ſelf than all the world can ſay of me or
by me; yet if I may be thought to know the inte-
rior motions and intentions of mine own heart
better than others, then I can truly and cordial-
ly teſtifie, that my ſoul is altogether inſcious and
innocent of any ſuch purpoſe. Doubtleſs I may
through miſtake and want of ability to diſcern
what is truth, and what is falſhood, what is true
learning, and what is but opiniative, painted and
ſeeming miſſe the way, and ſhoot far from the
mark; yet hath my will and affections no other
end but onely to hold out what is *Homogeneous* to
truth, and of real tendency to advance Science.

Others may imagine that confidence of ſelf-
ſufficiency, or hope of fame and vain glory, to
be ſaid to have attempted great things; or like
Scaliger with *Cardan* to think to gain credit, to
intermeddle with the ſplendor of the great name
of

of *Ariſtotle*; or to be ſo audacious, being but
as an *Ant* or *Pygmie*, to undertake to combate
with the Sons of *Anac*, in entring ſo boldly upon
an Examination of the *Academies*, which are,
and have been the Fountains of Learning, have
been the motives that have had the moſt principal impulſe upon my ſpirits in this iuterpriz·;
or that in the vain confidence of my abilities in
Oratory, I have plaid but *Agrippa's* Ape, to make a
declamation againſt the *approv'd Scholaſtick learning* thereby to be accounted more learned: To
theſe I plainly anſwer, my *own breaſt* is mine own
Sanctuary & let them judge what they pleaſe, for
if affection to ſimple and naked truth had had
no more influence upon my ſpirit than deſire of
fame and repute, I could have been willing to
have been ſilent untill I had been returned into
that univerſal ſilence into which all muſt goe;
and if I be not guilty of too much dubitation
with *Pyrrho*, I am not culpable of too much con-
ſidence with *Ariſtotle*. But I muſt needs confeſs,
as I never attempted any adverſary through the
incouragement of his weakneſs, ſo I never feared any becauſe of his ſuppoſed ſtrength; thoſe
that teach in the *Academies* are but as others, and
homo is a common name to all men.

 And if theſe men *underſtood* that I know better
how to live without the moſt men in the World,
than many in the world know how to live without me, they would never have judged me by
their own meaſure, nor have imagined that either fea r or favour, repute or diſrepute, could
have drawn me to this undertaking.   And my
                                                          un-

unskilfulnefs in *Oratory* is fo fufficiently manifeft in thefe unelegant lines, as it cannot be of much weight to beget a belief of gaining credit by that means, whereof I am abfolutely confcious I am utterly void; and if *Agrippa* have done well, why fhould I be troubled to be accounted his i-mitator?

Others will look upon me as an abfolute *Leveller*, and imagine that I would but have the Tree digged up by the roots, that if I get none of the main timber, yet I may have fome of the tops, or at leaft to warm my felf with the chips; And will fay, that as the *Presbyters* rooted out the *Epifcopants*, yet it was but to gather the Tythes into their own Barns; and as the *Independents* difmounted the *Presbyterians*, yet it was but to ride in their faddle: fo we that talk of reforming the *Academies* and *Schools*, do it but that we might divide fome of the fpoil, or ftep into the places of thofe that are turned out. Wel, it is an eafie expofition to expound other mens aymes by their own, and to judge what others intend to do, becaufe we our felves have either done or intend to do the like in like cafes; but facility and verity are not alwaies twins, others are not neceffarily corrupt becaufe we are fo, minds as well as faces may have the fame difference. But however I muft needs fo far own *Levelling*, that I hold plain dealing to be a jewel, and he that loves rugged, knotty and uneven paths may chufe them for me, I fhall not willingly follow him therein; fmooth and plain waies to me feem more amiable, fecure, and comfortable

fortable. For the *Prelacy* though it fought to bew me, yet it could not break me; though the *Presbyterian* pride did feem to threaten me, yet it could not hurt me, and the *Independent* forms could never inform me beyond the bafis of a better building than man can erect : nor can the fpoil of *Academies* ever pleafe my mind, nor fhall fill my purfe. And therefore I would have fuch to know that I am no *Dean* nor *Mafter, Prefident* nor *Provoft, Fellow* nor *Penfioner*, neither have I tyths appropriate, nor impropriate, augmentation, nor State pay, nor all the levelling that hath been in thefe times, hath not mounted nor raifed me, nor can they make me fall lower, *Qui cadit in terram, non habet unde cadat.* And he that would raife himfelf by the ruins of others, or warm himfelf by the burning of *Schools*, I wifh him no greater plague than his own ignorance, nor that he may ever gain more knowledge than to live to repent.

Some alfo will inquire who, and what I am, how bred and educated, that I dare be fo audacious and infolent to examine and oppofe that learning, which hath been received and approved for fo many years, affented unto, and extolled by fo many great wits and profound judgements, and defended, and patronized by all the *Academies* in the Univerfe : and will think it fit I fhould give an account of my felf, that the world may judge of mine abilities, left my fhoulders be found too weak to fupport fo ponderous a burthen. To all which I might return this, *Si refpondere noluero, quis Coacturus*

B   *fit?*

fit ? yet ſhall I not be ſo *Cynical,* but plainly tell them that *Hercules* is eaſily known by his foot, and the Lion by his paw, the Treatiſe it ſelf will ſufficiently ſpeak both my ſtrength and weakneſſe, my ſcience and ignorance, and cauſes are beſt known by their effects, and the tree by its fruits, and therefore they need no cleerer rules, or means to judge by, than the things herein laid down. And if I know little (as I am moſt conſcious that I only know this, that I know nothing at all, at leaſt as I ought to know) let not my education be blamed, but my negligence and ſtupidity; though I muſt confeſs I ow little to the advantages of thoſe things called the goods of fortune, but moſt (next under the goodneſs of God) to induſtry : However, I am a free born *Engliſhman,* a Citizen of the world, and a ſeeker of knowledge, and am willing to teach what I know, and learn what I know not, and this is ſufficient ſatisfaction to modeſt inquirers.

Furthermore ſome may object and ſay, that this Treatiſe is but like *Plato's Republick,* *Sir Thomas Moor's Utopia,* or the Lord *Bacon's* new *Athlantis,* fraught with nothing but *Heterodoxal* novelties, and imaginary whimſeys, which are not to be imitated, and are meerly unpracticable. To this I anſwer, that phantaſtical heads may very well be filled with ſuch roving thoughts, and conceited crotches, yet I would have them to know that in *Plato's Commonwealth,* and *Sir Thomas Moor's Utopia,* are more excellent things contained than figments

ments and impoſſibilities, though the general
blindneſs, and curſe upon the Sons of *Adam* keep
them frō ſeeing or practiſing any thing that may
break the yoak or remove the burthen : and for
the *arcana et magnalia naturæ*, aimed at by *Sir
Francis Bacon*, they might be brought to ſome
reaſonable perfection, if the waies and means
that he hath preſcribed, were diligently obſer-
ved, and perſued ; and if theſe poor lines of
mine contained but any treaſure comparable to
any of their rich mines, I ſhould ſet an higher
Character of eſteem upon them, than now I
ought, or they any way merit. And it is
true, that ſuppoſed difficulty, and impoſſibili-
ty, are great cauſes of determent from attempting, or trying of new diſcoveries, and enter-
priſes, for the ſloathful perſon uſually cryeth,
go not forth, there is a Lion or Bear in the way ;
and if *Columbus* had not had the ſpirit to have attempted, againſt all ſeeming impoſſibilities,
and diſcouragements, never had he gained that
immortal honour, nor the *Spaniards* been Maſters of the rich *Indies*, for we often admire
why many things are attempted which appear
to us as impoſſible, and yet when attained, we
wonder they were no ſooner ſet upon, and tried,
ſo though the means here preſcribed may ſeem
weak and difficult to be put into uſe, yet being
practiſed may be found eaſy and advantagious.
And I hope newneſs need not be a brand to any
indeavor, or diſcovery, ſeeing it is but a meer
relative to our intellects; for that, of which we
were ignorant, being diſcovered to us, we call

B 2   new,

new, which ought rather to mind us of our imbecillity and ignorance, than to be any stain or scandal to the thing discovered, for doubtlesly he said well that accounted *Philosophy* to be that, which taught us *nihil admirari*, and admiration is alwaies the daughter of ignorance.

And if some shall allege that here is nothing mine own but what is gleaned and collected from others, and so is nothing else but a transcription, and that if every bird take her own feather, I shall be but left naked and bare. Well, suppose all this be true, and that *nihil dictum quod non prius*, yet is this no more blameable in me than in others, for I confess the most of the Arguments I have used have been borrowed from those learned Authors whose names I have used, or whose writings I have cited, yet are there many things also of mine own, at least the methode and manner of arguing, so that I may say with *Macrobius*, *omne meum, nihil meum.* And if the things therein contained be hinted at and taught by others, then I only am not *Paradoxal* but they also, and I have produced their testimony, that the world may see how many valiant champions have stood up to maintain truth against the impetuous torrent of antiquity, authority and universality of opinion; and though they be not so numerous, yet are they no babes, but strong men, who fight not with the plumbeous weapons of notions, *Syllogism*, and putation, but with the steely instruments of demonstration, observation, and experimental induction, so that I hope I shall not

not be accufed of novelty and fingularity, feeing I have fo many noble *Heroes* to bear me company.

However I may be cenfured, I intend not to a-fperfe the perfons of any, nor to traduce nor ca-lumniate the *Academies* themfelves, but only the corruptions that time and negligence hath in-troduced there, but fimply to attempt (accor-ding to my beft underftanding) fome reforma-tion, not eradication of their cuftomes, and learning, which though I have (peradventure) but weakedly mannaged, yet I hope my poor mite, with the candid and ingenuous will be accepted, and for the reft I value them not, and I intreat the more able to fupply what my want of ftrength hath left incompleat, and imperfect.

Laftly, I have rather intended this as an effay to break the ice to fome more able judgement, than as fufficient of it felf to perform what is ai-med at, becaufe I have neither performed what I fhould have done, nor what I could, but only traced out fome few cleer things as a guide to higher and more noble undertakings: In a word, if I have faid or done any thing that may truely advance Science, I have mine end, if otherwife, blame the weaknefs, not the will of him, who fubfcribes himfelf,

*Octob.*21.   *Servant to all thofe that*
1 6 5 3.   *truely love Learning,*

Jo. WEBSTER.

Sa-

Sagaciſsimo et doctiſsimo Viro Johanni Webſterio carmen Acroſticon et Encomiaſticon.

J In an Ægyptian *darkneſſe men do live,*
O *O'recome with* Fancies *which the Schoolmen give ;*
H *High-building-Tower men, who ſuch notions make,*
N *Nothing but* Babel *we from them can take.*

W *Weave now ſuch damask,* Webſter, *that this age*
E *Eternize may thy Name with th'* Græcian *Sage.*
B *Build Thou a* School, *whoſe ſtrong foundation may*
S *Sacred remain, when Thou art laid in Clay.*
T *Time then ſhall write in brazen ſheets Thy Fame,*
E *Englands* Guard-Angel *ſhall preſerve Thy Frame,*
R *Rebuking Schoolmen with Thy very Name.*

R. H. N. & Medicus.

To

80

To the Reader concerning this Book, and his
Worthy Friend, the Composer of it.

WHo fears the fame of Academick sense
Must blame this Author, saying, a bonny sconce
Is fitter for him, than a weed that springs
In any Grove, that's shadowed by the wings
Of Pegasus, that nimble Horse that runnes
Among the Goths, the Vandals, and the Hunnes;
But we are Christians, say the men that bottle
All their Extractions out of Aristotle;
We are the men that must amuze the world
With what He hath broach'd, and still amongst us hurl'd:
But here's a man that tells the truth indeed,
And shewes our Human Learning but a weed,
A dream of yesternight, and no such thing
As men from Oxford, or from Cambridge bring.
Reader consider what he saies, and mark
What Artifice of mischief lyes i'th'dark,
How Ignorance hath brav'd it out, and still
Goes veil'd and mask'd under the name of Skill;
How men pretend to that which is Divine,
And yet discern not what is but Humane.
How earnest should we be, and valiant then
Against those Idols of the times, who when
They know not God, or what is taught by him,
Would yet in lower waters drink and swim
Of Human Learning? But how vain and odd
Is his conceit, that knowes neither man nor God,
And yet would fain perswade the world that he
Can handsomely unfold each mystery?
Away with fond conceits, let us lament
Our not perceiving what may us content,
Which lies not in the Creatures view, much less
Can any see it, who themselves do bless,
In groping after that which men enhaunce,
And yet what is it, but meer Nescience?
Well-fare the Author of this learned Book,
Whose pains from us frauds of this nature took.
　　　Φιλόθε⊙, φιλάνθρωπ⊙, φιλάρετος J.C. A.M.

The Contents.

A-

ACADEMIARUM EXAMEN,
OR THE
EXAMINATION
OF
ACADEMIES:

CHAP. I.

Of the general ends of erecting publick Schools.

T is a truth clearly evidential to all, who in a small measure have but convers'd with History, or are not absolute Infidels against the fidelity and facts of former ages, that there have been few Nations so feral and savage, who have not honoured literature, and in some way or other have not instituted means for the propagating of Learning. Which is sufficiently witnessed by the most Nations of note; for the *Indians* had their *Brachman's*, and *Gymnosophists*; the *Persians* their *Magusæi*, or *Magicians*; the antient *Gaules*, and *Britaines* their *Druides*; the *Jewes* their *Rabbies*, both *Cabalists* and *Talmudists*; and the *Græcians* their *Masters* and *Philosophers*. The *Ægyptians* also had their *Priests*, who were men of great learning, and did but account of the *Græ-*

C   *cians*

83

cians in point of knowledge as children, as one of them objected, *Vos Græci semper estis pueri* ; and this was that great learning, which *Moses* being skilled in, is commended by

Act. 7 22. S. *Stephen,* καὶ ἐπαιδεύθη μωσῆς πάση σοφία Ἀιγυπλίων, and Moses *was instituted from a boy in all the learning of the Ægyptians.*

Now these had their *Gymnasia* or publick *Schools,*
Philoſtrat. in vilà Apoll. Tyan. *Act.* 22. 3. wherein they inſtructed their youth, as *Apollonius Tyaneus* witneſſeth of the *Indians,* and ſo Sᵗ. *Paul* teſtiſieth of himſelf, *that he was brought up at the feet of Gamaliel.* And doubtleſs in imitation of theſe *Eaſtern* Nations the *Græcians* erected their *Schools,* and *Academies* ; for *Pythagoras, Democritus, Socrates, Plato* and others, having travelled into forein parts, to participate of their knowledge, and returning home abundantly inriched therewith, did open their *Schools* to inſtruct their Countrimen, and to let them in ſome meaſure taſt of the ſweet fruit of their far-fetched and dearbought Science. Yet had they not (as far as I can gather) any publick ſalaries, but their merit was their maintenance, and their excellency in arts, and diligent induſtry, the only Trumpet to blow abroad their fame, and to procure them both advancement, and auſcultators,

I ſhall not need to enlarge my ſelf to ſpeak of their antiquity, or the commendable ends of their firſt erection, it being manifeſt that the chief ends, in the inſtitution of them amongſt the Heathen, were firſt to inable men for their undertaking in the Commonwealth ; and ſecondly to fit them for the ſervice, or worſhip of their *Idols,* and imaginary gods ; which ends (though diverſified in the object) were (in all probability) the ſame that *Chriſtians* aymed at in ſetting up their *Schools* and Univerſities : The firſt of which was good, *Polirick,* uſefull and profitable, inabling men for all kind of undertakings, both military and civil, without which men do not much differ from brute animants ; the perfection of which is the greateſt acquiſition that men in this frail life can be partakers of, and in compariſon of which all other worldly treaſures are but as vapours and emptineſs.

But the other end, namely by theſe acquirements to fit

and

and inable men for the Ministry, and thereby to unlock the
sealed Cabinet of the counsel of God (as it hath been commonly received in judgement, and used in practice) hath
not onely failed of the principal end aimed at, but been
quite contrary and opposite thereunto. For every thing
stretched and elevated beyond its own proper sphear and acti-
vity, becomes not onely vain and unprofitable, but also
hurtfull and dangerous: *Boni oculi, & usui necessarii, sed*
cum sine lumine aspicere volunt, nihil eis species proficit,
nihil propria vis, sed affert nocumentum, The eies are
good, and necessary for use, but when they will see without
light, the species of things doth not profit, their own vertue
doth not profit, but bring nocument: So humane knowledge is good, and excellent, and is of manifold and transcendent use, while moving in its own orb; but when it will
see further than its own light can lead it, it then becomes
blind, and destroyes it self. So if the *Academies* had kept
within their own sphear, and onely taught humane science,
and had not in pride and vain glory, mounted into the Cha-
riot of the Sun like *Phaeton,* they had then neither disorde-
red nor injured *Theologie* that is above them, nor the things
of nature, which they account below them; nor had they
attempted to *send labourers into the Lords Vineyard,* which
none but he himself alone can do; nor been negligent in
that burthen, and labor, that was peculiar unto them, and
incumbent upon them. And to cleer this we shall only
touch some few arguments, because elsewhere we have
said more.

1. The chief scope and drift of the Gospel is to humble
the proud, and towering imaginations of lost man, and to
let him see that he is (notwithstanding the excellency of all
his acquisitions) utterly blind, and knows nothing as he
ought to know. And so while this vain tradition pretends
to enable man to understand the mysteries of the Gospel, it
makes him (through confidence in his attainments) uncapable of being taught them, as *Iobs friend* truly said, *vain*
man would be wise, though he be born as a wild asses Colt.
Tantò fit quisque vilior Deo, quanto pretiosior sibi, tantò
C 2 *pretiosior*

pretiosior deo, quantò propter eum vilior sibi, Every one
becomes so much more vile unto God, by how much more
he is precious unto himself, so much more precious unto
God, by how much more because of him he is vile unto
himself.

2. The end of the Gospel is to discover the *wisdome of*

1Cor.1.19,20   *the world* (in the height of its purity and perfection) *to be
meer foolishnes,* that so it may not be ballanced or compa-
red with those divine raies of Cælestial light that the Spirit of
God reveals in and unto man. *Hæc tota est scientia mag-*

Auguſt. ſup.   *na hominis scire, quia ipsa nihil est per se, & quoniam*
Pſal.70.   *quicquid est, ex deo est, et propter deum est,* This is
the whole knowledge of man, to know that it is nothing of
it self, and that whatsoever it is, it is of God, and for God.
But this opinion makes man confidently *walk on in the*

Iſa. 50.11.   *light of his own sparks,* and *by the fire that he hath kin-
kled unto himself,* and to prize it above the glorious and given light of the Spirit of Grace, and therefore (as faith the
Prophet) *to ly down in sorrow. Ad veram sapientiam*

Greg. lib. 9.   *pervenire non possunt, qui falsæ suæ sapientiæ fiduciâ*
Moral.   *decipiunt,* Those can never attain unto true sapience who
deceive themselves in the confidence of their own false wisdome.

Gal. 1. 1. 12.   3. The teaching of spiritual and Gospel knowledge is
Mat. 16.17.   onely and peculiarly appropriated and attributed unto the
Job 6.45.   Spirit of God, *It is neither of man, nor by man, flesh and
blood reveals it not,* but the Father which is in heaven;
and every Scribe fit for the Kingdome of heaven is taught
of God. *Doctus autem scriba, qui Magisterium uni-*

Nich. de cuſa.   *versalis scientiæ adeptus, habet thesaurum, de quo proferre*
de filiatione   *potest nova et vetera,* For the taught Scribe, who having
dei.   *attained the Magistery of universal science,* hath a treasury out of which he can bring new things and old. Now this
tenent doth attribute it to a fleshly power, contrary to the

1 Cor. 2. 14.   truth of God, which denies it to be in the power of humane
acquisition. *The natural man receiveth not the things of
the Spirit of God, for they are foolishnes unto him: neither can he know them, because they are spiritually discern-
ed.*

                 4. The

4. The weapons and instruments of a minister of the Gospel are of a more transcendent and sublime nature, than those that one man can furnish another withall, they are *not carnal, but spiritual, not mighty through us or our pow-* 2 Cor. 10 4 5. *er, but through Christ*, not for the elevating and blowing up, *but for the pulling down of strong holds, casting down imaginations, & every thing that exalteth it self against the knowledge of God, and bringing into captivity every thought* Vid. Chrysest. *to the obedience of Christ.* Now is it not manifest that all Sup. loc. the Science that men or Schools can teach is but carnal, and tends to exalt & not pull down the imaginations of man? and therefore true of them, as one of the Antients said, *Nugas* Hieronim. in *tenemus, et fonte veritatis amisso, opinionum rivulos con-* epist. de du- *sectamur, We hold trifles, and the fountain of verity being* obus filiis. *lost, we follow the rivulets of opinions.*

5. The Apostles and Disciples neither taught nor practised any such matter, but bad us *beware of Philosophy, which is after the rudiments of the World, and not after* Col. 2. 8. *Christ*: Nay the Apostle forbad us even to speak or declare the things of Christ in *the wisdome of mens words*, be- 1 Cor. 1. 17. cause thereby *the cross of Christ is made of none effect*, and 1 Cor. 2. 4, 5. thereby mens *faith doth but stand in the wisdome of man, and not in the power of God.* There is a very remarkable and apposite relation recorded by *Chrysostome* of two men disputing, the one a Christian, the other an heathen, and the question betwixt them was, whether *Paul* or *Plato* were more eloquent, the Christian arguing for St. *Paul*, and the heathen for his master *Plato*, of whom he affirms that the Christian had the argument that belonged to the heathen, and the heathen that which belonged to the Christian, and draweth this conclusion. *Si Platone disertior Paulus fuisset,* Chry. Hom. 3. *multi non immeritò asserere potuissent, non gratiâ vicisse* in 1 ad Cor. *Paulum, sed facundiâ; ex quo satis constat, non in sapientiâ* cap. 1. v. 17. *humanâ prædicationem factam esse, sed in divinâ gratiâ.* If Paul *had been more eloquent than* Plato, *many not unworthily might have asserted, that* Paul *had been Victor, not by grace, but facundity, from whence it is sufficiently manifest that the preaching of the Gospel was not made in the wis-*
dom

D

dome of man, but in divine grace. Therefore is this teach-ing and practice contrary to the Apostles rule and canon.

    6. All things that by the Spirit of Christ are revealed un-to, or wrought in man, are for this end, to take away from the creature totally all cause and ground of boasting or glo-rying, and to give the glory to God solely, to whom it is due. *He that rejoiceth, let him rejoice in the Lord, and let no flesh glory in his presence. Non confidat prædicator, vel auditor verbi divini, de acumine ingenii, de subtili-tate scrutinii, de sedulitate studii: sed magis confidat de bonitate dei, de pietate oraculi, de humilitate cordis intimi, Let not the Preacher or hearer of the divine word, trust in the acuteness of his wit, the subtilty of his scrutiny, the se-dulity of his study: but rather let him trust in the goodness of God, in the piety of the oracle, in the humility of his in-ward heart.* But this tenent of *Schools* inabling men for the Ministery, teacheth man to glory in his gotten learning, and acquired parts, and so is contrary to the truth of Christ.

    Object. 1. To this I know it will be objected, That *Schools* teach the knowledge of tongues, without which the Scriptures (being originally written in the *Hebrew* and *Greek*) cannot be truly and rightly translated, expounded, nor interpreted : and therefore it is necessary that *Schools* and *Academies* should teach these, as properly and mainly conducible to this end. To which I shall give this free and cleer responsion.

    Responsi. 1. It is not yet infallibly concluded, either which are the true original copies (especially concerning the *Hebrew*, and the *Oriental* languages) the *Iewish* tongue having been often altered and corrup ed by their several in-termixtures with, and transmigrations into other Nations; or that they have been purely and sincerely preserved unto our hands. For Languages change and alter, as fashions and garments. *Multa renascentur, qua nunc cecidere, cadent-que;* Neither have we any thing to assure us in this point, but bare tradition and history, which are various, perplex, dubious, contradictory and deficient. And that it which in

    it

Marginal notes:

1 Cor. 1. 29, 31.

Hug. de sanct. Victor. in Di-dalcalic.

t felf is dubious and uncertain, fhould be the means of ma-
nifefting the indubitable truth to others, feems not very probable or perfwafive.

2. Knowledge of tongues can but teach the *Grammatical*
conftruction, fignification, and interpretation of words, pro-
priety of phrafes, deduction of *Etymologies*, and fuch like;
all which tend no further than the inftamping of a bare literal
underftanding, and all this may be, the myftery of the Gofpel
being unknown, for the letter killeth, but the Spirit giveth life. 2 Cor. 3 6.
And *Saul* before his converfion, & the reft of the *Jewifh Rabbies*, underftood the *Hebrew* and *Greek* tongues, and yet
by them underftood nothing of the faving myftery of Grace,
for *they ftumbled at the ftone of offence*, and though
they were Princes in humane learning and wifdome, yet did
they not know God in his divine wifdome, *for had they
known it, they would not have crucified the Lord of Life.* 1 Cor. 2. 8.
And therefore is not tongues the right key to unlock the Scriptures, but the Spirit of Chrift, *that opens, and no man* Rev 3 7.
fhuts, and fhuts, and no man opens.

3. This is built upon no furer a foundation than a traditional faith, for *oportet difcentem credere, every man muft
believe his Teacher*, & therfore hath no more in this but what
is taught by man, who is not able to receive the things that
are of God, for they are fpiritually difcerned. So that in
this cafe he that underftands the original tongues, in which
the text was firft written, conceives no more of the mind of
God thereby, than he that only can read or hear read the
tranflation in his Mothers tongue: For the reafons are every
way pareil, and parallel; for what difference is there between him that relies upon his teachers skill, and he that relies upon the skill of a Tranflator, are they not both alike,
fince they are but both *teftimonia humana*, full of errors, miftakes and fallacies?

4. The errors and miftakes that ftill remain, and are dai-
ly difcovered in all tranflations, do fufficiently witnefs mens
negligence and ignorance, that in the fpace of fixteen hundred years, have not arrived at fo much perfection, as to
compleat one tranflation, to be able to ftand the hazard of

all

all essaies, and as the *Herculean* pillar with a *ne plus ultra*; especially if unto this be added, the uncertainty (if not deceit) of all or the most Translations, men usually pretending skill in the Original tongues, do draw and hale the word to that sense and meaning that best suited with their opinions and tenents, which is cleer in *Arrius* and those others that men have branded with the name of hereticks, (how justly God knows) and in those that many do call *Fathers,* as *Origen,* *Ambrose,* and many such; and in these times the *Papists,* *Socinians,* *Arminians* (as men have given them names) and those that have appropriated unto themselves the name of being *Orthodox :* these all pretending exact skill in the original tongues, do all wrest the Scriptures to make good their several tenents, and traditional formes, which plainly demonstrates the uncertainty, if not vanity, in boasting of, and trusting in this fleshly weapon, of the knowledge of tongues.

5. Lastly, while men trust to their skill in the understanding of the original tongues, they become utterly ignorant of the true original tongue, the language of the heavenly *Canaan,* which no man can understand or speak, but he that is brought into that good Land that flowes with milk and honey, and there to be taught the language of the holy Ghost, Jo. 3. 31, 32. for *he that is from heaven is heavenly, and speaketh heavenly things,* and all that are *from the earth, do but speak earthly things :* So that he that is most expert, and exquisite in the *Greek* and *Oriental* tongues, to him notwithstanding the language of the holy Ghost, hid in the letter of the Scriptures, is but as *Hieroglyphicks,* and *Cryptography,* which he can never uncypher, unless God bring his own key, and teach him how to use it, and otherwise the voice of Saints will but be unto him as the voice of *Barbarians, even as a sounding brass, and a tinkling Cymbal,* as not giving any *perfect or distinct sound.*

And therefore as nothing that I have spoken is intended against the learning and use of languages simply, so I am not averse to mens endeavours about the same, not their pains in perfecting translations, but could heartily wish it

were

were ten times more : yet principally I would have men to know, that it is the Spirit of God onely that freely gives men to underſtand the myſteries of the kingdom of heaven , and if any good or benefit accrew unto the truth and Church of Chriſt by the knowledge of tongues or tranſlations, it a riſeth not from their excellency, but ſolely and onely from the mercifull operation of his Spirit, who worketh all and in all, and *Rom 8. 28.* maketh *all things to co-operate for the benefit of thoſe whom he hath called according to his own purpoſe.*

Chap. II.

Of the diviſion of Academick learning , and firſt of that called School-Theology.

THere are three things concerning *Academies*, that do obviouſly offer themſelves to our examination ; Firſt, that Learning which is the ſubject of their labours. Secondly, their method in the teaching and delivering it unto others. Thirdly, their Conſtitutions and Cuſtomes, of which we ſhall ſpeak in order ; and firſt of that learning which they ſubjectively handle ; for they very proudly , and vaingloriouſly pretending to make men *Doctors* in divers Sciences , and *Maſters,* and *Batchelors* in or of Arts, it will be very neceſſary to conſider what theſe Sciences and Arts are , in or of which men are by them made Maſters, leſt it prove that when men vainly boaſt,& imagine that they are Maſters of arts, they be Maſters of none, but rather ignorant of all or the moſt. It is no leſs ingenuous than true , which the learned *Renatus des* Diſſerta. de *Cartes* acknowledgeth of himſelf; That having been from his Methodo. very young years ſtimulated with a mighty ardor and deſire lib.pag.3. of knowledge, and having run thorough the courſe and Curricle of the *Scholaſtick* ſtudies , after which by cuſtome and order he was to be received into the number of the learned, even then (ſaith he)*Tot me dubiis totque erroribus implicatum eſſe adimadverti, ut omnes diſcendi conatus nihil aliud mihi profeciſſe judicarem, quàm quod ignorantiam me-*
        D   *am*

am magis magisque detexissem, I understood my self
implicated with so many doubts and so many errors, that I
did judge all my desires of learning to have profitted me no
more, than that more and more I had detected mine own
ignorance. Memorable, faithfull, and vastly modest is that
free confession of that miracle of learning *Baptista van-Hel-
mont,* who when he had accomplished his course in *Philosophy,* and was to receive his degree of a Master of Arts, he
begun to examine what a great *Philosopher* he was, and
what science he had gained, saith, *Comperi me literâ infla-
tum, et veluti manducato pomo vetito planè nudum, præ-
terquam quod artificiose altercari didiceram. Tum prius
enotui mihi quod nihil scirem, et scirem quod nihili,* I
found my self puffed up with the letter, and plainly naked,
as though I had eaten of the forbidden apple, except that I
had learned artificially to chide. Then first it was known
to me, that I knew nothing, and what I knew was
of no value. And therefore modestly makes this
conclusion; *Peracto ergo cursu, cum nil solidi, nil
veri scirem, titulum magistri artium recusavi; nolens,
ut mecum morionem professores agerent, magistrum sep-
tem artium declararent, qui nondum essem discipulus,*
Therefore the course of my studies being finished, seeing I
knew nothing of solidity, nothing of truth, I refused the
title of Master of Arts, unwilling the professors should
play the fool with me, that they should declare me Master
of the seven Arts, who as yet was not a disciple, or taught.
And I could wish that all those that boast of being Masters of Arts had the true insight of their own self insufficiency,
then would they be more willing to learn, than to undertake
to teach.

Lib. Stud·
Author.
pag. 16.

The first usual division of *Scholastick* learning is into Divine and Humane; the first of which they commonly stile by
that improper and high-flown title of *School-Divinity:*
and sometimes more modestly and aptly, *School-Theology,*
and by some *Metaphysicks,* or *Natural Theology,* the Vanity, Uselessenesse, and Hurtfulnesse of which we shall shew
in some few clear arguments.

First, the Vanity of it appeareth in this, that men and *A-
cademies*

cademies have undertaken to teach that which none but the Spirit of Chrift is the true Doctor of, and fo contrary to the truth *call men teachers and masters upon earth*, when *we have but one father* (to teach thefe things) *which is in heaven*, and *one* true *Master* (who only can difciple us in thefe things) *even Chrift*, and fo ought not vainly (becaufe of mans pretending to teach us thofe things in the ordinary way of humane teaching) *to be called, or to call one another Rabbies ; for every good gift, and every perfect gift is from above, and commeth down from the father of lights, with whom is no variableneffe, neither fhadow of turning.* I do not deny nor envy men the titles of being called Doctors and Mafters for their knowledge in natural and civil things, and for to have a civil reverence and honour, but to have thefe titles given them as able, or taking upon them to teach fpiritual things, is vanity and pride, if not blafphemy : For I muft conclude with *Chryfoftome, Omnis ars fuis terminis non contenta, ftultitia eft, Every art not content with it own bounds, is foolifhneffe.* And therefore fober and Chriftian-like is that conclufion of *Cartefius* fpeaking of *Theology, Sed cum pro certo et explorato accepiffem, iter quod ad illam ducit doctis non magis patere quam indoctis, veritatefque à deo revelatas humani ingenii captum excedere, verebar ne in temeritatis crimen inciderem, fi illas imbecila rationis mea examini fubijcerem, et quicunque iis recognofcendis, atque interpretandis vacare audent, peculiari ad hoc dei gratia indigere, ac fupra vulgarium hominum fortem pofitieffe debere, mihi videbantur, But when I had received it for certain, and indubitable, that the path which leads unto it, is not more open to the learned than to the unlearned, and that the truths revealed of God do exceed the capacity of humane wit, I did fear left I fhould fall into the crime of temerity, if I fhould fubject them to the examination of my weak reafon, and whofoever did attend the handling and interpreting of thofe things, did feem to me to ftand in need of the peculiar grace of God for that work, and ought to be placed above the condition of vulgar men.* So that it is the proper and peculiar fcience and art of the holy Ghoft, which

D 2   none

Matth. 23. 9.
James 3. 1.

Jam. 1. 13.

Chryfoft. in
Ep. ad Cor. 1.
cap. 2. Hom. 7.

Renat. des
Cartes in Method:

none can teach but God onely, *vid. Cusan, in Apol. doctæ ignorantiæ, Bapt. van Helm. in promis. stud. author. et de venatione scientiarum, Paracels. lib. de fundamento scientiarum et sapientiæ, et in lib. de inventione artium, et alios.*

Secondly, from this putrid and muddy fountain doth arise all those hellish and dark foggs and vapours that like locusts crawling from this bottomlesse pit have overspread the face of the whole earth, filling men with pride, insolency, and self-confidence, to aver and maintain that none are fit to speak, and preach the spiritual, & deep things of God, but such as are indued with this *Scholastick.* & mans *idol-made-learning,* and so become fighters against God, and his truth, and persecutors of all those that speak from the principle of that wisedome, *that is from above, and is pure and peace-*
able : not confessing the nothingnesse of creaturely wisedom, but magnifying, and boasting in that which is *earthly, sensual,* and *devillish. Frustra enim cordis oculum erigit ad viden-dum deum, qui nondum idoneus est ad videndum seipsum, For in vain doth he lift the eye of his heart to see God, who is not yet fit to see himself.* And therefore these thinking themselves wise, they become fools, and proudly taking up-on them to teach others the things of God in the way of worldly wisedome, are not onely untaught of God, but are enemies to his heavenly wisedome. Excellent is that of the *Cardinal,* in his discourse between the *Doctor* and the *Idiot,* for the *Idiot* saith, *Hæc est fortassis inter te & me diffe-rentia, tu, te scientem putas, cum non sis, hine superbis; ego verò idiotam me esse cognosco, hinc humilior, in hoc fortè doctior existo, This perhaps is the difference be-twixt me and thee, thou thinkest thy self knowing, when thou art not, from hence thou art proud; I truly know my self to be an Idiot, from hence I am humbled, in this per-haps I am more learned.*

3. From this ariseth the dividing and renting of the seam-lesse Coat of Christ, which is indivisible, and admits no schism, but must pass all one way, according to the lot of the Father. But how have they attomized the unity and simplicity

Iam.3.15. 17.

Hug. lib. 3. de Anima.cap.6.

Nic. de Cusa. lib. idiotæ.

city of that truth ? when there is but *one Body, and one Spirit, and one hope in the calling of all Saints : one Lord, one Faith, one Baptifm, one God and Father of all, who is above all, and through all and in all.* For firft they have proudly under taken to define *Theologie,* as they have done other arts and fciences, and fo make it *habitus acquifitus,* and attainable by the wit, power and induftry of man, when it is peculiarly and onely *donum altiffimi,* and meerly the fruit of grace, and that alfo *gratis datum :* and yet fometimes they divide Sciences into two forts, Infufive, and Acquifitive, and number this as that which is infufed, and yet not remembring their own *Dichotomy,* do vainly pretend to teach men that which is onely inftilled and infufed by the Spirit of God : and therefore might more exactly keep their own divifion, to have left that infpired knowledge, which is onely infufed and given from above, to the teaching of the holy Ghoft. And if they would have confidered *Theologie* as natural, which is fuch a fpark of knowledge as can be had of God by the light of nature, and the contemplation of created things, which in regard of the object may be called *Divine,* in refpect of the information, *natural,* and fo kept it within its own bounds, it were tolerable ; for, *Hujus fcientiæ limites ita verè fignantur, ut ad Atheifmum confutandum, & convincendum, & ad legem natura informandam, fe extendant; ad religionem autem aftruendã non proferantur,* The limits of this fcience may be fo truly affigned or fet out, that they may extend themfelves to the confuting and convincing if *Atheifm,* and to teach the law or order of nature; but fhould not be brought forth to affert or build up Religion.

Eph. 3. 4 5 6.

Francif. Bacon. de Verulam. lib. de aug fcient. cap. 2.

Secondly, they have laid down pofitive definitions of God, who cannot be defined but by his own *Logick,* for with him is the fountain of life, and it is in his light that we fee light : and their own rules teach them that there cannot be a perfect definition, where there is not a *proxime genus* ; but he doth fupereminently tranfcend all their whole prædicamental skale, nay *the heaven of heavens cannot contain him,* how much lefs the narrow veffell of mans intellect, or the

Pfal. 36. 9.

1 King 8. 27.

weak

D*

weak and shallow rules of *Logical* skill? and therefore if
they had but humbly and modestly attempted no more, but
what is attainable by the poor scintillary glimpse of natural
light, and have confessed the same constantly and freely, and
that all their best descriptions of the immense and imcom-
prehensible one, were but infinitely weak and short to make
out his ineffable wisdome, power, and glory, and so have
used it but to convince *Atheists*, or to make manifest the
Cause of Causes, and Being of Beings, and not thereby to
have reared up an high-towring *Babell* of confused, notional,
fruitless and vain religion, it might have passed without re-
proof, and the *Schoolmen* without condemnation. For if
we could handle these high and deep mysteries of God, and
his Spirit, then ought we to have not the *spirit of the world*
1 Cor. 2, 10, 12. (which is carnal wisdome and reason) *but that Spirit which*
is of God, which searcheth all things, even the deep things
of God, that we might know the things that are freely gi-
ven to us of God: and so to go out of our selves, and out
of the weak and rotten vessel of humane reason, into that
ark of *Noah*, which guided by the divine *magnetick* needle
of Gods Spirit, can onely direct us to rest upon the mountains
Gen. 8. 4. of *Ararat*, even upon himself in Christ Jesus, *who is the*
Dan. 2. 34. *rock of ages, and the stone cut out without hands, that*
crusheth and breaketh in pieces all the strong images of
mans wisdome, power, strength and righteousness.

4. They have drawn *Theologie* into a close and strict *Lo-*
gical method, and thereby hedged in the free workings and
manifestations of the Holy one of Israel, who by his Spirit
Joh. 3. 8. *bloweth where he listeth*, like *the wind*, and men *may hear*
the sound thereof, but cannot tell from whence it cometh,
nor whither it goeth: as though the holy Ghost had not had
an higher and more heavenly method and way to teach divine
things in and by, than the art of *Logick* (which is meerly
humane, and mans invention) seeing *the foolishness of God*
1 Cor. 1. 25. *is wiser than the wisdome of men, and the weakness of God*
is stronger than men, when indeed the Spirit of God hath
a secrer, divine and heavenly method of its own, and onely
proper to it self, which none can know but those that are
                                        taught

taught it of God, and therefore they onely underſtand it, and ſpeak out the things of God, but not in the *words which mans wiſdome teacheth, but which the holy Ghoſt teacheth, comparing ſpiritual things with ſpiritual.* But theſe men accumulating a farraginous heap of diviſions, ſubdiviſions, diſtinctions, limitations, axioms, poſitions and rules, do chanel & bottle up the water of life (as they think) in and by theſe, and again powre it forth as they pleaſe, and this is ſpiritual ſorcery or inchantmeſt, like *Saul,* when God had left him, to ſeek for *Baal Oboth, the Lord in a bottle, or the Lord bottled up,* and not to look for his truth as a fountain of life, or as *a wel ſpringing up to eternal life;* and ſo forſook the Lord *the fountain of living waters, to draw water out of their own broken ciſterns that will hold no water;* theſe think *A-banah* and *Pharpar rivers of Damaſcus, better than all the waters of Iſrael, and that they may waſh in them and be clean;* and are not willing *to draw water with joy out of the wels of ſalvation,* and know not that there *is but one River the ſtreams whereof make glad the City of God, the holy place of the tabernacle of the moſt high:* when he that drinketh at any other fountain, *ſhall thirſt again,* but this ſhall be and ever is a well-ſpring unto eternal life.

1 Cor. 2. 13.

1 Sam. 28. 7.

Jo. 4. 14.
Ier. 2. 13.

2 Kings 5. 12.

Iſai. 12. 13.
Pſal. 46 4.

5. If we narrowly take a ſurvey of the whole body of their *Scholaſtick Theologie,* what is it elſe but a confuſed *Chaos,* of needleſs frivolous, fruitleſs, triviall, vain, curi-ous, impertinent, knotty, ungodly, irreligious thorny, and hel-hate'ht diſputes, altercations, doubts, queſtions and endleſs janglings, multiplied and ſpawned forth even to monſtroſity and nauſeouſneſs? Like a curious ſpiders web cunningly interwoven with many various and ſubtil intertex-tures, and yet fit for nothing but the inſnaring, manacling and intricating of raſh, forward, unwary and incircumſpect men, who neither ſee nor know the danger of that Cobweb-Net untill they be taken in it, and ſo held faſt and inchained. And while they pretend to make all things plain and perſpicu-ous, (by the aſſiſtance of their too much magnified *Logick*) puffing men up, by making them think themſelves able to argue and diſpute of the high and deep myſteries of Chriſt, and

97

and to conclude as certainly and *Apodictically* as of any other Science whatsoever; they do but lead and precipitate men into the caliginous pit of meer putation, and doubtfull opination; making the word of God nothing else but as a *Magazine* of carnal weapons, from whence they may draw instruments to fight with and wound one another; or like a tennis ball to be tossed and reverberated by their petulant wits and perverse reasons, from one to another, untill truth be lost, or they utterly wearied; while in the mean time the power and simplicity of faith lies lost in the dust of disputations, and they like Masters of *Fence* seem to play many doubtfull and dangerous prizes, seemingly in good earnest, and to the hazard of their lives, when in verity it is but to inhance their own reputations, and to suck money out of the purses of the spectators; so that their fit motto and impress may be, *Disputandi prurigo, fit ecclesiarum scabies.* Now how vain this is in it self, how pernicious, injurious, deadly and destructive to the truth of the Gospel, the Apostle sufficiently admonisheth us, warning *Timothy* to *keep that which is committed to his trust, and to avoid,*τὰς βεβήλας κενοφωνίας καὶ ἀντιθέσεις ψευδονήμου γνώσεως, *profanos illos, de rebus inanibus clamores, & oppositiones falso nominatæ notitiæ; prophane, vain bablings and oppositions of science falsly so called;* and also exhorteth to *eschew foolish and unlearned questions, which do engender strife,* and to *Titus,* that he should *avoid foolish questions, and genealogies, and contentions, and strivings about the law,* because *they are unprofitable and vain:* and therefore *Chrysostome* said well in the person of St. *Paul, Non veni syllogismorum captiones, non sophismata, non aliud quiddam hujusmodi vobis afferens præter Christum crucifixum ; I came not unto you bringing the subtilties of Syllogisms, nor Sophisms, nor any other thing of like sort, except Christ Crucified.*

Margin notes:
1 Tim. 6. 20.
2 Tim. 2. 23.
Tit. 3. 9.
Chrysost. in ep ad Cor. I. cap. 2.

6. The whole Scripture is given that man might be brought to the full, and absolute abnegation of all his wit, reason, will, desires, strength, wisdome, righteousness, and all humane glory and excellencies whatsoever, and that self-hood might be totally annihilated, that he *might live,*

yet

yet not he, but that Christ might live in him, and *that the life which he liveth in the flesh might be by the faith of the Son of God, who loved him, and gave himself for him.* But if man gave his assent unto, or believed the things of Christ, either because, and as as they are taught of and by men, or because they appear probable and consentaneous to his reason, then would his faith be statuminated upon the rotten basis of humane authority, or else he might be said to assent unto and believe the things, because of their appearing probable, and because of the verisimilitude of them, but not solely and onely to believe in and upon the author and promiser of them, for his faithfulness and truths sake, and nothing else; and so *his faith should stand in the wisdome of man, but not in the power of God, and so the cross of Christ should become of none effect.* But *Abraham believed God, and it was counted to him for righteousness*, though the things promised seemed neither probable nor possible; and therefore *Sarah*, who is the type of carnal reason, laughed at the promise, conceiving it impossible in reason that she should have a child; and therefore it is not that assent nor consent that reason gives unto the things of God, as they appear semblable and like, that is the faith of *Abraham*; but a simple and naked believing and relying upon the bare and sole word of the Lord, though reason & mans wisdom can see no way how possibly it can come to pass, but with *Mary* and *Nicodemus* question *how can these things be*; for reason is a monster, and the very root and ground of all infidelity; *for the carnal mind is enmity against God, and is not subject to the law of God, neither indeed can be*: but faith is that pure and divine gift and work of God that leads the heart of man in the light and power of the Spirit of Christ, with faithfull *Abraham even against hope to believe in hope, and not to stagger at the promise of God through unbelief; but to be strong in faith, and to give glory to God. Concludamus igitur* (saith learned *Verulam*) *Theologiam sacram ex verbo, & oraculis Dei, non ex lumine naturæ, aut rationis dictamime hauriri debere;* Therefore we conclude that sacred Theologie ought to be drawn from the word and O-

E racles

Gal. 2. 20.

1 Cor. 1. 17.
1 Cor. 2. 5.
Gen. 15. 6.

Gen. 18. 13.

Rom. 4. 18,
19, 20.

Lib. de Aug.
Scient 9. cap.
1.

racles of God, not from the light of nature, or the dictate of reason.

Chap. III.

Of the Division of that which the Schools call Humane Learning, and first of Tongues or Languages.

THose Sciences that the *Schools* usually comprehend under the title of Humane, are by them divided divers and sundry waies, according to several fancies or Authors; but most usually into two forts, *Speculative* and *Practick* : wherein their greatest crime lies in making some meerly Speculative, that are of no use or benefit to mankind unless they be reduced into practice, and then of all other most profitable, excellent and usefull ; and these are natural *Philosophy* and *Mathematicks*, both of which will clearly appear to be practical, and that in a few reasons.

1. Can the Science of natural things, whose subject they hold to be *corpus naturale mobile*, be only speculative, and not practical ? is there no further end nor consideration in *Physicks* but onely to search, discuss, understand, and dispute of a natural movable body, with all the affections, accidents and circumstances thereto belonging ? Is he onely to be accounted ——*Felix, qui potuit rerum cognoscere causas ?* Then surely we may justly conclude with *Seneca, Nostra quæ erat Philosophia, facta Philologia est, ex qua disputare docemus, non vivere* ! *That which was our Philosophy is made Philologie, from whence we teach to dispute, not to live.* Surely natural *Philosophy* hath a more noble, sublime, and ultimate end, than to rest in speculation, abstractive notions, mental operations, and verball disputes : for as it should lead us to know and understand the causes, properties, operations and affections of nature ; so not onely to rest there

there and proceed no further; But firſt therein and thereby to
ſee and behold *the eternal power and God-head* of him, who Rom. 1. 20,
hath ſet all theſe things as ſo many ſignificant and lively 21.
characters, or *Hieroglyphicks* of his inviſible power, providence, and divine wſdome, ſo legible, that thoſe which will
not read them, and him by them, are without excuſe; and not
to reſt there, but to be drawn to truſt in and to adore him, who
is the *Cauſa cauſans, ens entium,* and God of nature ; and
not to become like the Heathen, when *we know God, not to
glorifie him as God, neither to be thankfull; but to become
vain in our imaginations , and to have our fooliſh hearts
darkned.* And ſecondly, not onely to know natures power
in the cauſes and effects, but further to make uſe of them for
the general good and benefit of mankind, eſpecially for the
conſervation and reſtauration of the health of man, and of
thoſe creatures that are uſefull for him; for *ubi deſinit Phi-
loſophus incipit medicus ,* and is practicably applicable to
many other things; as we ſhall ſhew when we ſpeak of Magick.

2. Can the *Mathematical* Sciences, the moſt noble, uſeful, and of the greateſt certitude of all the reſt, ſerve for no
more profitable end, than ſpeculatively and abſtractively to
be conſidered of? How could the life of man be happily led,
nay how could men in a manner conſiſt without it? Truly I
may juſtly ſay of it as *Cicero* of *Philoſophy,* it hath taught
men to build houſes, to live in Cities and walled Towns; it
hath taught men to meaſure and divide the Earth; more facilely to negotiate and trade one with another : From whence
was found out and ordered the art of Navigation, the art of
War, Engins, Fortifications, all mechanick operations ,
were not all theſe and innumerable others the progeny of this
never-ſufficiently praiſed Science? O ſublime, tranſcendent,
beautifull and moſt noble Miſtreſs! who would not court
ſuch a *Celeſtial Pallas?* who would not be inamoured upon thy *Seraphick* pulchritude? ſurely thy divine and *Harmoniacal* muſick were powerfull enough to draw all after
thee, if men were not more inſenſible than ſtones or trees. Is
the admirable knowledge that *Arethmetick* afords worthy

E 2   of

of nothing but a supine and silent speculation? Let the Merchant, *Astronomer*, Mariner, Mechanick and all speak whether its greatest glory stand not principally in the practick part? what shall I say of *Geometry*, *Astronomy*, *Opticks*, *Geography*, and all those other contain d under them, as they are reconed up by that myrror of manifold learning Dr. *John Dee* in his Preface before *Euclide*? it were but to hold a candle to give the Sun light, to deny that they are practical. Nay are not all the rest also practical? what is *Grammar*, *Lodgick*, *Rhetorick*, *Poesie*, *Politicks*, *Ethicks*, *Oeconomicks*, nay *Metaphysicks*? if they serve to no other use than bare and fruitless speculation? I will onely conclude in this case as they do in that maxim of *Philosophy*, *frustra est potentia, si non reducitur in actum, In vain is power to speculate, if it be not reduced into action and practice.*

Therefore omitting the division of humane sciences, as either the *Academies* or others have ordered them; I shall proceed to divide them according to that way which I conceive most convenient and commodious for mine intended purpose, and so shall put them under a threefold consideration.

1. Those Arts or Sciences, that though they seem to confer some knowledge, yet is it in order to a further end, and so are instrumental, subordinate, and subservient to other Sciences. In the number of which I first reckon *Grammar*, or the knowledge of tongues, which in some sort and measure is instrumental, and subservient to all the rest. Secondly, *Logick* which I account instrumental, and helpfull to *Mathematicks*, natural *Philosophy*, *Politicks*, *Ethicks*, *Oeconomicks*, *Oratory*, *Poesie*, and all the rest as it especially teacheth a *Synthetical*, and *Analytical* method. Thirdly *Mathematicks*, which are not onely subordinate amongst themselves, but especially instrumental, and very usefull to *Physicks*.

2. Those Sciences that confer knowledge of themselves, and are not instrumental or subservient to others, as natural *Philosophy*, *Metaphysicks*, *Politicks*, *Ethicks*, and *Oeconomicks*.

3. Those that though they conferre some knowledg, and
have

have some peculiar uses, so they seem necessary as ornamental, and such I account *Oratory* and *Poesie.* Which divisions I put not so much because they agree in this order in their proper subjects , and ends, as to accommodate them to my present disquisition. And I shall speak in the order as I have put these, and first of the *Grammar.*

1. The knowledge of Tongues beareth a great noise in the world , and much of our precious time is spent in attaining some smattering and small skill in them, and so we do all *servire duram servitutem* before we arrive at any competent perfection in them, and yet that doth scarcely compensate our great pains ; nor when obtained, do they answer our longing, and vast expectations For there is not much profit or emolument by them, besides those two great and necessary uses, to inable to read, understand, and interpret or translate the works and writings of other men, who have written in several languages; so that in this regard they are as a key to unlock the rich cabinet of divers Authors , that thereby we may gather some of their hidden treasure ; and also to inable men to converse with people of other nations , and so fit men for forein negotiations, trade, and the like, which indeed are very useful and extremely beneficial to all mankind. Yet besides what I have formerly spoken of Tongues in relation to the interpretation of the Scripture , thus much also is evident, that if a man had the perfect knowledge of many , nay all languages , that he could give unto man, beast, bird, fish, plant, mineral, or any other numerical creature or thing, their distinct and proper names in twenty several *Idioms* , or *Dialects* , yet knows he no more thereby, than he that can onely name them in his mother tongue, for the intellect receives no other not further notion thereby, for the senses receive but one numerical species or *Ideal*-shape from every individual thing , though by institution and imposition, twenty, or one hundred names be given unto it, according to the *Idiome* of several nations. Now for a Carpenter to spend seven years time about the sharpning and preparing of his instruments , and then had no further skill how to imploy them, were ridiculous and wearisome; so for Scholars

to

to spend divers years for some small scantling and smattering in the tongues , having for the most part got no further knowledge , but like Parrats to babble and prattle , that whereby the intellect is no way inriched , is but toyllome, and almost lost labour. Excellent and worthy was that attempt of the renowned and learned *Comenius* in his *Janna linguarum* (if it had been as well understood, and seconded by others) to lay down a platform and seminary of all learning and knowable things , that youth might as well in their tender years receive the impression of the knowing of matter, and things, as of words, and that with as much ease, brevity and facility.

2. For *Grammar* which hath been invented for the more certain and facile teaching, and obtaining of languages, it is very controvertible whether it perform the same in the surest, easiest and shortest way or not ; since hundreds speak their mother tongue and other languages very perfectly , use them readily, and understand them excellent well , and yet never knew nor were taught any *Grammatical* rules , nor followed the wayes of Conjugations , and Declensions, Neun , or Verb. And it is sufficiently known, that many men by their own indestry, without the method or rules of *Grammar*, have gotten a competent understanding in divers languages: and many unletter'd persons will by use and exercize without *Grammatical* rules learn to speak, and understand some languages in far shorter time than any do learn them by method and rule, as is clearly manifest by those that travel, and live in divers Countries , who will learn two or three by use and exercize , while we are hard tugging to gain one by rule and method. And again, if we conceive that languages learned by use and exercize, render men ready, and expert in the understanding and speaking of them , without any aggravating or pussing the intellect and memory , when that which gotten by rule and method , when we come to use and speak it, doth exceedingly rack and excruciate the intellect and memory; which are forced at the same time, not onely to find fit words agreeable to the present matter discoursed of, and to put them into a good *Rhetorical* order, but

but muſt at the ſame inſtant of ſpeaking collect all the numerous rules, of number, caſe, gender, declenſion, conjugation,
& the like, as into one center, where ſo many rayes are united,
and yet not confounded, which muſt needs be very perplex-
ive & gravaminous to Memorative faculty; and theifore none
that attains languages by *Grammatical* rules do ever come to
ſpeak and underſtand them perfectly and readily, until they
come to a perfect habit in the exercitation of them,
and ſo thereby come both to loſe and leave
the uſe of thoſe many and intricate rules, which have
coſt us ſo much pains to attain to them, and ſo to juſtiſie the
ſaying, that we do but *diſcere dediſcenda,* learn things, which
afterwards we muſt learn to forget, or learn otherwiſe: when
thoſe that get them by uſe and exercitation, attain them in
ſhorter time, have a more perfect and ready way in ſpeaking
of them, and are freed from all theſe tedious pains and
fruitleſſe labour. Much to be commended therefore was
the enterpriſe of Doctor *Web*, who found cut a more ſhort,
certain and eaſie way to teach the *Latine* tongue in, than
the tedious, painful, intricate and hard way of *Grammar*,
and that by a brief and eaſie *Clauſulary method*, in farre
ſhorter time to attain perfection therein, and if it had
been well followed and improved, would have produced an
on incredible advantage to the whole nation; but we are in
this like tradeſmen, who all bandy and confederate together
to ſuppreſſe any new invention though never ſo commodious
to the Commonwealth, leſt thereby their own private gain
ſhould be obſtructed or taken away.

3. If the way to attain to languages by *Grammatical*
method and rule were the beſt and moſt certain, (which yet we
have made appear not to be ſo) yet the rules comonly uſed are
guilty both of confuſion and perplexity. How darkly and
confuſedly do they go to work? leading youth on in an intricate laborinth, wherein he is continually toyling like an
horſe in a mil, and yet makes no great progreſs, and all becauſe
the method is perplex and obſcure, void of evidential perſpicuity, rightly co-aptated to the tender capacities of young
years, which is the cauſe of the other, namely its prolixity, as
we

we can all witneffe by wofull experienc*e* ; and little hath
been endeavoured for a remedy herein , that hath not been
worfe than the difeafe , except the elaborate pains of our
Countreyman Mr. *Brinfley*, who therein deferves exceeding
commendation.

4. I fhall alfo touch fome of its material defe&s : How
probable, pleafant and ufeful is the *Hieroglyphical*, *Em-
blematical*, *Symbolical* and *Crytographical* learning, and all
relative unto *Grammar* , and yet therein nothing at all
touched of any of them ?   Was not the expreffions of things
by Emblems, and *Hieroglyphicks*, not onely antient ; but in
and by them what great myfteries have been preferved and
holden out to the world ? And who can be ignorant of the
admirable, eafie and compendious ufe of all forts of *Sym-
bolifms*, that have but any infight into *Algebraick Arithmetick* , or have but flenderly confulted with the learned
pieces of our never fufficiently praifed Countreyman Mr.
Oughtrede, or the elaborate tracts of the laborious *Harrigon ?* Or are the wonderful and ftupendious effe&s that *Po-
lygraphy*, or *Steganography* produce to be omitted or neglected ? which are of fuch high concernment in the moft arduous occurrents of humane affairs , of what price and value
thefe are , let that monopoly of all learning , the *Abbot
of Spanheim* fpeak , let *Porta* , let *Cornelius Agrippa*,
let *Claramuel* , let *Guftavus Silenus* , *Frier Bacon*, and
many others fpeak, who have written fo learnedly and accurately therein , even to wonder and amazement. *Vid.
Lib. Polygrap. Steganog. Trithem. Hen. Cor. Agrip.
de occult. Philof. lib. Jo. Claram. in lib. Trithem.
expofitio. Guftav. Silen. Crytomantices lib. Frat. Rog.
Bacon. de mirabili poteftate artis et natura lib. et alios.*

5. What a vaft advancement had it been to the Re-pub-
lick of Learning, and hugely profitable to all mankind , if
the difcovery of the univerfal Chara&er (hinted at by fome
judicious Authors) had been wifely and laborioufly purfu-
ed and brought to perfe&ion ? that thereby Nations of divers
Languages might have been able to have read it and underftood it, and fo have more eafily had commerce and trafick

one

Harrigon. lib.
Curf. Mathem.

Guft. Silen.
Cryrograph.
lib. 7.

106

one with another, and thereby the sciences and skill of one Nation, might with more facility have been communicated to others, though not speaking or understanding that language in which they were first written. This would have been a potent means (in some measure) to have repaired the ruines of *Babell*, and have been almost a *Catholick* Cure for the confusion of tongues: for do we not plainly see that those which are deaf and dumb have most pregnant and notable waies by signes and gestures to express their minds, which those that do much converse with them can easily understand and unriddle, and answer them with the like? that doubtlesly compleat waies might be found out to convey out notions and intentions one to onother, without vocal and articular prolation, as some have all ready invented and practised by *Dactylogy*, and doubtlesly might be brought to pass by the eies and motions of the face onely. Sir *Kenelm Digby* hath an apposite, though almost incredible story of one in *Spain*, which being deaf and dumb, was notwithstanding taught to speak and understand others, which certainly was performed chiefly by the eye; and though it may seem a *Romance* to some, yet whosoever shall seriously consider the vast knowledge, cautiousness, curiosity, sincerity, and punctual account of the relator therein, will be convinced of the possibility hereof. And it is recorded, and believed with Authors of repute and credit, that in *China*, and some other Oriental Regions, they have certain characters, which are real, not nominal, expressing neither letters nor words, but things, and notions: so that many nations differing altogether in languages, yet consenting in learning these Catholike characters, do communicate in their writings, so far that every nation can read and translate a book written in these common characters, in and into their own Countrey language. Which is more manifest, if we do but consider that the numeral notes, which we call figures and cyphers, the Planetary Characters, the marks for minerals, and many other things in Chymistry, though they be alwaies the same and vary not, yet are understood by all nations in *Europe*, and when they are read, every one pronounces them in their own Countreys language and Dialect. And to make it

F   more

Sir Kenelm Digbies Book of bodies and spirits.

Fr. Bacon de Au. Sci. l.6.c.1.

more evident, let a character denoting man be appointed, as
suppose this ✳, and though to perfons of divers languages, it
would receive various denominations according to their feveral vocal prolations, yet would they all but underftand
one and the felf fame thing by it: For though an *Hebrew* or
Jew would call it שיא, a *Gracian* Ἀνὴρ or Ἀνθρωπος, one
that fpeaks the *Latine Homo*, a *Frenchman Un home*, an
High German **Der Mann**, a *Spaniard Un Hombre*, and
the *Englifh, Man*, yet would the intellect receive but only
the fingle and numerical fpecies of that which it reprefen-
ted, and fo one note ferve for one notion to all nations.

6. I cannot (howfoever fabulous, impoffible, or ridiculous it may be accounted of fome) paffe over with filence,
or neglect that fignal and wonderful fecret (fo often mentiond
by the myfterious and divinely-infpired *Teutonick* , and in
fome manner acknowledged and owned by the highly-illu-
minated fraternity of the *Rofie Croffe*) of the language of
nature: but out of profound and deep confideration, muft ad-
umbrate fome of thofe reafons , which perfwafively draw
my judgement to credit the poffibility thereof.

1. For when I look upon the *Protoplaft Adam*, created
in the image, or according to the image of the great *Archetype* his father and maker, *Creavit deus hominem ad imaginem fuam, God created man in his own image*, and alfo
find the never-erring oracle of truth declaring evidently
what that image is, namely the only begotten fon of the father,
ος ὼν ἀπάυγασμα τῆς δόξης, ἡ χαρακτὴρ τῆς ὑποσάσεως ἀυτῦ,
*who being the effulgence or brightneffe of glory , and the
Character and image of his fubfiftence*: And this image
of his fubfiftence , being that out-flown , and ferviceable
word by *which he made the worlds , and that in the beginning was the word. and the word was with God , and the
word was God*; from this is manifeft that *Adam* made in this
image of God which is his eternal word , was made in the
out-fpoken word, and fo lived in, underftood, and fpoke the
language of the father. For the divine effence living in its
own infinit, glorious, and central being , having this eternal
word, or character of his fubfiftence, in and with himfelf, and
                                                        was

*Jac. Behem
Book of the
3 fold life of
man, and in
other places
of his works.*

Gen. 1. 27.

Heb. 1. 3.

Jo. 1. 1.

was himself, did by the motion of i·s own incomprehensible love, expand and breath forth this characteristical word, in which man stood, and so spoke in from, and through this out-flown language of the father , which is the procedure of the all-working and eternal *fiat*, in which all things live stand, operate , and speak out the immense and unsearchable wisdome , power and glory of the fountain and Abysse from whence they came , *the heavens declare the glory of God, and the firmament sheweth his handy work, and every thing that hath breath prayseth the Lord* , and so every creature understands and speaks the language of nature , but sinfull man who hath now lost, defac't and forgotten it. And therefore it is not without a deep and abstruse mystery, that the *Seraphical Apostle* speaks that *he knew a man caught up into the third heaven, into Paradise, and heard* ὄρρ᾽ητα ῥή-ματα, *ineffable words* , *which are not lawfull or possible to be spoken*, for this was the *Paradisical* language. of the out-flown word which *Adam* understood while he was unfaln in *Eden*, and lost after , and therefore the same illuminated vessel in another place mentions the *tongues of men and An-gels*, which would profit nothing, if they were not spoken in, and from the eternal word , which is the love-essence , or essence of love. For this *Angelical* and *Paradisical* language speaks and breaths forth those central mysteries that lay hid in the heavenly *magick*, which was in that ineffable word that was with God, and lay wrapped up in the bosome of the eternal essence , wherein were hidden and involved in the way of a wonderful and inscrutable mystery, all the treasury of those *ideal*-signatures , which were manifest and brought to light by the *Peripherial* exparsion and evolution of the ser-viceable word, or outflowing *fiat*, and so became existent in the matrix or womb of that generative and sætiferous word, from whence sprung up the wonderfull, numerous and vari-ous seminal natures, bearing forth the vive and true signatures of the divine and characteristical impressions : like so many *Harmoniacal* and *Symphoniacal* voices, or tones, all melodi-ously singing, and sounding forth in an heavenly consort, the wisdome, power, glory, and might of the transcendent central

F 2 *Abysse*

Abyſſe of unity, from whence they did ariſe, and all ſpeaking one language in expreſſing ſignificantly in that myſtical *Idiome*, the hidden vertues, natures and properties of thoſe various ſounds, which though one in the center, become infinitely numerous in the manifeſted, exiſtence and circumference, as ſaith the oracle of myſteries, *there are, it may be ſo many kinds of voices in the world, and none of them* Αφωνον *mute, or without ſignification.* Many do ſuperficially and by way of *Analogy* (as they term it) acknowledge the Macrocoſm to be the great unſealed book of God, and every creature as a Capital letter or character, and all put together make up that one word or ſentence of his immenſe wiſdome, glory and power ; but alas! who ſpells them aright, or conjoyns them ſo together that they may perfectly read all that is therein contained? Alas! we all ſtudy, and read too much upon the dead paper idolls of creaturely-invented letters, but do not, nor cannot read the legible characters that are onely written and impreſſed by the finger of the Almighty ; and yet we can verbally acknowledge, *praeſentemque refert qualibet herba deum*, but alas! who truely reads it and experiences it to be ſo ? And yet indeed they ever remain legible and indelible letters ſpeaking and ſounding forth his glory, wiſdome and power, and all the myſteries of their own ſecret and internal vertues and qualities, and are not as mute ſtatues, but as living and ſpeaking pictures, not as dead letters, but as preaching *Symbols.* And the not underſtanding and right reading of theſe ſtarry characters, therein to behold the light of *Abyſſal* glory and immortality, is the condemnation of all the ſons of loſt *Adam*; For the inviſible things of him from the foundation of the world are clearly ſeen, being underſtood by the things that are made, even his eternal power and divinity, ſo tha they are without excuſe. But if we look more narrowly into the great fabrick or machine, we ſhall find that it is a a *Pamphoniacal* and muſical inſtrument, and every individual creature is as a ſeveral cord or ſtring indued with a diſtinct and various tone, all concurring to make up a catholick melody, and every one of theſe underſtanding the ſound and

tune

1 Cor. 14. 10
Rom. 1. 20.

tune of each other , otherwise the *Harmony* would be dif-
cordant, and man himself makes up one string of this great
instrument , though in his faln condition he neither understands the sound of his fellow-strings , neither knows how
he concords with this musick , neither by his own will or
knowledge would concur in this heavenly consort, for to
him *the pipe is not understood*, neither distinguisheth he the i Cor 14. 7, 8.
tunes, and so knoweth not what is piped or harped.

2. Further, when I find the great and eternal being, speaking and conversing with *Adam*, I cannot but believe that
the language which he uttered , was the living and the ser-
viceable word, and that it was infinitely high, deep and glorious like himself, and that which was radically and essentially one with him . and proceeded from him , and was
indeed the language of the divine nature, and not extrinsecal-
ly adventitious unto him: and when I find *Adam* understanding this heavenly *Dialect* (which had been uttered in
vain if he had not understood it)I cannot but believe that this
was the language of nature infused into him in his Creation,
and so innate and implantate in him , and not inventive or
acquisitive , but meerly dative from the father of light,
from whom every good and perfect gift doth come and de- Jam. i. 17.
scend.

3. Again, when I find the Almighty presenting all the
Creatures before *Adam* to see what he would call them, and
whatsoever *Adam* called every living creature , *that is the* Gen 2 19, 20.
name thereof, I cannot but conceive that *Adam* did understand both their internal and external signatures, and that
the imposition of their names was adæquately agreeing with
their natures: otherwise it could not univocally and truely
be said to be their names , whereby he distinguished them;
for names are but representations of notions , and if they do
not exactly agree in all things, then there is a difference and
disparity between them, and in that incongruity lies error
and falshood: and notions also are but the images or *ideas*
of things themselves reflected, in the mind , as the outward
face in a looking-glasse , and therefore if they do not to an
hair correspond with, and be *Identical* one to the other , as

F 3   punctu-

&ctually and truly as the impreſſion in the wax agrees with the ſeal that inſtamped it, and as face anſwers face in a glaſs, then there is not abſolute congruency betwixt the notion and the thing, the intellect and the thing underſtood, and ſo it is no longer verity, but a ly, and falſity. And therefore if *Adam* did not truly ſee into, and underſtand their intrinſecall natures, then had his intellect falſe notions of them, and ſo he impoſed lying names upon them, and then the text would be falſe too, which avers that what he called them was their names. Alſo *Adam* was in a deep ſleep when *Eve* was framed of his bone, and yet when ſhe was brought before him being awaked, he could tell that *ſhe was bone of his bone, and fleſh of his fleſh*, and therefore *he called her woman, becauſe ſhe was taken out of man.* Now if it be denyed that he underſtood by his intrinſick and innate light, what ſhe was, and from whence ſhe was taken (which I hold altogether untrue) and that God by extrinſick information told *Adam* from whence ſhe was taken, yet did he immediately give unto her an adæquate name, ſuiting her original, which moſt ſignificantly did manifeſt what was her nature, and from whence it came, and doubtleſs the name being exactly conformable, and configurate to the *Idæa* in his mind, the very prolation, and ſound of the word, contained in it the vive expreſſion of the thing, and ſo in veritywas nothing elſe but that pure language of nature, which he then ſpake, and underſtood, and afterwards ſo miſerably loſt and defaced. And if it be objected, that if *Adam* did underſtand the internal natures, vertues, effects, operations, and qualities of the creatures, then he would have known that the effect of eating of the tree of the knowledge of good and evil, would have made him wretched, and diſcovered his nakedneſs, and then he would not have been ſo mad as to have taſted thereof: To this I anſwer, firſt, that God had plainly told him, that if he did eat thereof he ſhould ſurely dy, and yet notwithſtanding he did eat thereof, rather believing the *Serpent* and *Eve*, than the words of the Almighty. But if it be ſuppoſed, that if he had known the operation, and effect of that fruit, he would not have credited

dited

Gen. 2 23.

dited the word of the Serpent, more than his own evidential knowledge. To this, it is cleer, that though the Serpent denyed that the effect, or eating of it, would procure death, so likewise he cunningly affirmed and insinuated, that the eating of it would open their eyes, and that thereby they should be like Gods, knowing good and evil: and therefore it was the promise of *Deifying* them, that did inflame their desires, for *it seemed to the woman good for* Gen. 3. 5. 6. *food, and pleasant to the eyes, and a tree to be desired to make one wise, and therefore this made her put forth her hand, and eat of the fruit, and give also unto her husband, and he did eat.* But to answer this fully it is a deep mystery, and for man to eat of the tree of knowledge of good and evil, was to judge of God or his works, and creatures, by the creaturely, womanish, earthly, and Serpentine wisdome, and so to feed it self, and find both good and evil, and not to abide in the union, and to know all things in the light and image of God, and so to have seen them exceeding good, and to this the Apostle alludeth, saying, *A-* 1 Tim 2. 14: *dam was not deceived, but the woman being deceived was in the transgression.*

3. When I consider that the voices of birds, and beasts (though we account them inarticulate) are significative one to another, and that by the altering, and varying of those sounds, they express their passions, affections and notions, as well as men, and are thereby understood of one another, I cannot but believe that this is a part of the language of nature; for the Lamb knoweth the individual bleating of the Ewe that is the Dam, from all the rest of the Ewes; and the young Chickens will all run under the Hens wings, at a certain sound of the Cocks voice, and all the Hens will run unto him at a certain call, and therefore doubtless there is something more in that which *Cornelius Agrippa* relates of *Apollonius Tyaneus*, than every one takes notice of, that he understood the language of birds and beasts: And I cannot but admire how when we hear one laugh, and another howl and weep, though the sounds be not articulate, we can readily tell the one is the expression of sorrow, and

and grief, and the other of mirth and joy : now from
whence do we know this ? this is not acquired by us, or
taught us by others, for even Children cry immediately after
they be born, and though it be said to be by reason of the
sensation of cold which they felt not in the womb, it is true,
but then what is the cause that crying or weeping is in all
creatures the sign of sorrow, pain or grief, might not
some other kind of sound be the sign of it, or might it not
in several creatures be expressed by different and various
tones ? No truly, the mind receiveth but one single and simple
image of every thing, which is expressed in all by the same
motions of the spirits, and doubtlesly in every creature
hath radically, and naturally the same sympathy in voice,
and sound, but men not understanding these immediate
sounds of the soul, and the true *Schematism* of the internal notions impressed, and delineated in the several sounds,
have instituted, and imposed others, that do not altogether
concord, and agree to the innate notions, and so no care is
taken for the recovery and restauration of the Catholique
language in which lies hid all the rich treasury of natures admirable and excellent secrets.

Chap. IV.

Of Logick.

IN the next place I am to consider of that which they call
ars Dialettica, or most commonly *Logick*, the principal ends of which they make to be discovery of *Sophisms*
and fallacies, producing probability and opinion, and bringing forth of certitude and *Apodictical* Science, the last of
which being indeed its true and proper end : and so as to this
end is subservient to some other Sciences, but especially to natural *Philosophy*. I have formerly said something of the prejudice

judice that it hath done to *Theology*, where I treated of that
fubject, and therefore fhall onely now fpeak of it as it relates to humane and acquired Sciences, and fo lay out fome
of its chief defects, irregularities and abufes.

1. As it is now ufed in the *Schools* it is meerly *bellum
inteſtinum Logicum*, a civil war of words, a verbal con-
teſt, a combat of cunning craftineſs, violence and altercation, wherein all verbal force, by impudence, infolence,
oppoſition, contradiction, deriſion, diverſion, trifling,
jeering, humming, hiſſing, brawling, quarreling, fcolding,
fcandalizing, and the like, are equally allowed of, and accounted juſt, and no regard had to the truth, fo that by any
means, *per fas aut nefas*, they may get the Conqueſt, and
worſt their adverfary, and if they can intangle or catch one
another in the Spider Webs of *Sophiſtical* or fallacious argumentations, then their rejoicing and clamour is as great
as if they had obtained fome fignal Victory. And indeed it is
the counfel of the *Arch-Sophiſter* their Maſter, to fpeak am-
biguoufly while they difpute, to obfufcate the light with dark-
neſs, leſt the truth fhould fhine forth, nay rather to fpatter
and blurt out any thing that comes into the budget, rather
than yield to our adverfary, for he faith, *Quare oportet re-* Ariſtot. lib.
fpondentem non graviter ferre, ſed ponendo quæ non utilia Topic.2.
funt ad poſitionem, ſignificare quæcunque non videntur,
Therefore it behooves the refpondent not to take the bufineſs
grievouſly, but by putting thoſe things which are not pro-
fitable to the poſition, to ſignifie whatſoever doth not ap-
pear. O excellent and egregious advice of fo profound and
much-magnified a *Philofopher*! Is this to be a lover of verity, or indeed to play the immodeſt Sophiſter and Caviller?
Now how adverfe, and deſtructive to the inveſtigation of
truth thefe altercations and abjurgations are, is cleerly manifeſt, for as *Dionyſius* faid againſt *Plato, ſunt verba otio-
ſorum ſenum, ad imperitos invenes*, they are the words of
idle old men unto unexperienced youth, and nothing but
vanity and trifles can arife from this way of cavillati-
on.

2. *Logick* is ill applied, for the difcovery and finding
G   forth

forth of verity, and therein proceeds very præposterously : for seeing we know nothing in nature but *à posteriore* , and from the affections and properties of things must seek forth their causes, it required more powerful means , than verbal and formal *Syllogisms*, to find out , and denudate natures hidden operations.   And whereas the best part of *Logick* for that purpose is *Induction*, which backt with long experience and found observation , might be prevalent to discover the working of mother Nature;yet that hath been altogether laid afide , while the glory of *Syllogisms* hath been highly predicated : But *Syllogismus ad principia scientia-* Verulam. Nov. Org. Aph. 13. *rum non adhibetur, ad media axiomata frustrà adhibetur, cum sit subtilitati natura longè impar. Affensum itaque constringit, non res.*   *Syllogism is not applyed to the principles of Sciences, it is applyed in vain to the middle axiomes, feeing it is far unequal to the subtility of nature. Therefore it binds the affent or confent , but not things.* For whereas we should from particulars proceed to generals, this preposterously laies down universal axiomes without due proof of them, thereby to make good particulars.

3. The main defect of *Logick* is, that it teacheth no certain rules, by which either notions may be truly abstracted and gathered from things, nor that due and fit words may be appropriated to notions, without which it fails in the very fundamentals, and falls as an house built upon sand.   For , Verulam Nov. *Syllogismus ex propositionibus constat , propositiones ex* Org. Aph. 14. *verbis, verba notionum testera sunt: Itaque si notiones ipsa (id quod basis rei est) confusa sint, & temerè à rebus abstracta, nihil in iis, quae superstruuntur , est firmitudinis.*   *Syllogism consists of propositions , propositions of words, words are the special signs of notions: Therefore if notions themselves (which is the very bottom of the matter) be confused , or rashly abstracted from things, there is nothing of firmitude in those things that are superstructed.* So that un till a certain way and infallible rules be found out for the adæquation of notions and things, and fitting of genuine *Denominations* to notions, all the force and use of *Syllogisms*, as it should demonstrate, and bring forth science,

are

are but fruitleſs and vain. *Haud leve quiddam nominis im-* Plat.in Cratyl.
poſitionem eſſe, nec imperitorum, & quorumvis hominum
eſſe opus. Plato ſaith, *That the impoſition of names is no*
ſuch light matter, nor that it is the work of the unskilfull
and of any ſort of men.

4. Though *Logick* be as it were *Organon Organorum*,
an inſtrumental ſcience, they ſeem in ſome ſort to make it a
part of *Phyſicks*, and ſo intricate it with an innumerable
commixture of the moſt difficult diſputations, as any *Philo-*
ſophy hath : as though the unskilful and tender wits of young
men were to be overwhelmed with thoſe thorny queſtions
of univerſal, and *Metaphyſical* things. And as though
Logick (if it were neceſſary and uſeful) were not to be con- Petr.Gaſſend.
exer.Per.con.
Ariſt.exer.t.
tained in a few plain and eaſie precepts, and that it which
pretends to teach a ſhort, cleer, and eaſie methode applicable to all other ſciences, ſhould be ſo intricate and perplex
in it ſelf, as not to be able to reſolve of it ſelf whether it be
an art, or a ſcience? *Practical* or *Speculative*? whether
ens rationis, or ſomething elſe be the *ſubjectum* of it? So
that they do not ſee that they act as fooliſhly, while they
diſpute of the very art of diſputing, as he that endeavours Cor.Agrip.'li.
de van.Scie.c.
to ſee the proper viſion of his own eye. Moreover, that which
might be concluded in a plain, and ſhort propoſition, muſt be 7.& 8.deDial.
et Sophiſt.
drawn into mood, and figure, and after the framing, repea-
ting, and anſwering ſome ſcores of Syllogiſms, the matter is
further off from a certain and *Apodictical* concluſion than
in the beginning, and ſo moſt extremely becomes guilty of
Battology, and *Tautologie*, which it pretends to eſchew and
condemn. The grave *Seneca* ſaid well, ſpeaking of theſe
nugations. *Idem de iſtis captionibus dico : quo enim nomi-* Sen. Ep. 45.
ne potius Sophiſmata appellem? nec ignoranti nocent, nec
ſcientem juvant. I ſay the ſame of theſe Inſnarements: for
by what name may I rather call them than Sophiſms? they
neither hurt thoſe that know them not, nor help thoſe that
know them.

5. If we examine the *Logick* of the *Stagyrite*, who pretends himſelf the maſter of methode, and prince of perfection, we ſhall firſt find his *Organon*, which ſhould be his
G 2 great

great inftrument, and Mafter-piece, to be a confufed, and headlefs piece, wanting thofe lights wherewith all legitimate tractation (even *Plato*, *Cicero*, and other great men bearing teftimony) is made out, and illuftrated; for it wants a defi- nition of *Logick*, it wants the propofition of the fubject, it wants the diftribution and partition of the matter : and what fhould it want more neceffary than thefe ? And though fome may fay that thefe things are added by his interpreters ; that neverthelefs argues his defect, and befides the additions are not fo very compleat as might be defired. And fecondly, in his book *de Categoriis*, definitions are ufually wanting, for he defines not what a *Category* is, not what *Subftance* is, nor what *Quantity* is : but if any reply, and fay he could not define thefe becaufe they are the *fumma genera*, how could he define a *Relative*, or *Quality*, which are like- wife *fumma genera* ? Or to what end do the *Ariftotelians* define all the *Categories* ? Thirdly, in his book *de Interpre- tatione*, what a noife doth he keep about his *modal* propo- fitions, which he will needs limit neither to more nor fewer than four, that which is neceffary, impoffible, poffible, contingent ? But I pray you, why may there not be more ? For if that be a Mood, which doth modificate the propofiti- on, that is to fay, indicates how the prædicate is in the fub- ject, may not all Adjectives by the like right be Moods ? For if this be a modal propofition, It is a neceffary thing that man is a living Creature ; Thefe alfo are modal, It is an honeft thing that man fhould be ftudious of vertue, It is a juft thing that a Son fhould obey his Father, It is a gallant thing to die for ones Countrey ; but what fhall I fay more of many other defects, that may be feen even of a blind man? Thefe as inftances are enough, feeing they are but pleafant deceits, and cunning trifles; *Arcefilaus* the *Philofopher* us'd to fay, *Dialecticos fimiles præftigiatoribus calculariis, qui jucunde decipiunt*, *That Logicians are like to cunning jugglers, who do deceive pleafantly.* So I leave many other petty abfurdities, fuperfluities, defects, and miftakes, and pafs to things more material.

    6. Laftly I fhall fum up all in few words to efchew te- dioufnefs

Lip. in Epift.
Sen. 45.

dioufnefs. And firft of that principal part concerning **Definitions** as to matter and fubject (for we have faid fomthing of it formally as to methode and tractation) which is the bafis of all, wherein if there be a defect, the whole edifice falls to the ground; for whereas it determines all perfect Definitions to confift of the next *genus*, and a Conftitutive Difference, and fince there is fcarcely any other difference known, except rational, and irrational, that is fpecifical, and proxim to the individuals, the one of which is negative, and fo can pefitively prove nothing, and the other not only is, and may juftly be controverted, but alfo made apparent, that Brutes have tcafon gradually as well as man, how lame and dilacerate this member is, needs no further demonftration.

2. To fay nothing of Divifion, how defective, and imperfect it is, but to come to Argumentation, of all the 19 feveral forts of *Syllogifms*, feven onely conclude affirmatively, the other twelve negatively, and it is fufficiently known, that *de negativis non datur fcientia*, and therefore there is but narrow and ftraight room left for the certainty of demonftration : And it is undeniably true, that the knowledge of the Premiffes is more certain than the knowledge of the Conclufion, and therefore undoubtedly certain that the knowledge of the conformity betwixt the Premiffes and the Conclufion doth preexift in us, and is onely excited by Syllogifing, and therefore, *quid te torques, & maceras in ea quæftione, quam fubtilius eft contempfiffe, quam folvere?* why doft thou torment and macerate thy felf in that queftion, which is more fubtill to defpife than to diffolve.

Helm. F. Log.
inutilis dic.

Sen. Ep. 49.

3. *Ariftotle* forbids difpute, unlefs with thofe that do admit his principles, which he firft thinketh to be true, and yet notwithftanding from unlike principles, doth fometimes follow a ftrong Conclufion : as from falfe premiffes : *Nullum adorabile eft Creator : Omne fimulachrum et adorabile. Ergo, Nullum fimulachrum eft Creator :* Which is a true Conclufion. From whence it cannot be judged that the Conclufion of *Syllogifms* doth of neceffity compel affent, nor that the Conclufion doth neceffarily depend upon the Premiffes

E

misses. *Itaque prout in mendacio non continetur, aut latet veritas, ejusque cognitio: ita consequens est, quod in præmissis non claudatur necessariò conclusionis cognitio.* Therefore as the truth is not contained or hid in a ly, nor the knowledge of it: So the consequent is, that the knowledge of the *Conclusion* is not necessarily included in the Premisses.

4. It is cleer, that *Syllogizing*, and *Logical* invention are but a resumption of that which was known before, and that which we know not, *Logick* cannot find out: For Demonstration, and the knowledge of it, is in the Teacher, not in the Learner, and therefore it serves not so much to find out Science, as to make ostentation of it being found out; not to invent it, but being invented to demonstrate and to shew it others. A *Chymist* when he shews me the preparation of the sulphur of *Antimony*, the salt of *Tartar*, the spirit of *Vitriol*, and the uses of them, he teacheth me that knowledge which I was ignorant of before, the like of which no *Logick* ever performed: For, *Accurata Syllogismi forma, argumentoso, et luxurianti ingenio incongrua, inventioni adversissima, & res per se satis manifestas simplioi verborum texturâ, præceptorum impertinentium multitudine involuit.* The accurate form of Syllogism is incongruous to an argumentative, and luxuriant wit, most adverse to invention, and doth involve things manifest enough among themselves in the simple contexture of words, with the multitude of impertinent precepts.

5. It is true that *Syllogistical* disputations do bring forth Conclusions, but these conclusions beget but bare opinations, and putations, no infallible Science, and so all things remain but as probable and conjectural, not as firm and certain. And yet men are puft up with this vaporous, and airy sound of words, growing insolent and confident in the vain glory of *Syllogizing Sophistry*, and so are taken off from seeking any other more solid knowledge, *Causa verò & radix fere omnium malorum in scientiis ea una est; quod dum mentis hum ina vires falsò miramur, & extollimus, vera ejus auxilia non quæramus.* The cause truly, and root

Joh. Bap. van Hel. li. antecit.

Nic. Hil. l. de Phil. Epicur.

Verulam. Nov. Org. Aph. 9.

root almost of all evils in Sciences, is this one, *that while we falsly wonder at, and extol the force of humane understanding, we do not seek its true helps.* So that as *Cardan* said of his Countreymen, I may say of our *Logicians*, One may find three gods amongst them sooner than one man, so highly confident are they through these *Dialectical* delusions. *Cum quis illa quæ nescit, scire se putat, ab hac nimirùm omnes quæcunque nos fallunt opiniones, profiscuntur.* When any one thinketh he knoweth those things of which he is nescient, from this verily doth spring up all those opinions whatsoever that do deceive us. Neither is there any thing in the Universe that is more deadly and destructive to the progress and proficiency of Science, than the opinion and conceit of self-sufficiency, and with *Socrates* the more that we are sensible of the shallowness and nothingness of our knowledge, the more it will stir us up to inquire and seek after it, and therefore precious was that advice of the divine *Plato* his Schollar : *Decet sanè eum qui magnus vir futurus est, neque seipsum, neq; sua diligere, sed justa semper, sivè à seipso, seu ab alio quovis gerantur. Ex hoc ipso delicto accidit omnibus, ut ignorantiam suam esse sapientiam opinenter. Hinc fit, ut quamvis nihil (ut ita dicam) sciamus, scire tamen omnia arbitremur.* Verily it becomes him who should be great, neither to love himself, nor humane things, but to love alwaies things that are just, whether they be done of himself or any other; from this very fault, it hapneth unto all, that they opinionate their ignorance to be sapience. From hence it comes to pass, that although (as I may so say) we know nothing, yet notwithstanding we think we know all things.

6. And whereas *Raymund Lully* invented an *Alphabetical* way for *Syllogizing*, improved and opened by *Agrippa*, *Paulus Schalichius*, and others, in which *Picus Mirandula* and some did far excel, even to wonder and astonishment, which indeed is a far more certain, copious, easie, and compendious way for argumentation, especially to overcome all opponents, to be amply furnished to dispute *de omni scibili*, to answer all objections, and to confirm

Pla.l.de Soph.

Plat.Dialog 5. de Leg.

Cor.Agrip.li. in Art. brev. Lul.Paul.Sch. de Li. meth.

the

the mind in those opinions that it holds, and so deserves wondrous great praise and commendation: yet for all that it leaves the intellect nude and unsatisfyed, because it produces no certitude, nor evidential demonstration, and so fills the mind full of opinions, but not of *Apodictical* Science, and makes men *Parrat*-like to babble, argue, and say very much, but still to remain nescious, and ignorant, so vast is the difference betwixt putation and true knowledge.   *Huma-*

Marf. Ficin in Dia: 1. de Rep.

nam scientiam in negatione quadam falsi, potiùs quàm in veri affirmatione consistere.   It is true, *That humane science doth consist in a certain negation of falsity, rather than in the affirmation of verity.*   I will only conclude with that remarkable saying of the Lord *Bacon*, *Logica,*

Verulam. Nov. O.g. Aph. 12.

qua in abusu est, ad errores (qui in notionibus vulgaribus fundantur) stabiliendos, et figendos valet, potius quam ad inquisitionem veritatis, ut magis damnosa sit, quàm utilis.   Logick which is abused, doth conduce to establish and fix errors (which are founded in vulgar notions) rather than to the inquisition of verity, that it is more hurtful than profitable.

Chap. V.

Of the Mathematical Sciences.

FOr the *Mathematical* Sciences, the superlative excellency of which transcends the most of all other Sciences, in their perspicuity, veritude and certitude, and also in their uses and manifold benefits; yet in the general they are but either sleightly and superficially handled in definitions, divisions, axiomes, and argumentations, without any solid practice, or true demonstrations, either artificial or mechanical; or else the most abstruse, beneficial, and noble parts are altogether passed by, and neglected, which we

shall

shall discover in tracing over some of the several parts thereof.

1. For the prime and main stone in the building upon which all the rest of the Fabrick is erected, the noble Art of *Arithmetick*, so highly esteemed (and that not without cause) in the *Schools* of *Pythagoras*, *Plato*, *Euclide*, nay and of *Aristotle* himself, is quite rejected of our *Academick* Masters, who notwithstanding would be esteemed the great and most expert Master-builders, though they throw away the chief corner stone: And is not only sleighted and neglected as useless, and of no value, but transmitted over to the hands of Merchants and Mechanicks, as though it were not a liberal Science, or not worthy the study and pains of an ingenuous & noble spirit: And but that some private spirits have made some progress therein, as *Napier*, *Briggs*, Mr. *Oughtredge*, and some others, it had lain as a fair garden unweeded or cultivated, so little have the Schools done to advance learning, or promote Sciences.

2. And for the noble, and most necessary Art of *Geometry*, their handling of it hath been with the same superficial sleightness, and supine negligence, never bringing into perfect practice, nor clear demonstration, that which many years ago *Euclide* compiled with so much pains and exactness: and therefore are far from making any further discoveries therein, contenting themselves with the sole verbal disputes of magnitude, quantity, and the affections thereof, leaving the practice and application thereof to Masons, Carpenters, Surveyors, and such like manual operators, as though they were too good to serve so divine and noble a mistres. *Verul. lib. de Augm. Scient. 3. cap. 6.*

3. There hath been no more progress made in the *Optical* Art, which though it affords many, and wonderful secrets, both for profit and pleasure, for by it things far off are seen as at hand, minute and small things magnified, the wonderful intersection of various species, without confounding one another, demonstrated, the sight of men thereby succoured, the *Systeme* of the world thereby more perfectly viewed, and innumerable other rarities both of Art and Nature thereby

H by

by difcovered; yet have the Schooles proceeded no further therein, than to verbal difputes, and fome *Axiomatical* inftitutions and doctrines; and but for the noble attempts of fome few gallant men, fuch as *Galalæus, Scheiner, Aguillonius, Hevelius,* and the like, the grand myfteries of it had lain buried in oblivion, and this age never feen thofe ftupendious effects that through their induftry in this Art hath been brought forth.

4. As for *Mufick* it hath had fome little better fortune, for that vulgar and practical part, which ferves as a fpur to fenfuality and voluptuoufnefs, and feems to be the Companion of Melancholicks, Fantafticks, Courtiers, Ladies, Taverns, and Tap-houfes, that hath had fome pains taken about it, and fome honour done unto it, that the profeffors thereof might become *Graduats*: yet for the myfterious part thereof, which confifts in the difcovering the nature, quality, diftinction, fympathy, dyfpathy, fignificancy, and effects of all founds, voices, and tones that are in nature, thefe are altogether unknown and neglected; as alfo how far it might be ferviceable to Natural *Philofophy,* and the laying open of the univerfal *Harmony* of the whole *Mundane* Fabrick, that remains untried and unattempted.

5. The *Aftronomy* that the Schools teach being according to the *Peripatetick,* and *Ptolemaick Syfteme,* which they maintain with much rigor, feverity, and earneftnefs, is by hem extolled to the heavens, as an *Harmoniacal,* regular, and ftately *Fabrick,* which without any demonftration, or punctual obfervation they obtrude upon the tender underftandings of unwary youth: holding it forth with that Magifterial confidence, as though it would cleerly falve all the *Phænomena,* and render the true caufes, grounds, and reafons of the motions, and effects of all the *Cæleftial* Bodies, and as though no fault, exorbitancy, or defect could be found in this fo compleat, beautiful, and orderly ftructure. Yet I muft confefs, that in all the *Scholaftick* learning there is not found any piece (to my apprehenfion) fo rotten, ruinous, abfurd and deformed as this appears to be, and which

may

may from moſt evident principles be everted, and caſt down, and therefore I ſhall take the more time in enervating the ſame, and that from undeniable principles both of *Phyſicks* and *Mathematicks.*

1. They take that for granted, or at leaſt unproved, which is not onely controvertible and indemonſtrable, but untrue, namely that the Earth is the Center of the Univerſe, and that the Heavenly Bodies do in their motions ſo obſerve it, and from thence deduce the cauſes of gravity and levity; the contrary or uncertainty of which appears thus. Firſt, it is manifeſt that the Earth is not the Center of the moſt of the Planetary Orbs, becauſe by their own confeſſion, ſome of them, as ⊙ and ♂, are ſometimes in their *Apogæum*, and ſometimes in their *Perigæum*, that is ſometimes neerer and ſometimes further off from the earth; which they could not be if the Earth were their true and proper Center, becauſe according to the definition of *Euclide*, the Circumference of a circle is every where equidiſtant from the Center, and all lines drawn from the Center to the Circumference are equal, otherwiſe it would ceaſe to be a Circle, and one Circle can have no more than one Center, and therefore the Earth is not the Center of the Planetary Orbs. Secondly, if the Earth were the Center of the Orbs of the Planets, the diſſection of the Orbs would be needleſs into Excentricks and Concentricks, which being their own tenent, manifeſts that the earth is not their true, and proper Center.

Thirdly, if the Earth were their Center, the Æquinoctial line dividing both the Earth and Heavens into 2 equal parts, the *Sun* in his annual motion could not be longer time in the one half circle than in the other, unleſs he did not paſs over equal intervals, or ſpaces of the line, in equal times, and ſo ſhould intend and remit his motion, which is denyed of all: and therefore it being found by certain, and yearly obſervation, that he ſtaies ſome daies longer on the Northſide the *Æquator*, than on the South, it is manifeſt that the Earth is not the Center of his Orb.

Fourthly, there are divers Planetary Bodies that move circularly, that obſerve not the Earth as their Center at all, as

H 2 thoſe

those *Mediceal,* and *Jovial Planets* about *Jupiter*, and those about *Saturn*, *Mercury,* and *Venus* about the *Sun*, and the *Sun* about his own Center, and none of these respect the Earth, and therefore cannot be their Center, and so not the Center of the Universe.

Fiftly, for the eighth *Sphere*, no certain rules of Art can demonstrate that the Earth is its center, because it bears no sensible magnitude unto it, so that no angle can be assigned to know the distance, and the eye cannot be a certain, and proper judge, because it judges not of distance as its proper and immediate object, but to do that is the office of the common sense, and where the distance is great and vast, though the eye be far distant from the Center, yet the things seen will seem to stand in a Circle about it, though they be not truly and exactly so, and therefore this is rather a postulate than a proof, and may justly be denyed, because it cannot be proved: and that all the Stars that we call or account fixt (though we cannot prove that any of them are so) stand all in one Circle or Orb, cannot be true, for doubtless the difference of their apparent magnitude is a certain argument that they are not all equidistant from the Earth, and therefore is not the Earth the Center of the Universe.

Sixtly, for their arguments taken from gravity and levity, they do but therein usually *petere principium, beg the question,* and thereby commit a most palpable *Paralogism,* for they define gravity to be that *quod tendit deorsum, which tends downwards,* and if the cause is demanded why bodyes severed from the Earth do tend downwards thither again, they answer *quia gravia sunt,* which in effect is this, They tend to the Earth, because they do tend to the Earth, which is *idem per idem*: And if it were granted that the Earth Gal.Galal.lib. were the Center of the Universe, how could a Center any de Syst.mund. way understood be the cause of any motion at all, or locality which is defined to be a space void of bodies, and capable of them, have any power to give or cause motion in a body? These are the groundless *Chymæra's* of the *Schools,* Gil.l.de mag. not knowing that bodies separate from the Earth do move et lib. de thither again from an intrinsick *magnetick* quality, which in Phil. nov. the

the Earth is by way of attraction, and in the part separate by motion of Coition, besides some other clear reasons that may be given from *Statical* principles, which for brevities sake I am forced to omit: For from this is cleerly evident, that the Earth not being the Center of the Universe, the whole order and frame of the *Scholastick Systeme* is dissipated, and out of course.

2. And as they have mistaken the mark in making the Earth the Center of the Universe, they are as far wide in their determinations of the Circumference or Orbs, which they make to be of a *Quintessential* nature (as they term it) and so to be incorruptible, and free from change, and mutation: and it is believed that this opinion is chiefly grounded upon this, That the heavenly bodies remain still in the same state wherein they have been observed to be many ages before, and no sensible alteration could ever be perceived in them.

To which I answer, That this concludes nothing, because it argues from knowing to being, when being hath no dependance of, nor connexion with our knowing, for our knowledge is not the cause, nor measure of the Universe, nor of the things therein contained. *Falso enim asseritur, sensum humanum esse mensuram rerum; Quin contra, omnes perceptiones, tam sensus, quam mentis, sunt ex Analogia hominis, non ex Analogia Universi.* It is falsely asserted that mans sense is the measure of the Universe; but on the contrary, all perceptions, as well of the sense as of the intellect, are from the Analogy of man, and not from the Analogy of the Universe. — Vernlam. Nov. Org. Aph. 14.

Again, there may be many alterations in the *Cælestial* bodies, which by reason of their vast distance, we do not, nor can perceive, especially if we consider, that mutation is understood either as it relates *ad totum*, or *ad partes*, therefore there may be (and without doubt are) many alterations in the parts of the Heavenly bodies, though no change at all as to the whole of any of them: for the Earth is as immutable, and incorruptible, in relation to the whole, as any other of the *Starry* or *Planetary* bodies are, for the change — White Dial. de mundo.

that

E*

that appeareth in it, is but in the external and superficial
parts, and though sensible to us, yet is not perceiveable at a
great distance, for we can discern diverse mountains, and
parts of the Earth, far remote from us, yet cannot discern
the alterations that are in the parts thereof: and so if ones
eye were placed in the *Moon*, *Mars*, *Iupiter*, or any
of those Stars which we call fixt, we should perceive as
little change then here on the earth, as we being placed
here see in those Starry bodies.

Neither is it true that there appears no mutation in the
Heavenly Bodies or Orbs, because many men of great note,
experience and skill, have observed that *Comets* have been
above the Sublunary Orb, and evidently demonstrated the
same by there *Paralax*, as *Tycho Brehs*, *Copernicus*,
Kepler, *Galalaus*, and others, which clearly demonstrates
(beyond the refutation of *Logick*) that there are changes and
mutations in the heavens, and so they are not incorruptible
bodies as is falsely asserted: And the evidence that appears
to the eye in the use of the *Telescope* doth plainly evince that
there is an *Atmosphere* about the body of the *Moon*,
which could not be if the Heavens were unchangeable.

3. Another thing that they grossly maintain is, that the
heavens or Orbs are as hard as Steel, and as transparent as
glass, and yet have so many several sorts of solid Orbs,
Eccentricks, and *Concentricks*, *Epicycles*, and the like,
which are all concamerated one within another, the absurdi-
ties and impossibilities of which I shall demonstrate in some
cleer arguments.

For first, if they were solid bodies, and that every Star
were but *densior pars sui Orbis*, then either the convex superficies of the contained Orb, must exactly touch the concave superficies of the circumambient Orb, or else not, but
some space to intercede between, which must either be im-
plete with some other body, or else be a meer inanity and
vacuity; neither of which can possibly be according to their
own tenents, nor indeed according to the truth it self. For
if the convex superficies touch the concave exactly in all parts
and there be neither vacuity, nor body interjacent, then as
the

the *Mathematicians* truly fay, they muſt touch in infinite points, and ſo there could be no motion at all, becauſe there could be no appulſion, nor retroceſſion, and where there is neither of thoſe, it is impoſſible there ſhould be local motion, or lation; for two exact ſmooth, and equal ſuperficieſſes of hard and ſolid bodies joined together, the uppermoſt will if it be taken up, lift up the lower alſo, if the force of elevation be in the center of the ſolid bodies ſo fitted, as may be ſeen in Braſs, Marble, and the like, ſo that conſequently there could be no motion at all. And if there were any motion at all it muſt needs be with confrication, and attrition, and ſo without plenty of ſome oily ſubſtance, would not cauſe *Pythagoras* his ſpherical muſick, but an unheard-of rumbling noiſe, ſuch ſurely as poſſeſſed the brains of thoſe that were the fiſt Authers of this mad and extravagant opinion. And if they ſay there is a vacuity interjacent, then there could be no motion neither, becauſe according to the Schools *Motus in vacuo non datur;* and if they ſay there is ſome other body between, then what is it? for if it be any Elemental body, that cannot be, becauſe they have incarcerated them all within the concave ſuperficies of the *Moon;* and if there were ſome other body included between, then ſeeing according to *Ariſtotle* that *Motus eſt cauſa caloris,* how could it be but that body would be heated even to ignition? ſeeing that all heat doth continually rarifie, and the Orbs continually moving with ſuch an incredible ſwiftneſs, and no place for evaporation, but it cloſe pent in by the Superior Orb, how could all not be of a flame, or forcibly torn, and rent aſſunder? unleſs we muſt have all ſolved with that frivolous ſhift, that they are eternal, and ingenerable bodies, and are but *Analogouſly* like ours, and ſo ſuffer none of theſe things that Elemental bodies do: when they have cleerly ſhewed what that *Analogy* is, and wherein they are neither abſolutely like our Sublunary bodies, nor abſolutely different from them, then it will be time enough to return them a more plenary reſponſion, until then let this ſuffice.

Secondly, if the Orbs were ſolid, how could it poſſibly be

be that there could be *Eccentricks*, and *Concentricks*, the one having a more dense or thick part in one side of the Circle or Orb, and the other having so likewise on the parts opposite? now how these should have motions of their own, if they be solid, to me seems impossible; or how or which way *Epicycles* should be affixed to these extending onely from the concave Superficies, to the convex, how this should be in *Spherical* solids, or Orbs, without either penetration of dimensions, admitting of vacuity, or some other fluid body to be interjacent, to me seems more difficult to unloose, than the *Gordian* knot was to *Alexander*, and will never be untyed unless *Aristotle* have learned of his great Patron to cut that asunder which he cannot unty?

Thirdly if the Orbs were solid, and impenetrable, then could not possibly any Comets be above the superficies of the *Moons* Orb, or if it be certain that they have been observed above (which is true) then of necessity the Orbs are not solid, but fluid bodies: neither could any new Star ever appear if they were solid, but such have been known undoubtedly to be seen sometimes, and yet were no Comets, therefore of necessity they are fluid, and not solid bodies. And it is undeniably true, that if the Orbs were hard as Steel, and of such solidity as is alleged, then they could not possibly intersect or enter into the Orbs of one another; but it is certainly known by exact observation, and *Mathematical* demonstration, that when *Mars* is in the lowest part of his *Epicycle*, or in *Perigæo*, he is then within the Orb of the *Sun*, which he could not penetrate if it were solid, and therefore unquestionably they are not hard, but fluid bodies; and so the *Scholastick Systeme* is ruinous, and groundless.

Fourthly, I shall urge one *Optical* argument, which is this, That if the Heavens were all solid, and divided into so many Orbs, and they again subdivided into others, then it must follow necessarily that according to the multitude of Superficiesses, so must the multiplicity of refractions be, which in this case would be very numerous, and so none of
the

Kepler. Astro. Epit.

Philolai de Syst. mund. liber

White Dial. de mund. fol. 84.

Kepler. de Stella martis lib.

the Stars of Planets would ever be seen in their true places, but either confounded, or numerously multiplyed, which how abſurd, let the abbetters of this opinion themſelves judge.

4. From theſe they ground the motion of the tenth, ninth, and eighth *Sphere*, making the tenth *Sphere* move moſt rapidly from Eaſt to Weſt in that ſpace which we call 24. hours, and ſo ſnatcheth, and forceably whirleth about with it, all the inferior Orbs, which innately, and properly have a reluctancy, and contranitency againſt it. The abſurdity of which appears thus.

Firſt, that the Diurnal motions of all the Orbs in 24. houres, except the tenth *Sphere*, are meerly violent, and conpulſive, and only the motion of it natural, and proper. Now how could they conceive, who hold that *nullum violentum eſt perpetuvem*, that a motion that is violent could be perpetual in nature, eſpecially to theſe pure bodies which they hold to be eternal and immutable? or how can it be that the firſt *Sphere* ſhould communicate its velocity to all the inferiours, and the ſecond ſhould communicate none at all? Why is not *Jupiter* carried with the motion of *Saturn*? or the *Sun* with *Mars*? *Hoc mihi ſi ſolvas Oedipus alter eris.*

Secondly, if the extreme and incredible velocity of the tenth *Sphere*, be ſeriouſly conſidered, it will exceed all poſſibility of belief, nay even ſwifter than thought or imagination: for of diverſe Orbs moved about in the ſame ſpace of time, the leaſt moves the moſt ſlowly, and the greateſt moſt ſwiftly, for if it be computed according to the leaſt *Diametre* given unto it, and how it moves more ſwiftly than the Orb of the *Moon*, by ſo many times as it exceeds the greatneſs of its Circumference, it will be paſt all humane ſenſe, and underſtanding to imagine the extreme velocity of it, ſo that no Creature can believe it to be ſo, but alſo be compelled to confeſs, that it is moſt likely either to be ſet on fire, or elſe by the moſt vehement ſwiftneſs to be whirled into *Attomes.*

Thirdly, if the eight *Sphere* be conceived to move, wher-

I   in

in as they fancy to themselves that all the Stars are fixt, like
so many nayls in a wheel, or bowl, considering the im-
mensity of its compass, the exceeding velocity of its motion,
and that the earth (which they suppose the Center of it) to
bear proportion unto it, but as an insensible point or prick ,
then it could not possibly be but that it would appear all as an
inflamed light, or a concave globe of fire, because at one and
the self same instant the multitude of raies would all be u-
nited in this small Center, the Earth (or eye of the beholder)
and infinite rayes strike the eye successively in a manner, ere
the others passed from it, and so must of necessity appear all
intirely as fiery and luminous; so as we behold a piece of
wood whose end is fired, being quickly whirled about in
the air in a circular manner, doth appear to the eye as a true
Circle of fire or brightness: so that this would of necessity
follow upon the structure of their *Systeme*. By all which arguments may evidently appear, the impossibility of the truth
of that *Astronomical* composure which the *Schools* cry up
for so certain, neat, and beautiful, so that I may conclude
with a learned Author, *Non enim quæ de Arthuro et ipsius*

White Dial.
de mundo fol.
45.

*Equitibus finguntur, vel Homericas fabulas persuasu magis
difficiles opinor, quam illam Cælorum Compositionem,
quam proxima nos sæcula erudierunt.* For I think the
things that are feigned of Arthur, and his Knights of the
round table, or the fables of Homer, are not more difficult
to be perswaded, than that composure of the heavens,
which the age preceding us hath taught.

5. For the other parts of *Mathematicks*, some of them
are utterly unknown and unpractised in the Schools, and
some of them are taught there, but so sleightly, and superficially, that small or no profit doth redound from thence.
For they usually teach *Cosmography*, and the several species

Nath. Carpen.
Geograph.

thereof, as *Geography, Hydrography, Chorography,* and
Topography, yet whereas *Cosmography* is the whole, and
perfect description of the Heavenly and also Elemental part of
the world, and their *Homologal* application, and mutual
collation together, and so is no small or simple art, but high
and of manifold use, there hath little or nothing been done to
                                                    the

the perfection thereof, especially in the mutual correspon- Jo. Dee in his
dence and application of the heavens, and earth: neither Preface beare the other brought into practice, especially the *Theo-* fore Euclide.
remes of *Hydrography*, whereby men might be made able
and fit for Navigation. one of the most necessary imployments
and advantages of our Nation.

6. What shall I say of the Science, or art of *Astrology*,
shall the blind fury of *Misotechnists*, and malicious spirits, de-
ter me from giving it the commendations that it deserves ?
shall the *Academies* who have not only sleighted and neglected it, but also scoffed at it, terrifie me from expressing
my thoughts of so noble and beneficial a Science ? shall the
arguments of *Picus Mirandula*, and others, who have
bitterly inveighed against it, fright me from owning the
truth ? shall the thundering Pulpit men, who would have
all mens faith pinned upon their sleeves, and usually condemn all things they understand not, make me be silent in
so just a cause ? No truly, I must needs defend that which my
judgement evidences to me to be laudable, and profitable ;
not but that I utterly condemn the ignorance, knavery, and
impostorage of many pretending *Sciolists*, that abuse the
same; but shall the art of medicine or *Chymistry* be condemned, and rejected, because many ignorant *Empericks*,
and false *Alcumists* do profess them ? Surely no, let the
blame be upon the professors, not upon the profession it
self. For the art it self is high, noble, excellent, and
useful to all mankind, and is a study not unbeseeming the best
wits, and greatest Scholars, and no way offensive to God
or true Religion. And therefore I cannot without detract-
ing from worth and vertue, pass without a due *Elogy* in the
commendation of my learned, and industrious Country-
men Mr. *Ashmole*, Mr. *William Lilly*, Mr. *Booker*, Mr.
Sanders, Mr. *Culpepper*, and others, who have taken un-
wearied pains for the resuscitation, and promotion of this
noble Science, and with much patience against many unworthy scandals have laboured to propagate it to posterity,
and if it were not beyond the present scope I have in hand I
should have given sufficient reasons in the vindication of *A-*
stroloy.   I 2   7.

7. What shall I say of *Staticks*, *Archisecture*, *Pnea-matithmie*, *Stratarithmetrie*, and the rest enumerated by that expert and learned man, Dr. *John Dee* in his Preface before *Euclide*? What excellent, admirable and profitable experiments do every one of these afford? truly innumerable, the least of which is of more use, benefit and profit to the life of man, than almost all that learning that the Universities boast of and glory in, and yet by them utterly neglected, and never lookt into: but what huge, stupendious effects these can bring to pass, let our learned Countreyman *Roger Bacon*, let *Cardinal Cusan*, let *Galalæus*, let *Ubaldus*, let *Marcus Marci*, let *Baptista Benedictus*, and many others speak, who remain as a Cloud of Witnesses against the supine negligence of the Schools, who for so many Centuryes have done nothing therein: Is this to be the fountains of Learning, and wellspring of Sciences? let all rational men judge and determine.

CHAP. VI.

Of Scholastick Philosophy.

FOr the *Philosophy* which the *Schools* use and teach, being meerly *Aristotelical*, let us examine the ground and reasons why it should be imbraced and cryed up more than all other, or why he should be accounted the Prince of *Philosophers*, the Master-piece of Nature, the Secretary of the Universe, and such an one beyond whose knowledge there is no progression. Which however applauded to the heavens by his Scholars, who are *jurati in verba Magistri*, will upon exact and due test prove, both weak, groundless, false, unsatisfactory, and sterile, which we shall labour to elucidate in some clear Arguments.

r.

1. It will evidently appear that there is no reason why the *Aristotelical* Philosophy as it stands now received, according to the comments, glosses, expositions & interpretations of the Schools, should be preferred before any, or all others. Because *Aristotle* was but a man, and so might err as soon as others, neither was he more than other men any way privileged from human imperfections; nay considering him as an heathen, who did not know nor acknowledge the fountain of life, which is God, and therefore by so much less was able to teach the truth, by how much he was distant from the knowledge of the true God, who is the primary verity: so that what he hath written was rather by a *Diabolical* than a *Divine* instinct, for *Philoponus* recordeth that he begun to *Philosophize* by the command of the Oracle of *Apollo*, which the most acknowledge to have been uttered from the Devils advice and afflation.

2. Neither were his principles and tenents any whit differing from such *Diabolical* directions, for he makes God an animal in his *Metaphysicks*, and chained him to the exteriour superficies of the highest heaven, and made him bound to the laws and necessity of Fate, which his most obsequious and sworn Interpreters cannot deny. He denies in the twelfth of his *Metaphysicks* that God takes care of minute, and small things; in his books *de Cœlo* he makes the world eternal and increate; in his *Physicks* he teacheth that nothing can be made *ex nihilo*; in his books *de anima*, and of *Ethicks*, he denies the possibility of the resurrection of the dead, and in many places doth deny the immortality of the soul, so that *Lactantius* said truely of him, *Aristoteles Deum nec coluit, nec curavit*, and yet this is the man that is onely thought worthy to be the father of *Christian Philosophy*.

Arist. li. Phys. 8 prior: de Cœl. et de mund.

3. If the qualities and conditions of the man be lookt into, there will be found no such integrity in him, as may be any just cause of much confidence, nor such manners as may exroll him above the rest, for doth not *Eusebius* and others relate that he betrayed his Countrey to the *Macedonians*, and to blot out the infamy thereof that he prevailed with *Alexander*

lexander to reftore it again? And doth not *Pliny* relate, fpeaking of the poifon, *Cum id dundum Alexandro magno Antipater mitterit, magnâ eft Ariftotelis infamiâ excogitatum,* that he was guilty of adminiftring the fame? was he not accufed for being guilty of immolation to his meretricious miftris? was he not guilty of ingratitude (the worft of vices) againft his divine Mafter *Plato*, who therefore did juftly and fitly call him his Mule, becaufe he kickt againft the dugs from whence he fuckt his knowledge? what fhall I recount his avarice, which makes *Lucian* fo nippingly feign *Alexander* in hell upbraiding him, that he had conftituted riches a part of the chief good, that by that fpecious pretext he might obtain of him greater ftore of riches? Shall I recount his intemperance, voluptuoufnefs, and obfcæne manner of living? or his impious, doubtful or wicked end? no, let them be buried with his afhes. But thefe things do fufficiently declare, that there is no juft caufe fo much to efteem and applaud him above others, feeing it is impoffible to congeft fo many things againft *Plato*, *Zeno*, or *Epicurus*.

4. But I know they will fay, They refpect not his life fo much, as his moft excellent wit, great judgement, and laudable diligence; well, I eafily grant that he was fuch an one, but to prefer him notwithftanding before all others, cannot be done without too much temerity. And when arguments are comparative, between the abilities of one perfon and another, it behooves him that will judge, and determine rightly, thorowly to underftand and preponderate what there is of value and price in either of them. So when there is a queftion made of *Pythagoras*, *Thales*, *Democritus*, *Zeno*, *Plato*, *Phyrrho*, *Epicurus*, and others, it is fitting he fhould underftand whatfoever they all knew, or elfe he cannot difcern wherein *Ariftotle* doth exceed them all: unlefs he will give his fentence before the one party be heard fpeak. For how can any boaft to be more wife than all the other *Philofophers*, without being guilty of intollerable pride and arrogance? and truly I believe that *Socrates* who confeffed that he knew nothing, underftood far more than the

Stagyrite,

Stagyrite, who would hardly acknowledge himself ignorant of any thing.

5. But perhaps it will be said that he hath been received , and approved of by *Themistius, Abenrois, Thomas Aquinas, Scotus* and other men of great and vast learning, and knowledge ; well , it is truth he hath been so ; but who hath ever been the builder, or rayser of any Sect that hath not had multitudes to cry him up , to follow him , and earnestly to defend him ? have not the *Academicks* as much applauded *Plato,* as the *Peripateticks* have done *Aristotle?*

And have not the *Sceptists* as much extolled *Pyrrho?* and the *Epicureans,* their Master *Epicurus?* of whom it is said,

Qui genus humanum ingenio superavit, et omnes Præstrinxit, stellas exortus ut æthereus sol.

Nay is it not common to all, extremely and *Hyperbollically* to applaud the authors, and builders of their Sect ? neither hath he been, or is so generally received, and commended , but many men of as great note as any that have stood for him, have disceded from him, or opposed him ; for in his own times the whole *Schools* of the *Academicks* and *Stoicks* did oppugn him, *Epicurus* in many things did contradict him, and *Pyrrho* in all, nay his famous disciple *Theophrastus* (as *Themistius* relateth) did tax his master in many things: neither in all succeeding ages hath there wanted able and learned men who have strenuously opposed him, in many things if not in all , as *Thomas* himself, *Albertus Magnus, Scotus, Gregorius, Durandus, Harvæus, Maronæus, Alliacensis, Nicolaus Cusanus,* and many others; neither ought we therefore to follow or extoll him because multitudes have esteemed and adhered to him, for as *Cicero* well said, *Philosophia multitudinem consultò devitat, paucisq; est contenta judicibus. Philosophy consultively escheweth the multitude, and is content with a few judges.* And as *Seneca* witnesseth, *Hæc pars major esse videtur; ideo enim pejor est. Non tam bene cum rebus*

bus humanis agitur, ut meliora pluribus placeant. Argumenti peffimi turba eft. This part feemeth the greater, therefore it is the worfe. It goes not fo well with humane affairs, that the better things fhould pleafe the moft. The multitude is an argument of the worft. Neither if his *Philofophie* had been found and perfect, need his Sectators appeal to authority, and compliance of others, becaufe truth is able to ftand of it felf, without the authority of others: what is the caufe that fince the time that *Euclide* writ his Elements of *Geometry* there is not any one found that hath rejected them? or who hath not followed them? Truly becaufe the indubitable verity is in them, and it is impeffible the intellect fhould not affent unto them when they are known. And would not the fame thing have happened to the tenents of *Ariftotle* if they had been true, and indubious?

6. But they will urge further and fay, that he is praifed, and extolled of other famous men that were not of his Sect, as *Cicero, Plinius*, and *Quintilian*, and that he hath the teftimony of *Philip* and *Alexander* that were great, and knowing men. It is true, and no way to be denyed, for *Cicero* faith of him, *Quis doctior? quis acutior? quis in rebus vel inveniendis vel udicandis acrior Ariftotele unquàm fuit?* who hath been more learned? who hath been more acute at any time than *Ariftotle* either in the invention, or judging of things? And *Pliny* one while calls him *Summum in omni doctrinâ virum!* the chief man in all learning! fometimes he calls him *Virum immenfæ fubtilitatis*, a man of immenfe fubtiliy. And *Quintilian* faith, *Quid Ariftotelem? quem dubito feien a rerum, an feriptorum Copiâ, an eloquendi fuavitate, an inventionum acumine, an varietate operum clariorem putem.* What fhall I fay of *Ariftotle?* whom I doubt whether I might think more famous by his knowledge of things, or by his copioufnefs of writings, or by his fuavity of eloquence, or by the acutenefs of his inventions, or by the variety of his works. Well, admit all this to be true (as who would deprive him of his due honour) yet thefe are but the judgements of men that might err

as

as well as he; and what if others have thought otherwise? must we altogether stand to these mens judgements? or hath nature appointed them to be final and infallible determiners, from whose judgement there is no appeal? might not *Aristotle* and these men err in something? or were they privileged from the common frailty of all men? no, I believe not but that the proverb is true in them, and all men besides, *humanum est errare.* But shall we not find that the self-same men have given as great, or greater commendation to others? yes truely, for being Oratours they had all the liberty of a profuse and *Hyperbolical* stile, and often bringing in a commendatory catalogue of learned and worthy men, there was no cause why they should omit the noble *Stagyrite.*

But have they not often celebrated and preferred others before him? yes verily there is hardly any thing more vulgarly known, than that iterated saying of *Cicero*, when he was commending any of the *Philosophers*, alwaies added *semper excipio Platonem*, which manifested the high esteem that he had of him, accounting no other worthy to be compared with him, whom he judged superlative to all : and for *Pliny* we shall find him giving the precedence of wit and knowledge to *Homer* above all others, and calling *Plato Sapientiæ Antistitem*, than which *Elogy* I know not what can be given more illustrious, and also openly professing his repugnancy to *Aristotle*, and that he had added many things which that great man was ignorant of. And for *Quintilian* you may hear him preferring *Plato*, *Philosophorum quis dubitet Platonem esse præcipuum, sive acumine differendi, sive loquendi facultate divina quadam, et Homerica? ut mihi non hominis ingenio, sed quodam Delphico videatur oraculo instructus. Who doubteth that Plato is the chief of Philosophers, whether in the acuteness of disputing, or in a certain divine and Homerical faculty of speaking? That he seems to me instructed not with the wit of man, but with a certain Delphical Oracle :* And in a word, if thou wilt credit *Quintilian* thou shall find him extolling *Cicero* beyond *Aristotle*, *Plato*, or any other of the foregoing ages; so that the same mouths that com-

K   mend

mend him, do also prefer others before him.

But if the authority of men, the credit of the best esteemed, and the number of voices could certainly decide the truth, then what store of witnesses might be brought against him, and those also men of the greatest esteem and repute of any in the Christian world? For is not the whole *Peripatetick Philosophy* rejected of all the antient Fathers? what need is there to memorate *Tertullian*, *Irenæus*, and the more Antient? what need is there to mention *Lactantius* who so often carpeth at *Aristotle, tanqnam secum diffidentem, et repugnantia dicentem, et fentientem,* as one disagreeing with himself, and speaking, and thinking repugnant things? Why should I name *Justin Martyr*, who so often reprehendeth him? or *Hierome*, who with so open, and tart a word taxeth *verfutias ejus, his subtilties?* why should I recite *Ambrose*, *Augustine*, *Theodoret*, and the rest? who impugning humane *Philosophy* in general, have not intended to spare *Aristotle* alone. But in the name of them all hear *Gregory Nazianzen* who saith so elegantly, and truly, *Abjice Aristotelis minutiloquam fagacitatem, abjicite mortiferos illos fuper anima fermones, et univerfe humana illa dogmata. Throw away the minutiloquious fagacity of Aristotle; throw away those mortiferous Sermons of his upon the foul: and univerfally all those human opinions of his.* So that if the judgement of the Fathers be of any weight, the *Philofophy* of *Aristotle* is not much to be regarded.

As for that which is alleged concerning *Philip* chufing *Aristotle* for a Tutor to his Son *Alexander,* it merits but a flight confutation: for admit that *Philip* was a very wife and prudent Prince (as no doubt but he was) yet did the excellency of his skill principally confist in *Political*, and Military prudence, and knowing Arms better than Arts, was not adæquately fit to judge of the abilities of *Aristotle*, except by vulgar rumour, and common fame. And it is not to be denyed that in his time the fame of *Aristotle* was exceedingly blown abroad; but who is ignorant of the inconftancy and levity of the popular croud in propagating,

and

and spreading of rumours ?   But let it be granted that *Ari-stotle* did excell not only all the learned men in *Greece* that lived in his time, but all the men of the whole world that lived in the time of *Philip*; yet what is this to the number and abilities of those that have lived both before and since? or how comes the Judgement of *Philip* to oblige us who are not under his Empire, and who could not compel the minds of men, under the tyranny of one mind? for it is easier to inslave bodies than to captivate minds.   And for *Alex-ander*, though he had *Aristotle* in singular esteem, yet did he much value other learned men, as *Xenocrates*, whose æmulator *Aristotle* was, and also *Pyrrho*; so that both these received for gifts many Talents.

But this is not to be denyed, that the splendor of *Alexanders* name did bring much credit, and authority to *Aristotle* both living and dead : but this notwithstanding amongst the vulgar and those of vulgar wits, who as they are onely moved with external showes, so they think that a great Prince cannot but have a great Master : when for the most part Princes chuse not Tutors for Princes, either for their abilities in judging of the solidity of literature, or for the love they have to vertue , truth, or sincery, but rather for worldly or *Politick* ends; that their sons may be instructed, and fitted both to keep and acquire large Dominions, and Territories; and for the most part true Science scorns the bondage, flattery, and vanity of Courtly splendor.

2. Again, there is no reason why the *Peripatetick Philosophy* should have the palm and preheminence above all other, because there is a great uncertainty both of the books and doctrine of *Aristotle*, as we shall evince in some few reasons.

1. It is uncertain whether any book of *Aristotle*, or which owns him for author, be extant or no; for if it were not dubious to what end do his interpreters, as *Simplicius*, *Themistius*, and almost all the rest, which write in this age, prepose this question at the beginning of every book that they expound, *Sitne hujusmodi liber Aristotelis an non?* is this book *Aristotles* or not ? Certainly if this thing

were not dubious, there were no caule for propounding this queltion; for we ule not to lcruple about things that are certain, but about things that are doubful. For it is inquired concerning his book *de interpretatione*, whether it be his or no, the later men do affirm it, but long ago *Andronicus Rhodius* hath denyed it, whether therefore lhall we give our luffrage to thele modern men, or to him that is more antient? who by the verdict of *Boetius*, and *Porphyrius*, is laid to have brought *Aristotles* writings out of *Greece*, and to have digelted them into order; who lhall loole this knot? who lhall relolve this doubt?

2. Another argument ariseth from hence; that *Laertius* hath drawn the order and Catalogue of *Aristotles* books, and yet many are wanting which he enumerates, and we have many as 12 or 14. of *Metaphysicks*, 8. of *Physicks*, 4. *de Cœlo*, 2. *de generatione*, 4. *of Meteors*, and 3. *of the Soul*, which are not mentioned in his Catalogue, and therefore who need doubt but thele are Supposititious? For if they had been extant in the daies of *Laertius*, would he have concealed them? or could he have had no lulpition of them, who was lo diligent to know, and commit to polterity both the lives and books of the Philolophers? And it appears that when *Ptolomæus Philadelphus* did erect that huge Library at *Alexandria*, uling the help and pains of *Demetrius Phalereus*, who was a *Peripatetick*, This man, as he did promile great rewards in the Kings name to thole that brought books from any where, lo he hath not thought thole to be neglected which were laid to be *Aristotles*; And therefore *Ammoniu.* writeth, that many books were brought under the hope of gain bearing the title of *Aristotle*, that notwithltanding were lpurious and none of his: and therefore who can be certain in luch a caliginous *Labirynth*, to know whether thele that we have be truly his, or but falle and adulterate? leeing many of them are lulpected rather to belong to *Architas* than to *Aristotle*.

3. Seeing according to *Laertius*, and lome others, that there were many that bore the name of *Aristotle*, might

not

not eafily all their works be afcribed to this one *Stagyrite?*
as in other things it often falls out : for there were many
Jupiters, yet all things were afcribed to one fon of *Saturn,*
and there were many called by the name of *Hercules,* yet
all their labours made onely one fon of *Alcmen* famous.
And did not *Theophraftus* and others (who are faid to have
imitated the ftile of *Ariftotle*) compofe many books under
the fame title with thofe of his (as may be gathered from
Laertius Catalogues)& fo might not they in continuance of
time have the infcription creep in, one inftead of the other? And
is it not controverted whether the beginning of the *Metaphyficks* , and the books of plants, and others belong to *Theophraftus* , or to *Ariftotle?* And doth not *Cicero* in his
books *de finibus* witnefs that thofe books *Moralium Ni-
chomachiorum,* which are commonly afcribed to *Ariftotle* ,
are to be attributed to *Nichomachus* his fon?   And left any
fhould object (as they ufually do)that they are written in his
ftile and methode , doth he not conclude, *Non video, cur
non potuerit patri fimilis eft filius, I do not fee why the fon
might not be like the Father?*   And are there not fome
books amongft thofe vulgarly accounted the works of *Ariftotle* , as the book of plants, that of the world to *Alexander* , and others, that none dare pofitively affert to be
Ariftotles? Neither is this any new thing in him , for the
fame fuppofitition of books hath happened to *Plato, Cicero,
Seneca, Origen, Cyprian, Hierom, Auguftine,* and other
great men.

   4. Let it be concluded, that we have the books which
may juftly and legitimately be afcribed to *Ariftotle* , yet
notwithftanding how dubious is it to know in thefe books
what is properly and truly his, and what is not? For *Strabo,
Plutarch,* and others, do memorate that when *Theophraftus* had left *Neleus Scepfius* heir to his own, and *Ariftotles*
Library, their books lay long hidden in the ground and that
many years after, when they were corroded with worms, and
moths, and almoft confumed, and wafted , they were digged up and fold to *Apellicon Teius* , who took care to ex-
port them to *Athens* , and took upon him to amend and
correct

correct the defects according to his own mind: And when not long after *Lucius Sylla* had carried them to *Rome* forth of *Greece*, he committed them to *Tyrannion* the *Grammarian*, that he might correct and alter them; and so that he added detracted or changed what he judged *Appellicon* had depraved, or might better agree to the mind of *Aristotle*. And that afterwards succeeded *Andronicus Rhodius* who again turned all upside down and altered as he thought fit. Therefore how shall we believe that the pure text of *Aristotle*, passing the hands of so many Correctors (that I may not more truly say Corruptors, come to our hands without being viciated in innumerable places? first suffering by the injury of time, and then by the conjectures of so many Censurers. Especially if to this we shall add, the variety, oscitancy, and unskilfulness of transcribers, we shall find that in this author, which is common to almost all, that of one and the self-same place there will be various lections, that it will be hardly possible to divine, which are the primary and proper footsteps of the author.

5. But let this also be given, that there is nothing contained in his works but what is his own, yet the style and manner of *Aristotles* writing doth render his doctrine so uncertain, and obscure, that to fish out his meaning there is need of a *Delian* Urinator. For though he might be copious and elegant in easie matters, yet in things that are more difficult, and which require more perspicuous explication, he is so ambiguous, brief, lame, and intricate, that he seems from thence to have raised plenty of matter, and occasion to make his Sectators wrangle and conjecture. Therefore *Atticus* did worthily, and appositely compare him, and his writings, to that black humour poured forth by the Cuttle fish, under which lying hid she escapeth catching; for he seems to have spoken so on purpose, as though he be taken in some sense, yet in another he makes an escape, and so eludes the Catchers. And some of his followers do acknowledge that he hath used this kind of equivocal speaking of purpose; but what need we any further witness, behold *Aristotle* himself openly declaring that he used this

af.

affected obscurity in his *Physicks*, for labouring to confolate *Alexander* complaining that he had divulged them, he faith, *Scripfifti ad me de libris Aufcultatoriis, exiftimans in arcano cuftodiendos fuiffe. Scito igitur ipfos editos, et non editos effe. Cognofci enim, percipique ab iis tantum poterunt, qui nos audierint.* Thou haft written to me touching my books of *Aufcultation*, thinking that they were to have been kept in fecret. Therefore know that they are publifhed, and not publifhed. For they can onely be underftood, and perceived of thofe who have heard us. Which things being thus, we may marvail to what end they have called and accounted him as a *Dæmon?* for verily he hath imitated the cunning of a *Cacodæmon*, who is faid to fpeak by his Prophets and *Sibylls* after fuch a manner, that his words may be ufed in divers and contrary fenfes : is this the honour of *Ariftotle*, or the glory of the *Schools?*

6. But further let it be conceded that *Ariftotle* hath fpoken, and written perfpicuoufly, yet neverthelefs his doctrine is left very uncertain: For he for the moft part ftill ufeth a *Rhapfodie*, and is a great Compiler of other mens works, and that without taking time to digeft or cenfure all things in them, fo that it is difficult to difcern when he produceth any thing of his own, when of another mans. And therefore who is there, who when he perceives himfelf to be urged and preffed with any place in *Ariftotle*, may not oppofe, and fay, that it is not he that fpeaks there, but fome of the antients under his perfon, and fo never be without a fubterfuge, and way for evafion? Again, it is not feldome that he doth openly declare the fallacioufnefs, and uncertainty of his doctrine by inferting of Adverbs of doubting, as in his book of the *Categories* fpeaking of Relatives he faith, *Fortaffis autem difficile fit de rebus hujufmodi vehementer afferere:* Perhaps it is difficult to affirm any thing vehemently of fuch like matters. And further where he hath reckon'd up the four fpecies of quality, he addeth, *Fortaffis quidem igitur alius quifpiam apparuerit qualitatis modus, fed ferè qui maxinè dicuntur, hi funt.* For perhaps truly fome other mood of quality may appear, but thefe are almoft all

that

that are especially spoken of. There are many such like places which I omit, these being sufficient to manifest the man to be no other but such an one as the author of the censure commonly prefixt before his works, who after many commenda ions given him, saith, *Accedebat ad hæc, ingenium viri tectum et callidum, et metuens reprehensionis, quod inhibebat eum, ne proferret interdum apertè quæ sentiret. Jnde tam multa per ejus opera obscura, et ambigua.* There happened to these things, the closs wit of the man, and crafty, and fearing reprehension, which did inhibit him, that sometimes he durst not utter openly those things which he thought. From whence it is that so many things, throughout his works, are obscure and ambiguous.

7. But let us omit these, and give it for granted that *A-ristotle* hath uttered his opinion plainly, and doth speak altogether *Dogmatically*, and without hæsitation; will it not still remain of necessity that his doctrine is uncertain and obscure, seeing it is beset with continual altercations amongst the *Peripateticks* themselves, differing about the interpretation of his text? neither is there any possible hope of their reconciliation, but that we may sooner see a conjunction of the poles of heaven, one holding this, and another that, and yet all affirming that their meaning was *Aristotles* mind: for when they make the question, whether, and what kind of matter he did ascribe to the heavens, some affirm that he did attribute matter to the heavens, and some deny that he did attribute any: some hold that he appropriated the same matter to the heavens, that he did to the elements, and other some affirm that he gave them a divers matter. Wherefore suppose any one not preoccupated desired to be instructed in the *Peripatetick* doctrine, what should he do, or whither should he turn himself, when he should see about some one difficulty propounded, divers and sundry opinions differing one from another, and *Aristotle* wrested against himself? would he think it possible that *Aristotle* at one and the self-same time, did hold things absolutely contrary one to another?

8. And if all this were granted that the *Aristotelians*
did

did not disagree amongst themselves, and had a genuine interpretation of *Aristotles* mind, yet would there remain much doubt and uncertainty in his doctrine: because in it there are many things omitted, and insufficient, many things *Tautological*, and superfluous, many things false, impious, and calumnious, and many things repugnant, and contradictory, which we shall make out hereafter, and so pass them in this place.

3. Neither ought the throne be yielded to *Aristotle* alone, nor his *Philosophy* onely adored, and admitted, because in his writings innumerable things are wanting, and defective, that are essentially necessary to the compleating of *Physical knowledge*, which we shall something at large demonstrate.

1. I shall pass by the defects in his *Organical* learning, as having been touched before when we handled *Logick*, and onely come to open his defects in *Physicks*: And here first is required a definition of *Physick*, the declaration of the subject matter is wanting, a general partition, and distribution is required: neither is it shewn to what end, how or in what order he will proceed to speak of the heavens, the meteors, the animants, and the like, which all belong to *Physical* speculation, this is all the order of this great Methode-monger. And when he had said it was to be proceeded *ex notioribus nobis ad notiora naturâ*, and that even by common sense singulars are better known to us, and universalls more known in nature, yet presently after he preposterously concludes, *ab universalibus ad singularia procedendum*.

2. What a brave definition doth he give of Nature, to wit, *Natura est principium, & causa motus, & quietis ejus, in quo inest primò et per se, et non secundum accidens*, in which there are more defects and errours than words? For hereby nature is not distinguished from the efficient cause, art may be a principle as well as nature, and many more which I shall not stand to recite, seeing the most acute, and learned *Helmont* hath demonstrated no fewer than thirteen errors, or defects, in this so short a definition, and so concludeth,

Arist. l.2. Phy.

Hel. lib. Phys. Arist et Gal. ign.

L   deth,

Pet.Gaſ.exer.
5 contr. Ariſt.

deth, *Atque tandem valdè anxius, neſcit quid vocet, aut vo-care debeat naturam, naturalis auſcultationis ſcriptor.* And at the length being very anxious, the writer of natural au-ſcultation is ignorant what he ſhould or ought to call nature.

Ariſt.l.3 Phy.
cap. 3.

And alſo confutes ſome other deſcriptions of *Ariſtotle* with many pregnant and undeniable arguments: and in the moſt of all his diviſions and definitions, as may be ſeen in his definition of motion, and of alteration, and divers others, which were tedious and fruitleſs to reckon up.

3. His proofs and demonſtrations for the moſt part have the ſame lameneſs with the reſt, *ex uno diſce omnes.* He goes about to prove the world to be perfect, becauſe it doth contain bodies, and that a bodie is perfect becauſe it con-taineth trinal dimenſion, and that trinal dimenſion is per-fect, becauſe three are all things: but three are all things,

Ariſt. lib. de
Cœl.et Mun.
ca.1,2,3,8,9,
10, prim.lib.

becauſe if they be either one, or two, yet we have not named all things; but as ſoon as there are three, we may call them all things. O how egregious! O how ſuper-ſufficient is this proof! O how wonderfully beſeeming ſo great a *Phi-loſopher*! O how fit is he to be the Prince of Learning, and the *Dictator* in the *Academies*! And the ſame abſurdi-ties may be ſeen every where in his writings.

4. The like appears in his argumentations againſt the antient *Philoſophers*, whom he ſeems every where to con-fute, calumniate and contradict, but with the ſame imper-fections and defects, as to inſtance in two or three: He taxeth *Democritus, Leucippus,* and others very inſufficiently,

Ariſt lib. 1.de
Gen. et Cor.
cap.2,9.

who did hold that generation was by congregation, and that no continuum was compounded of indiviſible things, which they ſpeaking of *Phyſical* impartibilitie, he impugns as of *Mathematical.* Doth he not unworthily tax *Plato,* that beſides matter and Idæi, he had put no efficient cauſe of gene-ration? when he himſelf beſides matter and form, rather hath put privation, which is a *non ens,* than any efficient cauſe:

Helm.lib. an-
te citato.

Quapropter cum Ariſtoteles neſciat naturam, proprietates, itemque generationum cauſas, ac quidditatem; quis non judicaverit, ex aridis ciſternis Scholorum aquas Philoſo-phiæ hauſtas hactenus? Octo enim libri auſultationum Phyſicarum

Physicarum , somnia et privationes, pro natura cognitione expomunt. Wherefore seeing Aristotle *is ignorant of nature, proprieties , and also the causes , and quiddity of generations; who shall not judicate the waters of Philosophy hitherto drawn from the drie Cisterns of the Schools ? For the eight books of Physical auscultations, do expound dreams, and privations, instead of the knowledge of nature.*

5. This *Philosophy* is meerly verbal , speculative , abstractive, formal and notional , fit to fill the brains with monstrous and airy *Chymæras* , speculative, and fruitless conceits, but not to replenish the intellect with sound knowledge, and demonstrative verity, nor to lead man practically to dive into the internal center of natures abstruse, and occult operations: But is only conversant about the shell , and husk, handling the accidental, external and recollacious qualities of things , confusedly, and continually tumbling over obscure , ambiguous , general and equivocal terms, which are onely fit to captivate young *Sciolists* , and raw wits, but not to satisfy a discreet and wary understanding, that expects *Apodictical,* and experimental manuduction into the more interiour clossets of nature. Here in the *Schools* is found no such thing, but objurgations , and clamours , fighting and contending *Andabatarum more,* like blind, or madmen , not knowing where they wound others , nor where they are hurt or offended themselves.

6. And whereas names should truely express notions, and they be congruous to things themselves , the *Aristotelian Philosophy* leads us into an endless Labyrinth , having nothing in manner but *Syllogisms* , or rather *Paralogisms* to statuminate and uphold the Fabrick thereof : for they have altogether laid aside Induction as too mechanical and painful , which onely can be serviceable to Physical Science , and have invented and introduced words, terms, definitions, distinctions, and limitations consonant enough amongst themselves, but no way consorting or sympathizing with nature it self. *Scientia enim , quas nunc habemus , nihil aliud* Verulam.Nov. *sunt quam quædam concinnationes rerum antea inventa-* Org.Aphor.8. *rum; non modi inveniendi aut designationes novorum ope-*

L 2   *rum*

rum. For those Sciences that we have now, are nothing else but certain concinnation: of things formerly found out; not the wayes, or designations of inventing new works. And one thing more, instead of establishing the mind in Physical truths, most usually they confound the judgement with Mathematical terms, which in *Aristotles* writings is no small error: for though the Mathematicks be exceedingly helpful to Natural *Philosophy*, yet is confusion of terms very hurtful; for if a Mathematical point or superficies be urged in a Physicall argument it will conclude nothing, but onely obfuscate, and disorder the intellect.

7. This *School Philosophy* is altogether void of true and infallible demonstration, observation, and experiment, the only certain means, and instruments to discover, and anatomize natures occult and central operations; which are found out by laborious tryals, manual operations, assiduous observations, and the like, and not by poring continually upon a few paper Idols, and unexperienced Authors : As though we could fathome the Universe by our shallow imaginations, or comprize the mysteries of mother nature in the narrow compass of our weak brains; or as though she would follow us into our Chambers, and there in idlenesse communicate her secrets unto us; no verily, *Dii bona sua laboribus vendunt*, ease and idleness are not the way to get knowledge. Therefore here I shall shew what noble parts of Physical knowledge have been, and are neglected by the Schools, onely because they abhor taking of pains, and think they can argue Dame Nature out of her secrets, and that they need no other key but *Syllogisms* to unlock her Cabinet.

1. Therefore that noble, and almost divine Science of natural *Magick*, is by them not only repudiated, abominated, and prosecuted with fire and sword, but also the very name seems nauseous and execrable unto them ; so little have they done either to advance learning, or to vindicate truth. A great wonder that men that profess themselves almost ignorant of nothing, and think themselves the most skilful wordmen or *Logodædalists* in the world, should either not understand

underftand or be unwilling to acknowledge that the word *Magick* was in its primary and proper acceptation, taken in a good and honourable fenfe, and appropriated to thofe that the world accounted moft wife and learned : and never was abufively taken, until many Impoftors, and knaves did abufe and pervert that fo noble a fcience, as though the name of *Doctor* were difhonourable, or unworthy to be an epithite for the able and learned, who have juftly merited and taken that degree, becaufe every Montebank Emperick and Quackfalver, have ufually that title attributed unto them. Was not *Magick* amongft the *Perfians* accepted for a fublime Sapience, and the fcience of the univerfal confent of things? And were not thofe men (fuppofed Kings) that came from the Eaft ftyled by that honourable name Μαγοì, *Magic,* or *Wifemen,* (which the Holy Ghoft gives unto them, thereby to denote out that glorious myftery of which they were made partakers by the revelation of that fpirit of life and light. Neither do I here *Apologize* for that impious and execrable *Magick,* that either is ufed for the hurt and deftruction of mankind, or pretends to gain knowledge from him who is the grand enemy of all the fons of *Adam,* no, that I truly abominate, *Quia* (as learned *Mirandula* faith) *pendet ex manu hoftium primæ veritatis, poteftatum harum tenebrarum, quæ tenebras falfitatis male difpofitis intellectibus obfundunt. Becaufe it dependeth upon the hand of the enemies of the primitive verity, of the powers of thefe darkneffes, which do infufe the tenebrofities of falfity into evilly difpofed intellects.*

But that which I defend is that noble and laudable Science, *Quæ cognitionem formarum abditarum ad opera miranda deducat, atque activa paffivis conjungendo, magnalia naturæ manifeftet; which leadeth cognition of occult forms unto wonderful works, and by conjoining actives to paffives, doth manifeft the grand fecrets of nature. And indeed is that worthy, and wonderful fcience, not unbefeeming the nobleft perfon, or greateft Scholar, and is that fublime knowledge whereby the wonderful works of the Creator are difcovered, and innumerable benefits produced to*

Jo. Bapt. Port.
mag. natu. l. 1.
cap. 1.

Matth. 2. 1, 7.

Jo. Pic. Miran.
Con. mag. no.
26.

Verul. l. 3 de
Aug. Sci. ci. 5.

to the poor Creatures. *Mirabilia artis Magicæ non sunt* Jo. Pic. Miran.
loco citato. *nisi per unionem & actuationem eorum , quæ seminalitèr, & separatæ sunt in natura.* The wonderful things of Art Magick are not brought to pass, except by the union, and actuation of those things that are seminally, and separately in nature : So that indeed, *Magicam operari, non est aliud nisi maritare mundum.* To operate by Magick is nothing else but to marry the world, that is, fitly and duly to join ard connex agents to their patients, masculines to fæminines, superious to inferiours, Cælestials to Terrestrials, that thereby nature may act out her hidden and latent power. And this is that which the greatest Doctor need not be ashamed of, whether *Physician* or *Philosopher*, but that which is commendable both before God and man, and that wherin if the Schools had been exercised, their works and fruits would have been more manifest, and they then owned not as the disseminators of vain controversies, and frivolous disputes, but as the true interpreters of nature, Patriots of true learning, and benefactors to mankind. But I pray God they may repent and amend, and imbrace the truth , and also practise it.

2. The next thing I shall mind them of, as one of their greatest defects, is that sublime, and never-sufficiently praised Science of *Pyrotechny* or *Chymistry*; which though it hath suffered much through the corruption of time, and the wickednesse of covetous Impostors, and ravenous Harpies, who gaping after mountains of Gold, do either suck the purses of others as greedy as themselves, or else do willingly suffer themselves to be deluded , and circumvented by these broilers and smoak-sellers, and so bring an injust infamy upon this so profitable and laudable an art. And though in former times it was had in honour by *Trismegist, Geber, Raymund Lully, Arnoldus de villà novâ, Roger Bacon,* and many others, yet was it for many ages in a manner buried in oblivion, or banished to the Monastick cells, until *Basilius Valentinus, Isaac Hollandus,* and *Paracelsus* that singular ornament of *Germany*, did revive and restore the same, and since more cleerly manifested by him, who is
justly

justly stiled *Philosophus per ignem*, and many other famous men. The benefits of which are now so openly known, especially the common and vulgar part of it (though the grand mysteries are hid in the brests of those who are truly called *Adepti*) and so much written by the elaborate pens of many learned and industrious men therein, that it would be needless to relate its transcendent uses, and excellencies: it being in a word that Art that doth help more truly and radically to denudate, and discover the secret principles and operations of nature, than any other in the world, and I dare truly and boldly say, that one years exercise therein to ingenious spirits, under able Masters, will produce more real and true fruit, than the studying *Aristotelian Philosophy* hath brought forth in many centuries. O that the Schools therefore would leave their idle, and fruitless speculations, and not be too proud to put their hands to the coals and furnace, where they might find ocular experiments to confute their fopperies, and produce effects that wou'd be beneficial to all posterities. I will onely mind them of this one rule. *Discendæ primum ergo digestiones, distillationes, sublimationes, reverberationes, extractiones, solutiones, coagulationes, fermentationes, fixationes, & omne quod ad opus hoc instrumentum requiritur, cognoscendum est usu, prout vitra, cucurbita, circulatoria, gallinarum ova, terrea vasa, balnea, furni ventales, reverberatorii similesq̃, nec non carbones atque tenacula: sic in Alchimia medicinaque proficere poteris.* Neither despise this counsel because the author is no friend to *Aristotle*, nor be ashamed to cast off thy fine clothes to work in a laboratory, for without this thou mayest wax old in ignorance, and dy with guilt, because thou hast served thy generations with no better stuff than *Aristotles* dreames, and *Scholastick* fables. *Nam ut ut naturale ingenium, & acumen judicii, Philosophus habeat, nunquam tamen ad rerum naturalium radicem, aut radicalem scientiam admittitur, sine igne.* For howsoever a *Philosopher* may have a natural wit, and acuteness of Judgement, notwithstanding he is never admitted to the root, or radical *Science* of natural things, without the fire.

Paracel. li. de. Tinct. Phys.

Helm li. Phys. Arist. et Gal. ign.

3.

3. Another thing of no less weight than the former I shall denote unto them, which is that part of natural *Philosophy*, that concerns medicine, which of all other is most necessary, and ochooful for conserving and restoring the health of man; and yet is no less imperfect, and defective than any of the rest.

For first it is turned into a way of meer formality, flattery, cunning, craft and covetousness, nothing being so much sought after by its professors as popular applause, repute, and esteem with rich and mighty men, that thereby the larger fees may be drawn from them, while in the mean time, the poor are neglected and despised. Is this the office of a Physician? is only riches got by hook or crook, whether the Patient receive benefit or none, live or dy, the sole end of their profession? and must these things have the countenance of Law, and confirmation by Charters? must these things be applauded and cryed up, while the sincere and faithful endeavors of simple and honest-meaning men, are disdained and trampled upon? But the world hath alwaies loved deceivers, and therefore must be deceived.

Secondly, the rule being most sure, that *ubi definit Philosophus, incipit medicus,* it must of necessity follow, that if *Philosophy* be false, uncertain, and ill bottomed of it self, then the medicinal knowledge that is built thereon and drawn from thence, must needs be faulty and ruinous. Now how false the *Aristotelian Philosophy* is in it self is in part made cleer, and more is to be said of it hereafter, and therefore truth and experience will declare the imperfection of that medicinal knowledge that stands upon no better a basis. For *Galen* their great *Coryphæus* and *Antesignanus* hath laid down no other principles to build medicinal skill upon, than the doctrine of *Aristotle*, as that all bodies mixt are compounded of the four Elements, and that the total parity or disparity, temperament, complexion, and constitution of all bodies do arise from the equal or unequal conflux and commixture of these four: and that from these do result four prime qualities, and four humours, and that the abounding; defect, repugnancy, or alteration of hese are
the

the caufes of all difeafes. *Mirum fane, quantum in his* Jo. Bapt. Van
rixatum, et fcriptum fit: ac miferandum, quantum hæc Hel·li. Elem·
laxa nugarum fomnia, mundum hactenus circumvene-
rint. *Truly it is a wonder how much hath been difputed*
and written in thefe things: and it is to be commiferated,
how much thefe loofe dreams of trifles, have hitherto cir-
cumvented the world.

For this fame author makes it good by undeniable arguments and experiments, that there are not four Elements, nor
humours, in *rerum natura*, and hath faid enough, fufficiently to confute and overthrow the whole Fabrick of the
Galenical learning, which here I forbear to infert. And
therefore it is very ftrange that the Schools, nay in a manner
the whole world, fhould be inchanted and infatuated
to admire, and own this ignorant *Pagan*, who being
ambitious of erecting his own fame, did traduce, and
darken the writings of thofe that preceded him, and pretending to interpret and open the doctrine of learned *Hippocra-*
tes, he altogether obfcured and perverted the fame: And
yet can the Schools be fo wilfully mad to adore this Idol, and
follow this blind guide.

Thirdly, if the ground of *Galenical Phyfick* had been
found and firm, and that it were the true and certain way
both to find out the caufes, and to cure difeafes, yet notwithftanding hath it been but loofly profecuted, and fmally
promoted, feeing for the fpace of fo many hundred years,
there is not by the Schools found out any more certain, fafe,
or eafie way to cure difeafes than was in the daies of *Hippo-*
crates, and *Galen*: It is very ftrange that it fhould grow up
and flourifh with them, and never fince come to any more
perfection, when it is ufually obferved that nothing is *fimul*
& femel invented and perfected. For it is plain that in *Bo-*
tanical knowledge nothing of value is found out or difcovered fince the daies of *Diofcorides*; for though fome plants be
now found out that were not then known, and many fpecies
of others alfo, and their cuts and figures more perfected, as
befide much confufedly heaped up concerning their qualities
of heat and cold, drinefs and moifture; yet is nothing more

M added

added by real experience, and diligent observation of their specifick vertues, and intrinsick properties, so that in regard of the vegetable Kingdom the art of medicine hath got little advance.

Fourthly, though medicinal knowledge have received some melioration especially in the *Anatomical* part, wherein men have laboured with much acuteness, diligence, and observation, so that this part seems to be growing, and arising towards the *Zenith* of perfection, especially since our never-sufficiently honoured Countryman Doctor *Harvey* discovered that wonderful secret of the bloods circulary motion : yet for all this there comes small advantage by it in practice, and application, for the more certain, safe, and easie curing of diseases : for though it bring great satisfaction to a speculative understanding, and help to cleer many intricate doubts, yet doth it little to remove dolor, danger, or death.

And moreover though it be grown to a mighty height of exactness, in vulgar *Anatomy* and dissection of the dead bodies of men, or the living ones of beasts, birds, and fishes ; yet is it defective as to that vive and *Mystical Anatomy* that discovers the true *Schematism* or signature of that invisible *Archeus* or *spiritus mechanicus*, that is the true opifex, and dispositor of all the salutary, and morbifick lineaments, both in the seminal *guttula*, the tender *Embrio*, Rob. de Fluct. and the formed Creature, of which *Paracelsus*, *Helmont*, lib de Anato-and our learned Countryman Dr. *Fludd*, have written most mia mystica. excellently.

Fiftly, the most excellent art of *Chirurgery*, though much advanced by the help of *Anatomy* in all that belongs to manual operation, or the use of instruments; yet in the curing of great and dangerous sores, as the *Lupus*, *Cancer*, *Fistula*, *Carcinoma*, *Elephantiasis*, *Strumaes*, virulent and malign Ulcers, and the like, it is much defective, and can perform little, without mineral and *Chymical* medicaments. Not because nature and providence have ordained no remedies for them, but because of the sloathfulness and negligence of professors and artists, who sit down contented with *Galeni-cal*

cal medicaments, thinking there is nothing of greater virtue, and operation than they; and so become slaves and captives to some few Authors, whom they think it not lawful to relinguish, or that natures whole mysteries were comprized in their paper Monuments, and no search further to be made: Not knowing that their scrutiny should be through the whole *Theatre* of nature, and that their only study and labour ought to be to acquire and find out salves for every sore, and medicines for every malady, and not to be inchained with the formal prescriptions of *Schools, Halls Colleges*, or Masters, but to seek continually that these things might be made known unto them, and not to imagine it is sufficient to have served an appenticeship to it as to a trade, except they arrive at higher attainments. *Quia me-dicus ad imaginem dei agere ac laborare jussus est, constat ipsum non nugacibus rebus, sed secretioribus Magiæ ac Cabalæ studiis operam suam locare debere: non enim ut Jurisconsultorum vel Physicorum scientia, sic et Medicina humanis speculationibus comprehendi potest, cum ipsa supra omnes artes admirabilis ac occulta existat.* Because the Physician is commanded to act, and labour according to the image of God, it is manifest that he ought not to place his pains in trifling things, but in the more secret studies of *Magick*, and *Cabalistick Science*: for not as the knowledge of Lawyers and Naturalists, so also can Medicinal skill be comprehended by human speculations, seeing it is admirable and occult above all arts. Therefore what great error, and how haynous a crime is it to leave the great book of the *Macracosm*, nay and the writings of others, only to adhere to the doctrine of ignorant, wicked, malicious, and blind *Pagans*? I shall onely add this, *Adeoque cum omne donum bonum, nedum virtutum, sed & cognitionum, descendat a patre luminum; quis poterit a Scholis Gentilitiis scientia medica tesseram ediscere? Dominus enim creavit medicum, non Schola.* Therefore seeing every good gift, not onely of vertues, but also of Sciences, doth descend from the Father of lights; who can perfectly learn the sum of Medicinal knowledge from the heathenish Schools?

Paracel. lib 4. de caus. Luis Gal. Cap. 9.

Hel. de prom. Author.

M 2

Schools? For the Lord hath created the Physician, not the Schools.

4. There remaineth diverse excellent discoveries of many mysterious things in nature that do properly belong to *Physicks*, which yet the Schools take small or no notice of, and as little pains in, either to know, teach, or improve them; and so are a witness against them of their sluggishness, and deficiency of their too-much-magnified *Peripatetick Philosophy*.

As first, they pass over with a dry foot that laudable, excellent, and profitable science of *Physiognomy*, which hath been admired, and studyed of the gravest and wisest Sages that have been in many generations: which is that Science which from and by certain external signs, signatures, and lineaments, doth explicate the internal nature and quality of natural bodies either generally or specifically. And this so necessary a knowledge both in the genus and species of it is altogether omitted by the School; they understand and teach nothing of Cælestial signatures, which are in some measure made known by the quantity, light, colour, motion, and other affections of those bodies: They teach nothing of *Subcælestial Physiognomy*, whether Elementary, *Meteorological*, or *Mineralogical*, but are utterly ignorant in all these, as also in *Botanical*, and *Anthropological Physiognomy*, contenting themselves with a few frivilous, false and formal definitions, and notions, and so never seek to penetrate into the more interiour nature of things, by which it comes to pass that they know little in the vegetable, and animal kingdomes, and least of all in the subterranean, or mineral; and but that *Paracelsus*, *Crollius*, *Quercetan*, *Baptista Porta*, and some others had taken pains in it, there had no footsteps of it almost been visible. And my Lord *Bacon* doth reckon also as defective the interpretation of natural dreams; for though *Aristotle* himself hath said something of this, yet those that pretend most to admire and honour him, have taken as little pains in this as the rest, to improve it to the glory of their great Master.

Secondly, they are as ignorant in the most admirable,
and

Verul·lib·4·de Aug.Sci.ca. 1.

Arist. lib. de Som. et vig. cap.3.

and soul-ravishing knowledge of the three great *Hypostatical* principles of nature, *Salt*, *Sulphur*, and *Mercury*, first mentioned by *Basilius Valentinus*, and afterwards clearly and evidently manifested by that miracle of industry and pains *Theophrastus Paracelsus.* Which however the *Schools* (as hating any liquor that is not drawn out of their own Cask, and despising all things that come by toyl and labor) may sleight and contemn it, and please themselves with their ayery *Chimæra* of an abstracted and scarce intelligible *materia prima*, or *Hyle*, which is neither *plane ens*, *nec non ens*, and think to make fools believe their Masters description of it, that it is *neque quantum, neque quale, neque quid, neque quicquid eorum quæ cernuntur*, and so the *Delphick* devil cannot expound it, nor *Sphinx* nor *Oedipus* be able to unriddle it; Is notwithstanding so cleer, certain, and *Apodictical* a truth, that all the *Academies* in the Universe will never be able to eradicate, and whose verity is made so evident by *Pyrotechny*, that he must needs distrust his own senses that will not credit it; but what avails it to sing to a deaf man? And though *Helmont* with the experiments of his *Gehennal* fire, and some other solid arguments labour the labefactation of this truth, yet doth he not prove that they are not *Hypostatical* principles, but onely that they are not the ultimate reduction that the possibility of art can produce, which he truly proves to be water; yet are the most compound bodies in the universe to be reduced into them, and by that introversion is the secrets of nature more laid open than by all the *Peripatetick Philosophy* in the world, and if this be not so, let experience speak,

    Thirdly, what shall I say of that wonderful and most beneficial discovery of the *Magnetical Philosophy*, by our worthy, learned, and industrious Countreyman Doctor *Gilbert?* what rare and unheard-of mysteries doth it disclose? what huge light, and advantage doth it bring to Natural *Philosophy*, and the *Mathematicks?* What helps to Navigation, and almost all other arts, and trades? How vastly is it improved, inlarged, and adorned by those great wits, and unwearied persons, such as *Ridley, Carpenter, Barlow,*
Ca-

Beguin. Tyr. Chy. c 2.

Par. de Trib. princ.

Gilb. de mag.

F*

Cabæus, and the grand gatherer of all kind of learning *A-*
thanasius Kercherus? Can the Schools say, or make it
good, that in the space of fifteen hundred years they ever invented any such like thing? nay it were well if they had not
been, and still were the opposers, contemners, and condem-
ners of all new discoveries, how transcendent, useful, or profitable soever they were.

Fourthly, what shall I say of the *Atomical* learning
revived by that noble, and indefatigable person *Renatus des*
Cartes, and since illustrated and improved by *Magnenus*
Regius, *White*, *Digby*, *Phocyllides*, *Holwarda*, and
divers others? Hath the Schools any thing of like firmness,
do they demonstrate after *Euclides* most certain and undeniable way, as *Democritus revivifcens* doth? no surely, all theirs
is but like dross and chaff in comparison of this. What shall
I say of that notable conceit of the most happy *genius* these
latter ages have had, *John Kepler*, of the Continued Emis-
fion of raies from the body of the Sun, that causeth all the
reft of the Planets to move? Deferves this no further inveftigation? What shall I say of the *Epicuræan Philofophy*,
brought to light, illuftrated and compleated by the labour of
that general Scholar *Petrus Gaffendus*? Surely if it be rightly
examined, it will prove a more perfect, and found piece,
than any the Schools ever had, or followed.

4. The *Philofophy* of *Ariftotle* maintained by the *Schools*
ought not to be prifed fo much above others, becaufe
in it there are many things fuperflucus, *Tautological*, frivolous, and needlefs, as we fhall in a few inftances make cleerly
evident.

For firft, omitting many fuperabundant reiterations, and
repetitions in his *Organicks* and *Animafticks*, I fhall only
touch fome few contained in his *Phyficks*: as in that much
celebrated definition wherein nature is faid to be *Principium*,
& caufa motus, & quietis ejus, in quo ineft primò, & per fe,
& non fecundùm accidens. 1. This particle *caufa* feems to
be put fuperfluoufly; feeing every caufe is a principle. 2.
That of *quietis*; feeing the faculty of Contraries are the
fame, for that which is the faculty of fpeaking, and holding
ones

ones peace, is the same. 3. That *ejus, in quo est*, seeing also art is the principle of the motion of the artificer, in whom it is. 4. That *primò*. 5. And that *per se*; for also art is the cause of artificial motion, primarily, and by it self, *quatenus* as far as it is of this sort. 6. That particle, *& non secundùm accidens*, is needless; for wherefore was that necessary seeing before he had put *per se*? I shall omit the rest of his nauseous *Tautologies* in the 3, 5, and 7. chapters of the forecited book, and in the most of the books of *Physicks* following, as obvious to every one that will take pains to examine and consider them.

Secondly, in his book *de Cœlo* he reiterates this, *Simplicis corporis simplex est motus, & simplex est motus simplicis corporis*, as though these two were much different : and there twice or thrice is repeated the probation, that Circular motion doth agree to some body according to nature. The like to which may be seen in the 5, 6, 7, 8, 9, and 12. chapters of the same book, and in all the books following of the same subject. I shall onely name one other, and so pass this point, *in lib. 1. De ortu, et interitu, cap. 6.* He propounds the question of the Elements, whether they be, or they be not? and whether they be sempiternal, or not ? As though they had not been agitated in his third *book de Cœlo*, and at last brings in that vain repetition, *est igitur tangens ut plurimùm id, quod tangit tangens : apparet tangens tangere quod tangit, necesse videtur esse quod tangitur tangere*, &c. O how egregiously is this disputed of him who must needs be accounted the *Prince of Philosophers*! O how excellent needs must those disciples be that are taught by so worthy a Master !

5. This *Philosophy* ought not so much to be magnified above other, because in it are very many things that are apparently, and absolutely false, to make which appear, I shall onely name two or three manifest particulars.

First he affirms that nothing is contrary to substance, which he again asserts in his *Logick*, and repeats elsewhere, which to me seems absolutely false : for certainly the substance of the fire is contrary to the substance of the water. But thou wilt

Arist. l. 1. de Cœl. et Mun. cap. 2.

Arist. lib. 1. Phys. cap. 6.

wilt say the Contrariety is solely in the Qualities.   But seeing these qualities are every one proper to their Substances, and do arise out of them, and accept their *esse* from them: and therefore doth not this also argue contrariety in them ? For let the substance be of the same nature on both sides; from whence is it that these qualities do arise rather than others which are contrary unto them ? And again in the same chapter it is false that he teacheth that contraries cannot suffer of themselves: For do not cold things strive with hot, and moist things with dry ? And do not these qualities mutually beat back, and expel one another.

Secondly, it is false which he affirms *lib.* 2. *Phys. cap.* 7. That the formal, final, and efficient causes are coincident, to wit in respect of the same effect: for how can the father be the same with the essential form of the Son ? And it is also false which he defends in the eighth chapter, That art doth not deliberate; otherwise artists do all things rashly. But although the Mason do not deliberate, whether he ought to prepare a foundation rather than an house, Therefore doth he not consult, whether he shall build it now rather than at another time ? or whether of this matter, rather than of other ? or whether in this manner, rather than in another ?

Thirdly, how false is that which he laies down in the 6, and 7. chapters of the third book of *Physicks*, that no number can be given, than which a greater may not be excogitated: but that a magnitude may be given, to wit the world, than which no greater can be excogitated ? I pray you why may it not be lawful and possible to conceive a magnitude greater than this world ? nay ten thousand times greater, wherein lies the impossibilitie ? He also defines there *infinitum* to be that beyond which something alwaies may be taken; but how is that possible to be infinite that hath something *extra se* ? or that it can be made infinite by something without it self ? These are brave fancies, and fine dreams.

Fourthly, in the 8. book, besides innumerable falsityes that may be observed in the 5, 6, 7, 8, and 9. chapters, that

is

is a moſt ſignal one, which in the firſt chapter he labours to build up, of the eternity of motion : that thereby he may make out the ingeniture, and eternity of the world. Let us therefore ſee with what reaſons he can evince, and perſwade it. 1. Is this, Motion is the act of a movable thing : Therefore that which is movable hath preceded Motion. I pray you doth he not wound himſelf with his own weapon, and ſtrangle himſelf by his own conſequence ? For if any thing hath preceded Motion ? Therefore motion is not eternal. 2. He argues, The thing moving, and the thing moved are either made, or are eternal; But neither can be ſaid to be ſo. But wherefore cannot the one or both be eternal, and neverthelefs without motion ? He adds, becauſe this is abſurd. An egregious inſtance truly, and indeed *Philoſophical*! for where appears this abſurdity ? He further urges : If the thing movable had preceded motion, then it had reſted : and ſo another motion had been neceſſary before, of which that reſt had been a privation. Verily as though he who is born blind, ought to have ſeen in the womb, that blindleſs might be accounted the privation thereof. 3. He proceeds, Power ought to be neer to the Act. As though ſtones that have lain hid from the framing of the world under the earth, had not as well power to be framed into an houſe which is made to day, as they have a few daies before they be digged up. 4. He ſaith, Time is eternal, therefore Motion alſo : He confirms the *Antecedent*, 1. Becauſe all *Philoſophers*, except *Plato*, do affirm it. As though the matter were pleaded in the Court, where voices are numbred? yet ſome have accounted *Plato*'s judgement more than a thouſand ; but this were to try things by authority, not by truth. 2. Becauſe time is not *ſine nunc* : but every *nunc* is the beginning of the ſequent, and the end of the præcedent time. As though there could not be a *nunc* firſt, and laſt; if either the motion of heaven hath begun, or alſo if we believe that motion is not meaſured by time, which were not hard to demonſtrate.

5. I ſhall onely inſtance in one place more, and that is *lib.*1. *de Cœlo cap.*3, *cap.*4. There he aſſumes, and endeavours

N

vours

vours to prove, that Circulary motion hath nothing contrary unto it: what if of two wheels or orbs, the one were moved towards the Orient, and the other towards the Occident, were they not to be said to be moved towards contrary parts? and is not this to have something contrary unto it? nay may not the motion of something in a straight line, be contrary to motion that is circular, seeing all motion is considered in relation unto the term, or point from whence, and unto which it moves? and how this cannot be possible, to me seems neither probable nor possible. And though I have but taken these few things to instance in, yet were it no hard matter (but that it belongs not to my present purpose) to evert the whole ground and fabrick of his *Philosophy*, and that with arguments unanswerable, and infallible, but these are sufficient for this place and purpose.

6. *Aristotle's ipse dixit*, or the *School's sic habet Aristoteles*, ought no longer to pass for oracles, nor his tenents for truths before others: because innumerable things in his *Philosophy* do contradict, and are *diametrically* contrary; and that I may make out what I say, I shall call in for witness his own words, and instance in some few particular places, that it may be manifest how inconstant and wavering he was in his own opinions.

First, in his book of *Categories* there is plain contradiction, seeing he makes ten: and notwithstanding elsewhere sometimes three, sometimes six, sometimes eight. He saith the first substance is rather substance than the second, and not long after he affirmeth that the property of substance is to receive more and less. He makes Time a species of Continued quantity: and notwithstanding in the 4 book of *Physicks*, he will have it to be Number, which is Discrete quantity. He also indeavours in the 1 *book Priorum Analyticorum*, to demonstrate the definition of the figures, and in the 2 after teacheth that definition cannot be demonstrated. In the 1 *book Posteriorum* he will have us in Demonstration to proceed from things more known to us: and for all that he defines demonstration to be that which proceeds from Causes, but causes are more unknown to us than effects; and in the

same

same books he hath many such like, which for brevity I omit.

Secondly, in his first book of *Physicks* he impugneth that immovable principle of *Parmenides*, and *Melissus*: and after in the 8 book he proveth that there is one immovable principle of motion. He teacheth in the fifth chapter, that Contraries are not made, by course, of themselves, and not long after he holdeth, that whatsoever is generated, is generated of its contrary, and that whatsoever is corrupted goes into its contrary. In the second book, and seventh chapter, he disputeth against *Empedocles* affirming that the works of nature are made by chance; And yet confesses that Monsters are the misses and lapses of nature: And in the seventh book of *Metaphysicks* the seventh chapter, he holdeth that those things that do grow without seed are made casually, from whence also in the 3 *de Animâ* the 1 2. *chapter*, he saith, *Quæ naturâ sunt, propter aliquid sunt, aut casus eorum, quæ sunt propter aliquid.* And many other of the like sort, from which I purposely supersede, these being sufficient to make good the assertion.

Thirdly, one more may be joined to these out of his book *de Cælo* the 2 *chapter*, where he saith, that every natural body is movable: And yet for all that in the third chapter, and more expresly in the fourteenth of the second book, he contendeth that the earth doth rest immovable in the center of the world. In the seventh chapter in the words cited not long before he altogether supposeth the heaven not to be animated: and notwithstanding he expressely saith it is animated in the second book, and second chapter; and also the first *de anima* the third chapter, and elsewhere. In the second book, and second chapter, he holdeth that a sempiternal motion is in God: and in the eighth of the *Physicks* he maintaineth the *primum movens* to be immovable, which is God: In the eight he saith the heaven is not an Organical body, and notwithstanding (as it is already seen) he hath made it to be indued with a Soul: For the soul, as he defines it, is the act of an organical body: as also in the twelf he saith, *Actionem astrorum talem esse, qualis est plantarum, & animalium.* N 2 But

But of thefe things enough; by all which (I conceive)
it is cleerly manifeft that the *Peripatetick Philofophy* ought
not to be preferred before all other , nay rather to be utterly
exterminated, and fome better introduced in the place therof,
and that is the thing was attempted to be proved.

C H A P. VII.

Of Metaphyficks , Ethicks, Politicks, Oeco-nomicks , Poefie, and Oratory.

THough there be fomething in the moft of thefe, that
might tollerably pafs, yet are many things in them fo
ufelefs, falfe, uncertain, fuperfluous, wicked and defective,
that they ftand in need of reformation , melioration, or eradication , as we fhall fhew of every one of them in their order.

    1. For the *Metaphyficks,* which they call their *Philofo-phia prima* , and do ufually define it to be *Scientia entis ,
quatenus ens eft* , the abufe and vanity of it appears in this :
That it being nothing elfe but an abftract confideration of
things by way of prefcifion, or cutting off from all other co-
comitant cogitarions , and fo to weigh and examine the
things nudely and barely under the refpect of their being ,
all other notions thereabout being feparate from it , doth
bring no better inftruments , nor effective means for the difcovery of truth, than the weak and bare operation of the Intellect, or indeed of Phantafie, or the Imaginative faculty, and
therefore no marvail that it hath fpider-like weaved forth
fo many flie and cunning Cobweb-contextures of flender
conceits, and curious niceties, fit for nothing but to infnare
and intangle : and hath been fo luxurioufly petulant in the
fœtiferous production of fo many monftrous, fruitlefs, and
                                          vain

vain Chimæras. For they holding the foul to be *tabula ra-
fa*, in which nothing is infculpt, and that Science comes
not by *reminifcence*, or *refufcitation*, but meerly acquifi-
tively *de novo*, and that there is nothing in the Intellect that
hath not firft fome way or other been in the Senfes, then muft
it needs follow that the operations of the Intellect are but
weak means to produce *Scientifical* certitude, and fo *Metaphyfical* learning but barren and fruitlefs.

2. It hath neither laid down, nor affumed any certain
principles, that are neceffary or helpful to promote Science; for whereas it obtends this for a maxim, That not
any thing can be, and not be at the fame inftant of time,
what fruitful products was there ever yet drawn from this unprofitable fundamental? neither ever hath it proceeded fo
far as to find a fure, and ultimate refting place, which notwithftanding the learned *Renatus des Chartes* hath happily
performed, having gone back to the very bafis of all, which
is, that there is *mens cogitans*, which can no way feign, or excogitate it felf not to be, which is a more certain and undeniable principle than ever the Schools invented, or built upon.

3. It is of no ufe nor advantage to other Sciences, nor
ever hath brought any good or profit unto the fons of men,
but onely feduced them into ftrange labyrinths of notional
Chymæras, and fpeculations, like idle and vain dreams,
filling and feeding the fanfie, but yielding nothing of folidity to inrich the Intellect, nor any thing of ufe or profit
to accomodate mankind: except that may be accounted an
advantage, to obfcure the truth, and lead the phantafies
of men into the crooked *Meanders* of conceit, and nutation,
and fo with the affiftance of its Twin *Logick* (both fifters
of the fame mother *Nox*) bring men to imagine and argue
much, but in truth and verity to know little.

4. If it had been able (as it proudly pretends) to have
taught any thing truly and certainly of thofe things that are
Metaphyfical, or fupernatural, that either are not corporeal
or materiate, or elfe much tranfcend the nature of *Phyfical*
bodies both Cæleftial and Elementary, then might it juftly
be

Renat. des
Chart. de
method.

be received, and have its due commendation.   But alas!
what weak, frivolous and groundless opinions hath it produced concerning God, Angells, separate substances, and

Verul. de Au
Scient. lib. 3
cap. 2.

the like? not seeing so much in these things as the *Ethnicks*,
who, in the fable of the Golden Chain, did affirm, that neither men, nor the Gods could draw *Jupiter* from heaven to
the earth, but that *Jupiter* could easily draw men from the
earth to heaven. *Quare frustra sudaverit, qui Cælestia
religionis arcana, nostræ rationi adaptare conabitur.*
Therefore he in vain sweats, who indevours to fit the heavenly mysteries of religion to our reason.

5. What shall I say of those strange, vain, and poisonous

Vid. Meta-
physc. Campa-
nel. et Pet.
Gassend. con-
tra Arist.

Cockatrice eggs that it hath hatched, full of nothing but
useless questions and altercations, to as little purpose as the
disputes *de Lanâ caprinâ*, or Moonshine in the Water?
What shall I say of it, is it not altogether defective of all
solid, and fruit-bearing knowledge? doth it not superflu-
ously abound with vanities and follies? was ever any made
either wise or happy by it? and yet this is the *Schools* prime
Philosophy or *Metaphysical* learning, which is nothing but

Aug. Alstem.
de nobil. in-
stitut.lib.

vain opination, void of *Scientifical* demonstration, and cleer
verity. *Fateamur, rerum divinarum paucissimarum de-
monstrationes habemus, omnia fere opinionibus desinentes.*
*We must confess, we have the demonstrations of very few
divine things, defining all things by opinions.*

In the next place comes the *Ethicks* to be considered of,
which how fruitless and vain they are may appear in a few
reasons.

For 1. how can he be supposed to be the fittest teacher
of that art, who was himself an heathen, and neither knew
nor acknowledged God, who indeed is the *summum bonum*, and so placed felicity in fading, and momentary
things, as riches, and honour: or at the best made but Vertue the chief good, which cannot however be happiness it
self, but at the most but the way and means to attain it? And
it must necessarily follow that he that understands not the
real, and true end, cannot teach the indubitate means that
leads to that end, and therefore must needs be a blind guide,
                                                    especially

especially to Chriſtians, as *Lambertus Danæus* hath ſufficiently manifeſted; and yet the Schools muſt needs follow, Lamb. Danæ.
and prefer the dark Lamp of a blind *Pagan*, before the de Ethick.
bright-ſhining Sun of the Prophets, and Apoſtles. Chriſt.lib.

2. Though the Schools have diſputed much of the Chief
good, of vertues, and of vices, yet have they either taught
nothing at all that is practicable, whereby vertue might be
obtained, and vice eſchewed, or felicity enjoyed, or but
touched it very ſlenderly, perfunctorily, and unprofitably
as though it were ſufficient to teach a Pilot the many dangers
of his voyage in reſpect of tempeſts, ſtorms, winds, ſands, Verulam. de
ſhelves, rocks, and the like, and to make a large commen- Aug. Scient.
dation of the peace, plenty, fruitfulneſs, and happineſs of lib.7.1.
the place to which his journey were intended; yet leave him
altogether ignorant and untaught how to eſcape thoſe dangers, and unfurniſhed with means to attain to the harbour
unto which his navigation is purpoſed.

3. They have choſen to themſelves ſuch a way, whereby
the maſs of *Ethical* knowledge might be ſet forth as a ſplen-
did and beautiful thing, bearing forth the brightneſs of wit,
and vigour of eloquence, rather than any truth in the matter, or benefit to the readers and hearers, and ſo have made
it facilely diſputable, but difficultly practicable, ſeeking
themſelves, more than truth, or the benefit of others; as
Seneca truly ſaith, *Nocet illis eloquentia, quibus non rerum facit cupiditatem, ſed ſui: Eloquence hurteth thoſe,
to whom it cauſeth not the deſire of things, but of themſelves:* for water is better in an Earthen veſſel, than poiſon
in a golden cup, and he that ſpeaks truly and to profit others
is to be preferred before him that ſpeaks *Rhetorically*, and
elegantly to ſmall profit or purpoſe.

4. It cannot but be matter of much wonder to all ingenuous men that ſhall more ſeriouſly perpend, and weigh the
buſineſs, why not onely the Moral *Philoſophy* of *Ariſtotle* ſhould take place above that which is deduced from
principles of Chriſtianity; but alſo why he ſhould have
therein the preheminence above *Socrates*, *Plato*, *Zeno*,
and many others, who truly taught many divine and pretious
things

things for the eradicating of vice, the planting of vertue, and the eſtabliſhing of mental tranquillity, and moral feliciý, which *Ariſtotle* and all his *Sectators* never either underſtood, or had fruition of.   What ſhall I ſay of that man of men the ſevere *Seneca?* are not his writings about vertue, tranquillity, and curing the minds diſeaſes, infinitely beyond all thoſe needleſs, fruitleſs, vain and impertinent diſcourſes of the proud *Stagyrite?* Let all that ever loved vertue and tranquillity, and have peruſed the one, and the other, ſpeak, and declare their judgements: nay doth not that one little *Enchiridion* of *Epictetus* contain more pretious treaſure, than all the great volumes of *Ariſtotle?* let vertue ſpeak, and truth determine.

Ariſt. Nich.l.
l.cap.5.

Pet. Gaſſend.
con. Ariſt ex.
7.

Now for the *Political* and *Oeconomical* learning taught by the Schools out of *Ariſtotle*, as it hath many things of ſingular uſe, and commoditie in it, ſo is it not without its chaff, and tares, deſerving rather purging, and refining, than the eſtimation of being compleat and perfect: For as there are many things in it frivolous, obſcure, immethodical, ſuperfluous, and falſe, ſo alſo is it very defective, and imperfect; for if we look upon what *Plato* hath written *de legibus*, and *de Republica*, though there may be found many things unpracticable, and incompleat, yet compared with the other, it is no way inferiour, but deſerves as great, if not an higher commendation; and ſo the writings of *Bodin*, nay *Macchiavel* and divers other modern authors may duly challenge as much praiſe in this point, as that of *Ariſtotle*, which the *Schools* do ſo much adhere to and magnifie, yea even our own Countreyman maſter *Hobbs* hath pieces of more exquiſiteneſs, and profundity i n that ſubject, than ever the *Grecian* wit was able to reach unto, or attain; ſo that there is no reaſon why he ſhould be ſo applauded, and univerſally received, while more able pieces are rejected, and paſt by.

Laſtly, for *Rhetorick*, or *Oratory*, *Poeſie*, and the like, which ſerve for adornation, and are as it were the outward dreſs, and attire of more ſolid ſciences; firſt they might tollerably paſs, if there were not too much affectation towards

towards them, and too much pretious time spent about
them, while more excellent and neceffary learning lies neglected and paffed by: For we do in thefe ornamental arts, as
people ufually do in the world, who take more care often
time about the goods of fortune, than about the good of the
body, and more nice and precife follicitoufnefs about fafhi-
ons and garbs, than either about the body it felf or the goods *Verul. de Au-*
of the mind, regarding the fhell more than the kernel, and *Sci. l. 6 c. 3.*
the fhadow more than the Subftance. And therefore it was
not without juft caufe that *Plato* (though by fome cenfured
for it) did reckon *Rhetorick* amongft the voluptuary arts,
for we moft commonly ufe it either for the priding and plea-
fing of our felves that we may appear eloquent, and learned
to others, or elfe ufe it cunningly and fophiftically to captivate, and draw over the judgements of others to ferve our ends
and interefts: and thereby make falfe things appear true, old
things new, crooked things ftraioht, and commodious
things unprofitable, as *Auguftine* faith, *Imperitior mul-*
titudo, quod ornate dicitur, etiam vere dici arbitratur,
The more unfkilful multitude thinketh that what is fpoken
elegantly, is alfo fpoken truly. And therefore *Seneca* faith, *Sen. Epift. 115.*
Seeft thou a man neat and compt in his language, then is his
mind occupied in minute things.

2. Both Eloquence and *Poefie* feem rather to be numbred amongft the gifts of nature, than amongft the difci-
plines, for thofe which excell much in reafon, and do dif- *Aug. Alft. de*
pofe thofe things which they excogitate in a moft eafie me- *nobil. inftitut.*
thod, that they may be cleerly, and diftinctly underftood,
are moft apt to perfwade, although they did ufe the language of the *Goths*, and had never learned *Rhetorick*: and
thofe that are born to invent moft ingenious figments, and *Ren. der Char.*
to exprefs them with the greateft elegance and fuavity, are *de method.*
to be accounted the beft *Poets*, although they are ignorant
of all the precepts of the *Poetical* art; for *nafcitur, non fit*
poeta; and therefore *Plato* moft truly concludeth, *Omnes*
itaque carminum poetæ infignes, non arte, fed divino af-
flatu, mente capti omnia ifta præclara poemata canunt.
Therefore all the famous makers of verfes, do not fing all

O   *thofe*

thefe excellent Poems by art, but by a divine afflation, being carried above themfelves.

3. Though *Ariftotle* were a great Mafter in *Oratory*, and a very eloquent man, yet in that point might juftly give the palm to his Mafter *Plato*, unto whom all the attributes of honour in that particular are worthily accumulated, of whom it is faid, That if *Jupiter* would fpeak in mans language, he would fpeak in that of *Plato*.

Thus have I briefly run over fome of the faults, and defects of *Academick* learning, but am far from having touched all, for to have done that would have reached beyond both my time, and purpofe, and alfo mine abilities; for *Benardus non videt omnia*: yet if the Lion may be known by his paw, and *Hercules* by his foot, then I hope there is enough faid to make it clear, that the *Ariftotelian*, and *Scholaftick* learning, deferves not the preheminence above all other, nor thofe great commendations that the corruption of times, and floathful ignorance of the moft have afcribed unto it, but that a great part of it doth deferve eradication, fome of it reformation, and all of it melioration, and fo I proceed.

Chap. VIII.

Of their Cuftomes, and Methode.

HAving hitherto fpoken of the fubjective learning that the *Schools* handle, it follows in order to examine their cuftomes and methode, not that I mean to meddle either with their manners, or maintenance, but leave that to the judgement of others, left it happen to me, as *Erafmus* faid of *Luther*, that it was dangerous to meddle with the *Popes* Crown, and Monks bellies: but only to note fome
                   things

things in the way, and methode of their teaching, which are obvious to my weak obfervation, and fo fhall lay them down as they prefent themfelves to my low apprehenfion.

1. Though in one *Academy* there be ufually divers *Colleges*, or houfes, yet muft all the Scholars in thofe feveral places be tyed to one methode, and carried on in one way, nay even bound to the fame authors, and hardly allowed fo much liberty, and difference, as is between *Ariftotle*, and *Ramus Logick*: As though they in the way of their teaching had arrived at the higheft point of perfection, which could no way be improved, or no o:her as profitable could be difcovered and found out, and fo are all forced like carriers horfes, to follow one another in the accuftomed path, though it be never fo uneven or impaffable.

2. Their *Scholaftick* exercifes are but flenderly, negligently, and floathfully performed, their publike acts (as they call them though but verbal digladiations) being but kept four times in the year, that is in the terms, which if one fhould tell them in plain terms, are but ufually idle termes : as though time of all other things here below, were not to be accounted moft pretious, and that there can be no fuch detriment done unto youth, as to lofe or mifpend it.

3. Their Cuftome is injurious, and prejudicial to all thofe that defire to make a fpeedy progrefs in learning, nay unequal, and difproportionable in it felf, namely to ty men to a fet time of years, or acts, befote they can receive their *Laureation*, or take their degrees: as though all were of one capacity or induftry, or all equally able at their matriculation, and fo the floathful, and painful, the moft capable, and moft blockifh, fhould beth in the fame equal time have an equal honour, which is both difproportionable and unjuft. For fome will attain to more in one year than fome in three, and therefore why fhould they not be refpected according to their merits and proficiency, and not bound to draw in an unequal yoak ? and what matter were it whether a man had been there one moneth or feven years, fo he had the qualification required, and did *fubire examen*,

O 2   and

and perform the duties of the place, surely it is known that *gradus non confert scientiam, nec cucullus facit monachum.*

4. Their custome is no less ridiculous, and vicious, in their histrionical personations in the performance of their exercises, being full of childishness, and scurrility, far from the gravity, and severity of the *Pythagorean* School where a five years silence was enjoined: using so much lightness as more befits stage-players than diligent searchers of Science, by scoffing and jeering, humming and hissing, which shewes them like those animals they imitate, nay rather hurtful Geese, than labourious Bees, that seek to gather into their Hives, the sweet Honey of Learning, and Knowledge.

5. What is there in all their exercises, but meer notions, and quarrelsome disputations, accustoming themselves to no better helps for searching into natures abstruse secrets than the *Chymæras* of their own brains, and converse with a few paper Idols? as though these alone were sufficient keyes to open the Cabinet of Natures rich treasurie, without labour and pains, experiments and operations, tryals and observations: Surely if he that intends to prove a proficient in the knowledge of *Agriculture*, should onely give himself over to contemplation, and reading the books of such as have written in that Subject, and never put his hand to the plough, nor practise the way of tilling and sowing, would he ever be a good husbandman, or understand thorowly what pertains thereunto? Surely not, and no more can they be good Naturalists that do but onely make a mold and *Idæa* in their heads, and never go out by industrious searches, and observant experiments, to find out the mysteries contained in nature.

6. Their custome is no less worthy of reprehension that in all their exercises they make use of the *Latine* tongue, which though it may have custome, and long continuance to plead its justification, and that it is used to bring youth to the ready exercise of it, being of general reception almost through the whole world: yet it is as cleerly answered, that custome, withou

without reason and benefit, becomes injurious, and though it make them ready in speaking the *Latine* while they treat of such subjects as are usually handled in the *Schools*, yet are they less apt to speak it with facility in negotiations of far greater importance. And in the mean time, the way to attain knowledge is made more difficult, and the time more tedious, and so we almost become strangers to our own mother tongue, loving and liking forein languages, as we do their fashions, better than our own, so that while we improve theirs, our own lies altogether uncultivated, which doubtless would yield as plentiful an harvest as others, if we did as much labour to advance it: *Neque hodiè ferè ulla est natio, qua de idiomatis sui præstantia non glorietur, aut contendat.* And therefore were the *Romans* so careful to propagate their language in other nations, and to prohibit the *Greek* language or any other to be spoken in their publike contentions: And so likewise *Pythagoras, Plato,* and *Aristotle* did teach in their own mother tongues, and *Hippocrates, Galen, Euclide,* and others writ in the vulgar language of their own nation, and yet we neglecting our own, do foolishly admire and entertain that of strangers, which is no lesse a ridiculous than prejudicial custome.

Aug. Alp. de nobil institut.

7. Another is no less faulty and hurtful than the precedent, and that is their too much admiring of, and adhering to antiquity, or the judgement of men that lived in ages far removed from us, as though they had known all things, and left nothing for the discovery of those that came after in subsequent ages; It was appositely said of *Seneca, In re maximâ, & involutissimâ, in quâ cum etiam multum actum erit, omnis tamen ætas quod agat inveniet.* In the greatest, and most intricate thing, in which when also much is done, notwithstanding every age shall find what it may further do; and so profoundly censures those great men that went before us, to be as our leaders, but not our masters, and so most excellently concludeth, *Multùm restat operis, multumque restabit: nec ulli nato post mille sæcula præcludetur occasio aliquid adhuc adjiciendi.* Much work doth remain, and much will remain: neither will the occasion

be

Verul.de An.
Scient.l.1. et
Nov.Org. lib.
Aphor. 84.

be cut off to any born after a thousand ages, still of adding something. And indeed we usually attribute knowledge and experience to men of the most years, and therefore these being the latter ages of the world should know more , for the grandævity of the world ought to be accounted for antiquity , and so to be ascribed to our times , and not to the Junior age of the world, wherein those that we call the antients, did live , so that *antiquitas saculi, juventus mundi.*

8. They usually follow another hurtful Custome not unlike to this preceding, which is too much to bind in themselves with the universality of opinions, and multiplicity of voices, as though it were not better to stand single and alone with truth, than with error to have the company of the multitude, or as though the multitude could not err , or that the greater number must necessarily be in the truth, when as the wiseman saith the number of fools are infinite , and *Aristotle* himself tells us, that though we speak as the most , yet we should think as the fewest , and *Cicero* informs us that *Philosophy* is content with a few judges, and *Seneca* most egregiously saith, *Nihil magis præstandum est, quàm ne pecorum ritu sequamur antecedentium gregem, pergentes non quo eundum est, sed quò itur:* Nothing is more to be performed, than that we may not , according to the manner of cattel, follow the flock of those that went before, not following whither it ought to be gone, but whither it is gone. And again, *Nulla res nos Majoribus malis implicat, quàm quod ad rumorem componimur, optima rati ea, qua magno assen u recepta sunt :* Nothing doth insnare us with greater evils, than that we compose our selves to rumours, supposing those things the best, which are received with great assent.

9. Consonant to this is that other of their adhering to authority, especially of one man, namely *Aristotle,* and so do *jurare in verbi Magistri*, when according to their own tenents, arguments drawn from authority , are numbred amongst the weakest , and what could *Aristotle* know more than all other, that his opinions should be received as oracles?

he

both might and did err, as well as other mortals: And may not we as juftly recede from him as he from his Mafter *Plato*, and the reft of the antient *Philofophers*? Is it any thing but a juft liberty that we ought to maintain, and purfue, thereby to be admitted into the Court of Lady Verity? for which all chains ought to be broken, and all fetters fyled off.

10: Neither is their methode, and order in teaching any whit lefs vicious than the reft, for whereas *Ariftotle* himfelf prefuppofeth his Aufcultator or Scholar in *Phyficks* to have been already trained up in the *Mathematical* Sciences (which are indeed inftrumently fubordinate to natural *Philofophy* as intreductive thereunto) the Schools immethodically, and prepofteroufly teach youth *Logick*, and natural *Philofophy*, not having at all tafted the very rudiments of *Mathematical* knowledge, which how much out of due order and methode, nay contrary unto it, I leave to all judicious perfons to judge and confider.

CHAP. IX.

Of fome expedients, or remedies in Theologie, Grammar, Logick, and Mathematicks.

I Know it will be objected, that *facile eft reprehendere*, *it is an eafie thing to find fault*, but difficult and arduous to repair and amend, and that one fool may mar, and fpoil that in an hour, which many wife men cannot make right again in many ages: and the moft ignorant may eafily diforder, and deface the mafter-piece of the moft curious artift,

tift, when he is not able to repair the leaft part of it. And therefore that it is not fufficient to demolifh an antient, and goodly Fabrick, upon pretence that it is either unprofitable in the fite, and figure, or that the materials are ruinous, and decayed; unlefs we bring better in their room, have laid a better platform, and know certainly how to erect a better Fabrick.

To which I anfwer, by a cleer confeffion, that before we throw down we fhould know wherewithal, and how to build, and that it is far more eafie to demolifh, than to erect a fufficient and compleat Structure, and efpecially for a fingle perfon (and he alfo of the loweft, and leaft abilities) which is & ought to be the work of many, nay all perfons and ages: for as I verily believe that what I have produced for demonftrating the groundlefnefs, ruinoufnefs, and compofure of the *Scholaftick* Fabrick of learning is not far from the truth, fo alfo am I confident of mine infufficiency to erect a better in the place thereof, yet *in magnis voluiffe fat eft*, I fhall do mine endeavour, hoping that thofe that are more able will put to their hands to help to fupply my defects, and fo fhall offer the beft materials and art that I have to erect a new, and better building, and in the fame order that I have handled the fevtral parts.

1. Therefore for *Theology* which is a fpeaking of God, or a fpeaking forth the things of God, it is expedient that men fhould lay afide the fuffering of themfelves to be ftyled by that blafphemous title of *Divines*, which is fuch an impropriety of language as all their learning will never be able to juftify, it being an attribute that doth onely predicate effentially of the being of God, and is indeed incommunicable to the Creature, who hath nothing that is divine or fpiritual but by participation; for though the text faith that *Saints* are partakers of the divine nature, yet will it not follow that becaufe they are faid to be partakers of divine things that therefore they are divine, becaufe participations do not truly predicate of thofe effences to which they are communicated, but of that being from whence they flow: for men participate of the light and heat of the Sun, but

but it cannot be truly predicated of men that either they are the Sun, nor truly and univocally that they are of a *Solary* nature, but onely that participating of its influences and operations, they may be truly said to be heatned, and inlightned: for though it be in the *English* translated *Iohn the Divine*, whereby those that understand not the *Greek* are misled, and thereby drawn to give that title to their *Priests*, who blasphemously assume it to themselves, yet I hope there is much difference betwixt Θεόλογος, and Oς̃τος, one that speaks of God or divine things, and one that is divine, the *Scots* therefore have a more apposite and warrantable *Epithite*, who seldome or never call their Ministers *Divines* but *Theologues*, and we have many could cry out against the *Bishops* for having the title of Lord, or Grace given them, and yet they themselves can swallow this title of being *Divines*, which is more unseemly, unfit, and unwarrantable.

2. Another expedient that I shall offer in this case is, That the Scriptures which are as the seamless Coat of Christ may not be rent and torn with the carnal instruments of mans wit and reason, nor modell'd, or methodiz'd as an humane art or science, but laid aside in *Scholastick* exercises, as a sacred and sealed book, lest they offering strange Lev. 10. 1,2. fire upon Gods altar, perish as others have done: for in the day of mans light the Tabernacle of the Lord will be covered with a cloud, and in the night of his darkness there will be fire; therefore let not men journey until the cloud be taken Exod 40.36, up, or the fire appear, otherwise they must know the Lord 37,38. doth not lead them nor go before them. And indeed, whatsoever the proud and deceitful heart of man may imagine, the Scriptures are a sealed book, for so the prophet saith, *The* Isa.29.11, 12. *vision of all is become as the words of a book that is sealed, which men deliver to one that is learned, saying, Read this I pray thee: and he saith, I cannot, for it is sealed. And the book is delivered to him that is not learned, saying, Read this I pray thee, and he saith, I am not learned.* What can be more plain than this, that it is as a sealed book both to the learned, and unlearned ? and this is it that is sealed

P with

Rev. 5. 1,2,3,
4, 5. with seven seals, and no man in heaven, nor earth, nor in the Sea, that is found worthy to open this book, and to un-close the seaven seals thereof, but only the strong Lion of the Tribe of *Iuda*, and therefore let *Schools* not touch it, lest it be their destruction. For unless they leave the Lords own work to himself, and cease to sit in the seat of the scornful,

Psalm 1. 7. *The Lord will laugh them to scorn, and vex them in his sore displeasure*, neither will he bless them in their labours, nor prosper them in their exercises : Nay, until all the Magi-strates, and Elderships of the earth that profess his name, take off their Crowns, and lay them at the feet of the Lamb, and learn to practise, and put in execution our Saviors coun-sel, *To give unto God the things that are Gods, and to Cæsar the things that are Cæsars*, and not at all to intermed-dle with the things of God, misery and destruction will fol-low them to the grave, and of them shall be required the blood of all the Saints.   O therefore that they would

Psal. 2. 12. *Kisse the Sonne lest he be angry, and so they perish from the way of everlasting truth : for when his wrath is kin-dled but a little, blessed are all they that put their trust in him.*

   3. The last expedient I shall present in this subject is, That what can be discovered of God, and supernatural things, by the power of Reason, and the light of Nature, may be handled as a part of natural *Philosophy* (unto which it doth belong) because it is found out by the same means and instruments that other natural Sciences are : and what may from thence cleerly be demonstrated, and deducted, may be holden forth as a means to overthrow *Atheism, Gentilism*, and the like, but not to statuminate, or build up any thing in religion, nor like a wild bore to enter into the Lords vine-yard to root up and destroy it.

   In the next place are languages, and *Grammar*, which is the means or instrument by which they are taught, unto which I shall offer these few helps.

   1. That care may be had of improving, and advancing our own language, and that arts and sciences may be taught in it, that thereby a more easie and short way may be
had

had to the attaining of all forts of knowledge: **and** that thereby after the example of the *Romans* we may labour to propagate it amongft other nations, that they may rather be induced to learn ours, than we theirs, which would be of vaft advantage to the Commonwealth, in forrein Negotiations, Trading, Conqueft and Acquifitions, and alfo of much domeftick advantage within our own territories. For if we fhould arrive at any extraordinary height of learning, and knowledge, though we fhould but fpeak and write in our own mother tongue, then would other nations be as earneft in learning it, and tranflating our books, as former ages have been in labouring to attain the language, and tranflate the books of the *Græcians*, and *Romans*, and we at this day of the *French*, and *Germans*.

2. That fome compendious way for both teaching and learning forein languages, may be eftablifhed by ufe and exercife, without the tedious way of rule, or *Grammar*, which doubtlefs upon diligent, skilful, and exact tryal, would prove more fhort, eafie, certain, and beneficial, as is manifeft by ordinary people that never knew any thing of *Grammatical* order, being kept in families that fpeak another language, and having none to converfe with that fpeaks their own, will in a wonderful fhort time learn to fpeak, and underftand it; for when neceffity is joined with induftry, it produceth great and ftupendious effects.

3. That in the way of teaching languages the order prefcribed by *Comenius* in his *Janua linguarum* may be practifed, and means ufed to improve it, that both words and matter, names and things, may be learned together, which may be done both with the fame facility, and in the fame fhortnefs of time; that fo the tender intellects of young children may not onely inbibe the names, but alfo the natures and qualities of things

4. That in the methode of teaching *Grammar*, mafter *Brinfleys* way laid down in his *Grammar School* may be put into practice, that children may be taught in their mother tongue to know perfectly the feveral parts of Speech, declinable

clinable

clinable, and indeclinable, and punctually to vary the declinable parts, especially Noun, and Verb, and to construe and parse in their own tougue, that so they may be ready to make use, and to apply it when they learn the *Latine*, or any other language, without which they shall never have any sure foundation, nor proceed in any way of ease and certainty, nor arrive at any height of perfection, for none learns more than what the intellect clearly comprehends, and what it knows how to practise, and make use of.

5. In the *Grammatical* way of teaching it is a most certain axiom, that what is one part of speech in one language, is so in all, and four parts being indeclineable, it is manifest that they are learned by no rules, but only by use and exercise, as the memory can congest and record them. so that there remains but other four to be obtained by rule, and two of them, which is Pronoun and Participle, either are but very few, as the Pronoun, and so are easily known wherein they agree or differ from the Noun & Verb; or the Participle, which hath nothing but what agrees either with the Noun, or Verb, or with both: So that the whole difficulty is in the Noun and the Verb, of both which some are regulars, and some are irregulars, *Anomala*, defectives, or *Heteroclytes*. Now for the irregulars, the best, easiest, and shortest way were to learn them by use and exercise, without rule, which for the most part is done, and the rules usually are but superfluous and render the way more perplex and tedious; and this being observed, the way of regulars would be facile and brief, as being but one rule for all. And this I suppose being observed would render the way of *Grammar* teaching of more bevity, facility, and certainty, but greater experiences may know better waies.

It may be imagined that I should proffer some auxiliary means for the promoting of *Symbolical*, and *Cryptographical* learning, as being a part of *Grammar*, but therein I must rather acknowledge mine inability, and onely wish that so much of it as is discovered, and made clear by others, might be put in practice, then would the benefit of it be better
understood

underſtood by uſe, than I can demonſtrate in words. And for the univerſal **Character** that would require a peculiar Tract, not a curſory touch: and for the language of nature, I fear it is not acquiſitive but dative, and therefore ſhall not be ſo weak in that particular, to preſcribe a rule, which none hath power to follow, or ſtrength to perform.

Next in order followeth *Logick*, which being that art or Science that ſhould adminiſter expedients and helps for the promoting and finding out of all other Sciences, doth notwithſtanding ſtand in need it ſelf : from whence then ſhould it have it? truly it is hard to determine, for it is ſuch a groundleſſe, intricate, and perplex piece, that it is very doubtful from whence it had its original, and therefore moſt difficult to know how to find its remedies; yet ſhall offer my beſt aſſiſtance to its regulation and amendment.

1. It is neceſſary that its radical ground be found forth in nature, and likewiſe its extent, without which it is not poſſible to lay open its nature and efficacy; for though it undertake to reaſon and argue of all things, yet bears it forth but little light and evidence of its own power and ſtrength. And therefore in the firſt place it is requiſite to inquire, what reaſon and ratiocination are in their intrinſick nature, and what they can operate, and effect, both ſolely by themſelves, and conjunctively with the ſenſes, becauſe it is clear that the work of Reaſon is poſterior to that of Senſe, and doth but compound, divide, and compare the ſeveral ſpecies that are received by the ſenſes, and make Deduction, and draw Concluſions from them, and this is neceſſary that its diſtinct power and efficacy may be known. Alſo it is expedient to examine wherein man in reaſon exceeds other animants; for though man to maintain his unjuſt tyranny over the other fellow creatures (excuſe the phraſe it is no ranting term, for *Job* confeſſeth, *I have* Job 17. 14. *ſaid to corruption thou art my father, to the worm thou*
                                                                    art

art my mother and my sister) hath assumed to himself the
title of being Rational, and excluding all other living Creatures from that prerogative, when it is certain that many o-
ther Creatures excell man in the acuteness of some Senses,
and it is questionable that some exceed him in Reason too,
though therein he be to be preferred before the most,
so that if it be diligently searched into, it will be found
that there is no specifical but a gradual difference.

2. Before any great good can be effected with *Logick*,
especially with the *Syllogistical* part, it will be very expedient that its principles be demonstratively cleared and proved,
either in some other Science from whence they are taken, or
be briefly and compendiously laid down, and defined, that
they may more certainly be assented to, and the grounds
known, as in the *Mathematicks*, where a few Definitions, *Petitions*, and *Axioms*, serve to demonstrate the
whole operations by, with such certitude, that none since
the daies of *Euclide* have denyed, or rejected them, that so
by this means the Conclusions in *Logick* may be certain and
profitable.

3. That some prevalent way might be found out, for discovering and rectifying the delusions and fallacies of the
senses, and for drawing adæquate, and congruous notions
from things, and giving apposite and significant denominations to notions, that so the fountain may be made cleer
at the head, and rise of it, that all the several rivulets, and
streams that run from thence may be lympid and pure, without which it will be but as a muddy puddle, whose streams
cast forth dirt and myre.

4. That the chiefest and most beneficial part, which is
Induction, may be improved, that it may be serviceable
and helpful for the discovering of Science, which cannot be unless some carefull, diligent, and exact means
be brought into practice, for the making, trying, and
                                        observing

obferving of all forts of experiments, both frugiferous, and luciferous, that time may not be vainly fpent in needleffe altercations, difpurations, fpeculations, and notions, but in reall, and profitable experiments, and obfervations; That fo the end of *Logical* labour may not be to bring forth opinion, and errour, but certainty of Science, and folidity of truth.

The *Mathematicks* fhould now come in order, but of them I need fay little, as to their advance, becaufe they contain fufficient expedients in themfelves for the progreffe of their promotion, and indeed do want nothing but diligent and faithful profecution, and practice, that they may arrive at a compleat period. And therefore the onely help I fhall offer in this cafe, is, to defire that this fo noble, and excellent a Science, with all the parts of it, both general, and fpecial, vulgar, and myftical, might be brought into ufe and practice in the Schools, that men might not idlely lofe their time in groundleffe notions, and vain *Chymæras*, but in thofe reall exercifes of learning that would both profit themfelves, fucceeding generations, and other Sciences.

And I could alfo wifh that the found, and *Apodictical* learning of *Copernicus*, *Kepler*, *Ticho Brahe*, *Galilæus*, *Ballialdus*, and fuch like, might be introduced, and the rotten and ruinous Fabrick of *Ariftotle* and *Ptolomy* rejected and laid afide.

CHAP.

Chap. X.

Of some helps in Natural Philosophy.

NOw when I come to lay down some expedients for the reformation and promotion of *Physical* knowledge, two things (I know) will be questioned, and inquired of.

And first, Whether all the whole body of the *Aristotelian Philosophy* should be eliminated, and thrown away.

To which I answer, No; for there are many things in his *History* of *Animals*, and some things in his *Politicks*, *Ethicks*, *Logick*, *Metaphysicks*, and *Rhetorick*, that are commodious and useful, yet do they all stand in need of reformation and amendment: But for his Natural *Philosophy*, and his *Astronomy* depending thereon, it admits of no reformation, but eradication, that some better may be introduced in the place thereof. And for his Expositors, and Commentators, they instead of reforming what was amisse in his writings, carried with a blind zeal to make him the onely oracle of truth, have increased the corruption, and not supplyed the defects, nor removed the errouts.

Secondly, it will be urged, That if the *Peripatetick Philosophy* which the Schools maintain, should be taken away, where would any such perfect, compleat, and methodical piece be found to supply the place thereof.

To which it is answered, That I have already demonstrated, and laid open the faults and defects thereof, that there is no such perfection in it at all as is supposed, and therefore no inconvenience to remove it. And admit there were

were no such compleat piece, as were requisite to substi-
tute instead of the *Aristotelian* learning being taken away,
the greater were the shame of *Academies*, that within the
compass of so many Centuries have done no more for the advancement of learning, for the greater the defect is, the more
it ought to stir up all mens endeavours to repair, and make
good the same. And also there are some pieces of *Philosophy* more compleat than *Aristotles*, as I shall shew in the
following expedients.

1. It cannot be expected that *Physical* Science will arrive
at any wished perfection, unlesse the way and means, so
judiciously laid down by our learned Countreyman the Lord
Bacon, be observed, and introduced into exact practice;
And therefore I shall humbly desire, and earnestly presse,
that his way and method may be imbraced, and set up
for a rule and pattern: that no *Axioms* may be received
but what are evidently proved and made good by diligent
observation, and luciferous experiments; that such may be
recorded in a general history of natural things, that so every age and generation, proceeding in the same way, and
upon the same principles, may dayly go on with the work,
to the building up of a well-grounded and lasting Fabrick,
which indeed is the only true way for the instauration and advance of learning and knowledge.

2. How unfit, and unsuitable is it, for people professing
the Christian Religion to adhere unto that *Philosophy* which
is altogether built upon *Ethnical* principles, and indeed
contrary and destructive to their tenents? so that I shall
offer as a most fit expedient, that some *Physical* learning
might be introduced into the Schools, that is grounded
upon sensible, rational, experimental, and Scripture
principles: and such a compleat piece in the most particulars of all human learning (though many vainly and
falsely imagine there is no such perfect work to be found) is
the elaborate writings of that profoundly learned man
Dr. *Fludd*, than which for all the particulars before mentioned (notwithstanding the ignorance and envy of all opposers) the world never had a more rare, experimental and perfect piece.   Q   3.

3. That the *Philosophy* of *Plato*, revived and methodized by *Franciscus Patritius*, *Marsillius Ficinus*,
and others; That of *Democritus*, cleared, and in some measure demonstrated; by *Renatus des Cartes*, *Regius*, *Pho-
cylides Holwarda*, and some others; That of *Epicurus*,
illustrated by *Petrus Gassendus*; That of *Philolaus*, *Empedocles*, & *Parmenides*, resuscitated by *Telesius*, *Campanella*, and some besides; and that excellent *Magnetical
Philosophy* found out by Doctor *Gilbert*; That of *Hermes*, revived by the *Paracelsian* School, may be brought
into examination and practice, that whatsoever in any of
them, or others of what sort soever, may be found agreeable
to truth and demonstration, may be imbraced, and received;
for there are none of them but have excellent, and profitable
things, and few of them but may justly be equallized with
Aristotle, and the *Scholastick* learning, nay, I am confident
upon due and serious perusal and tryal, would be found far
to excel them.

4. That youth may not be idlely trained up in notions,
speculations, and verbal disputes, but may learn to inure
their hands to labour, and put their fingers to the furnaces,
that the mysteries discovered by *Pyrotechny*, and the wonders brought to light by *Chymistry*, may be rendered familiar unto them: that so they may not grow proud with the
brood of their own brains, but truly to be taught by manual operation, and ocular experiment, that so they may not
be sayers, but doers, not idle speculators, but painful o-
perators; that so they may not be *Sophisters*, and *Philosophers*, but *Sophists* indeed, true Natural *Magicians*,
that walk not in the external circumference, but in the center of natures hidden secrets, which can never come to pass,
unless they have Laboratories as well as Libraries, and work
in the fire, better than build Castles in the air.

5. That the *Galenical* way of the medicinal part of *Physick* (a path that hath been long enough trodden to yield so
little fruit) may not be the prison that all men must be inchained in, and ignorance, cheating and impostorage maintained by Lawes and Charters; but that the more sure, cleer
and

and exquisit way of finding the true causes, and certain cures of diseases, brought to light by those two most eminent and laborious persons, *Paracelsus*, and *Helmont*, may be entertained, prosecuted and promoted; that it may no longer be disputable whether medicine (as it stands in the common road of use and form) be more helpful than hurtful, or kill more than it cures; and whether the *Republique* of *Rome* were more happy in the health of her Subjects which wanted *Physicians* for five hundred years, than we that have them in more abundance than Caterpillers, or Horseleaches. And unless these few expedients be put in practice, we may wax old in ignorance, and never see *Physical* knowledge arrive at any height of perfection; and so I pass to the others following.

The next is *Metaphysicks*, to help which I shall only offer this expedient, that it might be reduced to some certain grounds and principles, from whence demonstrations might be drawn, that men might proceed with some certainty, and not wander in the dark they know not whither, and so that the most sure way of *Renatus des Cartes* may be brought into use, and exercise, who hath traced it unto the head of the Spring, and shaken off the loose and superfluous questions, notions, and frivolous *Chimæras* thereof: That so it might become useful and beneficial, which as it now stands, and is used (or rather abused) serves for little else but only to amuse, and amaze the understanding, to blow up the Phantasie with ayrie and empty notions, and to make men vainly and fruitlesly wast their most pretious time, which should be bestowed in things of more necessary use, and of greater concernment.

As for *Ethical* knowledge, I suppose it better taught by president and practice, than by words and precepts, for seeing vertue doth consist in action, it must of necessity be far more laudable. that men be brought up to live vertuously, than to talk and dispute of vertue, and therefore could wish it more practical and less speculative. And yet could desire that the nature of passions and affections, vertues and vices, might be more radically demonstrated, and sought into, than they

Q 2
are

are in the Scholaſtick way, and therefore ſhall onely propoſe that what *Melancthon* and *Carteſius* have diſcovered of them, might be made documental , and practicable, and that the doctrine of them might be made more conſonant to that Chriſtian Religion which men ſo much profeſs, and glory of , and that *Seneca* and *Epictetus* might not be ſleighted , and neglected , while *Ariſtotle* is only applauded and imbraced, betwixt whom there is no ſmall difference.

Laſtly for *Rhetorick* and *Poeſie*, I ſhall preſcribe nothing, but leave every man to the freedome of his *genius*, only to add this, that Emperours and Kings can make and create Dukes, Marqueſſes, and Earls, but cannot make one Orator or Poet , and ſo ſhall conclude with the *Lyrick* Poet, *Tu nihil invitâ facies, diceſve, Minervâ.*

Chap. XI.

Some Expedients concerning their Cuſtome, and Method.

IN order to the preſcription of remedies concerning their Cuſtomes and Method, though (as in the reſt) I cannot do what ſhould or ought to be done in ſo weighty a matter, yet ſhall I contribute what lies in my weak power, and at leaſt expreſſe my good will, if not my skill.

1. And ſo ſhall firſt deſire that men may no be tyed up all to one method or way, leſt as it may keep them in a good path, ſo it may hinder them from imbracing , or following a better : and it is cleer that there may be many waies to one place , and divers methods for the attaining the ſame end of knowledge , ſo as we would not exclude men from tryals that they may find out the beſt, ſo we would not ty them to any one, leſt it prove the worſt.

2:

2. That above all other things care may be had that time be not mifpent, or trifled away, which is an irreparable lofs, and utterly irrevocable, and therefore I could wifh that *Apelles* motto might be had in everlafting remembrance, *Nulla dies fine linea*; and therefore long vacations, relaxations and intermiffions are to be looked upon as *Scylla* and *Charibdis*, the rocks and fhelves whereon youngmen may eafily fuffer Shipwrack.

3. I fhall tender this, that all fhould not be tyed to one term or time, but every one have his honour according to his induftry and proficiency, that therby thofe that are painful may be incouraged, and thofe that are idle and fluggifh may be afhamed. And that none may be debarred of his degree or grace, how fhort a time foever he hath been there, if he be but able to perform the requifites and exercifes injoined, by which means merit, not years, fufficiency, not formality, fhall take place and be rewarded.

4. That their exercifes may not only be verbal and difputative, but practical and operative, that they may not onely be tryed what they can fay, but what they can do, not only what they opinionate, but what they can perform, that as nature hath given them two hands, and but one tongue, fo they may learn to work more and fpeak lefs.

5. That their exercifes may be in the *Englifh* as well as other tongues, that while they labour to make other languages familiar unto them, they become not altogether ftrangers unto their own : and that fcurrility, and childifhneff may be laid afide, and all things performed with more fobriety and gravity.

6. That neither antiquity nor novelty may take place above verity, left it debarre us from a more diligent fearch after truth and Science: Neither that univerfality of opinion be any prefident or rule to fway our judgements from the inveftigation of knowledge; for what matter is it whether we follow many or few, fo the truth be our guide? for we fhould not follow a multitude to do evil, and it is better to accompany verity fingle, than falfity and errour with never fo great a number. Neither is it fit that *Authority* (whether

ther of *Aristotle* or any other) should inchain us, but that there may be a general freedome to try all things, and to hold fast that which is good, that so there might be a *Philosophical* liberty to be bound to the authority of none, but truth it self, then will men take pains, and arts will flourish.

7. As to the order to be observed in teaching the Arts, and Sciences, doubtless there can be no better method, than leading them into the fair fields of *Mathematical* learning, which by reason of its perspicuity and certitude would so settle and season the understanding, that it would ever after be sufficiently armed to discern betwixt truth and opinion, demonstration and probability: and render it more fit and able to proceed in Natural *Philosophy*, and other Sciences, and so to proceed to the Tongues, then to *Physicks*, and so to *Logick*, *Metaphysicks*, and the like, which order without question, would prove more advantagious, than that which the Schools have pursued for so many years with so little fruit.   And these are the Expedients that for the present I have to present, hoping they may be acceptable until better be found out; and if any thing herein may appear to be erroneous, let it be but candidly made manifest, and he will be willing either to give further satisfaction, or to reclaim his mistakes, who in these things judgeth himself but as the meanest of men, and so no way privileged from frailty and infirmity.

FINIS.

Vindiciæ Academiarum

CONTAINING,

Some briefe Animadverſions upon

Mᴿ *WEBSTERS* Book,

STILED,

The Examination of Academies.

Together with an Appendix concerning what M. *Hobbs*,
and M. *Dell* have publiſhed on this Argument.

May 26.

OXFORD,
Printed by *Leonard Lichfield* Printer to the Univerſity,
for *Thomas Robinſon.* 1 6 5 4.

SIR,

THERE came lately to my hands fince I came to this place a Difcourfe ftiled the *Examination of Accademies*, (which I herewith fend you) It pretends to the reforming of Publick Schooles, and the promoting of all kind of fcience. I muft confeffe my felfe at firft fight, very much pleafed with the undertakeing, as being fuitable to my owne frequent wifhes, and what I conceived might with fome reafon be hoped for in this inquifitive age. And therefore I came to the reading of it, with great expectations of finding fomewhat anfwerable to the nobleneffe of the attempt.

But I quickly difcovered, that I was like to be much difappointed in that hope, & that befides a Torrent of affected infignificant tautologies with fome peevifh unworthy reflections, & the repetitions of fome old & trite cavills, together with feverall bundles of groffe miftaks there was litle elfe to be expected from this Author.

Two grand incapacityes for fuch a worke, he quickly difcovers himfelfe guilty of, that are not to be pardoned or excufed in fuch an undertaker.

1. His ignorance of the prefent ftate of our Univerfityes which he pretends to reforme.

2. His Ignorance in the common grounds of thofe Arts and Sciences which he undertakes to advance and promote. In both which refpects he muft needs fall under that cenfure of *folly and* Prov: 18.13. *fhame*, which *Solomon* doth afcribe unto thofe that will venture to judge of a matter *before they underftand it*.

1. For the prefent ftate of the Univerfityes. He fuppofes and takes it for granted, that they are fo tyed up to the Dictates of *Ariftotle*, that whatfoeuer is taught either againft or befides him by way of refutation or fupply, they do by no meanes admit of, fo much as to any confideration or debate, but are wholy ignorant of it.

Which is fo notorioufly falfe, that I fhould very much wonder

A 2   with

with what confidence he could suppofe it, if I did not finde Mr *Hobbs* likewife guilty of the fame miftake. Whereas thofe that underftād thefe places,do know that there is not to be wifhed a more generall liberty in point of judgment or debate, then what is here allowed. So that there is fcarce any Hypothefis , which hath been formerly or lately entertained by Judicious men, and feemes to have in it any cleareneffe or confiftency, but hath here its ftrenuous Affertours, as the Atomicall and Magneticall in Philofophy, the Copernican in Aftronomy &c.

And though we do very much honour *Ariftotle* for his profound judgment and univerfall learning, yet are we fo farre from being tyed up to his opinions, that perfons of all conditions amongft us take liberty to difcent fom him,and to declare againft him, according as any contrary evidence doth ingage them,being ready to follow the Banner of truth by whomfoever it fhall be lifted up.

Witneffe the publick *Lectures of our Profeffors*, the Pofitions or Queftions maintained in the *publick Exercife of the Univerfitie* for Degrees,& in the *private Exercifes of Colledges*, befides the *Inftructions and readings of many Tutors*,wherein the principall things which this Author doth accufe us to be ignorant of, and enemies unto, are *taught* and owned, and I can affure him they are fo well *learnt*, that for all his contempt of the Univerfityes,we have here many young boyes(who have not yet attained *to that very proud & vainglorious title of Bachelours of Art*, (as he is pleafed to phrafe it) that are able to reforme this Reformer, in thofe things, wherein he thinks us all fo ignorant, and himfelfe fo great a Mafter.

2 . And for his ignorance in the common grounds of thofe things which he undertakes to advance and promote , his whole Difcourfe doth not fo clearly prove any thing elfe, (not that which he intends by it,) as it doth prove this.

Let any ferious man but confider the two firft Chapters of it, wherein he endeavours to prove, *Univerfities are not in any kind ufefull to fit men for the Miniftry, but oppofite thereunto*, pag. 3. *And that thofe Syftems of Theology, which are therein taught are not only ufeleffe but hurtfull*,pag. 10.

One might reafonably expect that upon flinging out his Gauntlet for the defence of fuch pofitions as thefe, this Author fhould mufter up his forces, and appeare at leaft with fome feeming ftrength and reafon. And yet he doth nothing leffe.

His Arguments to this purpofe being generally fo triviall, coincident, inconfequent,that we fhould looke upon it as a figne of

very

very great negligence or ignorance in many of our young Boyes, if they fhould debate matters in fo impertinent and loofe a manner. And I muft obferve by the way, how this Author doth herein give fufficient warning what we are to expect from him in the *Reforming of Logick*, of the ufe of which he himfelfe underftands fo little, that will teach a man how to *define* and *diftinguifh*, to underftand *Confequences* and *Method*, and by this meanes to fpeake *cleanly*, ftrongly and *plainly*: To which he is altogether a ftranger. Nor is it to be much wondered at, if he appeare an enemy to Syllogifmes, (as he afterward profeffes) confidering how wildly his own arguments would looke, if they were to be put into that dreffe.

He fuppofes in both thefe Chapters, that the Univerfities doe undertake to teach fpirituall knowledge, and to furnifh men with fuch gifts, as do only proceed from the Spirit of God. And this is the chiefe foundation that he doth erect his following heap of Arguments upon, then which nothing can be more groundleffe or falfe. There being no man, (that ever I heard of) who hath believed or afferted any fuch thing. And I cannot think it any great prefumption to believe that I underftand the tenets of the Univerfity in this point as well as he. I am fure it hath been the common opinion amongft them, that there are three kind of gifts materially requifite to compleat a man unto the Minifteriall function.

1. Something to be infufed by the Spirit of God, which muft illuminate him to underftand the mifteries of the Gofpell, and affect his heart with an experimentall favour, and acquaintance with thofe facred truths wherein he is to inftruct others.

2. Some naturall abilityes in refpect of folidity of judgment, ftrength of memory, warmenes of affection, readineffe and volubility of fpeech, by which he may be rendered much more ferviceable in that worke, then thofe that want thefe abilities.

3. Something to be acquired by our own induftry and the teaching others; Namely, a diftinct and methodicall comprehention of the feverall fubjects to be treated of, together with the meanes or advantages that helpe to facilitate the worke of inftructing others.

In which refpect it may be of fingular ufe for a man to be acquainted with the feverall Scriptures and Reafons, that are more immediately pertinent to any particular head in Theologie, as concerning God, his Attributes, Workes: The fal on eftate of man, the meanes of his reftitution &c. The dutyes of the Law and

A 3

Gofpell

Gofpell together with many particular cafes of Confcience which
are incident to the various ftates and bufineffes of life.

Concerning all which things, fure it can be no hinderance to
a man (as this Author fuppofes) to have all the moft materiall
notions upon any fubject, put together, cleared up and ftated by
the concurrent labours of many wife and good men, after much
confideration and experience about them. And this is that Theologie, which the Univerfities do pretend to teach, and though it
doth not exceed the fphere of thofe common gifts which meer
naturall men are capeable of, yet is it of fuch fingular ufe to
enable a man to fpeake diftinctly unto feverall points, to confirme
truth, to cleare up difficultyes, anfwer doubts and confequently
to help in the worke of informing others. That I am not able to
imagine any reafon, why an eminent ability in *this kind* might not
be fufficient to make a man capable of a civill degree, as well
as fkill in any other faculty.

I am fure the preparatory ftudies required to the profeffion of
Phyfick or Civill Law, are not more then for this Theology, nor
is it leffe copious for its extent, or of leffe importance and ufefulneffe for its end, then either of the other Faculties.

Now unleffe this Author will fay, that he who has grace, and
is without thefe gifts, is better able to Teach, then he that hath
both grace and thefe gifts too, he hath no reafon to complaine of
the ufelefneffe and danger of Academicall education, in reference
to the worke of the Miniftry.

Whereas he doth object that *thefe common gifts are a Tempta-*
tion to pride, confidence, boafting : That is meerely accidentall:
So is health too, and liberty, and all other naturall or acquired a-
bilities, and he may upon as good grounds, hope to perfwade men
to love fickneffe and flavery, as to preferre Ignorance before that
Knowledge of this kind that is to be learnt in the Univerfities: the
beft things that are (even Grace it felfe) may be accidentally
hurtfull by the abufe of them, but that is no argument againft
their proper ufefulneffe.

Coff. 2. 8.   As for his objecting that place of the Apoftle, where he bids to
beware of Philofophy: If that prohibition be to be underftood
abfolutely, and without limitation, why doth he here pretend fo
much to the knowledge of it himfelfe, and to the Advancement of
it in others? The fame anfwer that he will make for his own vindication, will ferve for his Objection. But befides if he confider
the place better, he will find the words to be, Beware leaft any *man*

fpoile

fpoile you through Philofophy and vaine deceit. Where 'tis the abufe and not the ufe that is prohibited.

I cannot paffe over this fubject without taking notice of the neare affinity betwixt his third and fourth Argument againft fchoole Theologie, *pag.* 14, 15. In one he quarrells with it becaufe tis drawn into a *ftrict Logicall Method*. And in the next, becaufe *tis a confufed Chaos*. Are they not judicioufly put together ? And is not the man very quarrellfome ? That out of zeale to contradict his Adverfaries, takes no care of contradicting himfelfe.

What a loofe and wild kind of vapouring is that *Cap.* 3. about *Cryptography*, and the *univerfall Character* wherein he fuppofes the Univerfities to be wholly ignorant, *none of them having fo much as touched at thefe things. pag.* 24.

But above all, the man doth give me the freeft profpect of his depth and braine, in that canting Difcourfe about the language of nature, wherein he doth affent unto the highly illuminated fraternity of the *Rofycrucians* In his large encomiums upon *Jacob Behem*, in that reverence which he profeffes to judiciall Aftrologie, which may fufficiently convince what a kind of credulous fanatick Reformer he is like to prove.

How wretchedly doth he abufe fome ingenious opinions by his ignorant managing of them, particularly the copernican Hypothefis; In the defence of which he urges fuch pittifull arguments as are enough to fright a ferious man from the beliefe of it, & to breed a prejudice againft it in fuch as are that way inclined.

It is enough to naufeate and make a man fick to perufe his crude and jejune Animadverfions upon *Logick, Mathematicks, Phyficks, Metaphyfickes*, &c. with the expedients or remedyes which he propofes, wherein he has abufed fome good Authors, by his ill managing the notions that they have fuggefted to him.

I muft needs confeffe that at the firft fight of this Book, I had a very great defire to know what the perfon was who had put himfelfe forward to fo noble an attempt, as reforming all Schooles, and advancing all Arts. But for that he doth in his *Epiftle* at the beginning referre wholly to his Booke, whereby he faith he will difcover himfelf *as Hercules doth by his foot & the Lion by his pawe*. But if I were to judge of him by the impreffions which he therein makes of his foote or pawe, I fhould not by that gueffe him to be either a *Hercules* or a *Lion*, but fome more weake and leffe generous Animal.

I

I have heard from very good hands that he is fufpected to be a Friar, his converfation being much with men of that way, And the true defigne of this Booke being very fuitable to one of that profeffion, Befides that his fuperficiall and confufed knowledge of things is much about that elevation.

I fhould have been apt to have conjectured him to be fome obfcure perfon, whofe peevifh malecontented humour had brought him into the gang of the vulgar Levellers: Amongft whom his ability to talke of fome things out of the common road, hath raifed him to the reputation of being τις μέγας, fome extraordinary perfon; and by that meanes hath blowne him up to fuch a felfeconfidence, as to think himfelfe fit to reforme the Univerfityes.

And thus Sir have I given you my fuddaine thoughts upon the curfory reading of this Examen. And though the Booke will appeare unto all Judicious men but flight and contemptible, yet becaufe it may light into the hands of fome weaker perfons, who may be apt to take accufations for convictions: It would not be amiffe if for their fakes fome body would vouchfafe more particularly to examine this Examiner, and to difabufe fuch as may be feduced by him. It is part of that Scholaftick imprudence, which men of our profeffion are fubject unto, to fit downe and fatisfie our felves in our owne knowledge of the weakeneffe of fuch Adverfaries, without taking any paines to fatisfie others, who are not fo well able to judge.

I fhoud think that Mr Alex: Roffe might in fome refpects be very fit to enter the lifts with this Champion. But I know not how farre he may at prefent be engaged in the Confutation of fome better Booke. I am very fure Sir there are many of your acquaintance, who if their leifure and patience would permit, are able to play with this Hercules, and I fhould think it a good recreation for fome of their fpare howers. And the hopes that you may be inftrumentall for this is, the chiefe occafion that provoked me to trouble you with fo large an account of my prefent thoughts upon this fubject.

It may feem fomewhat odde and ftrange to confider what feverall kinds of Adverfaries have of late appeared againft the Univerfityes. Mr Hobbs, Mr Dell, Mr Webfter.

The firft of them being a perfon of good ability and folid parts, but otherwife highly magifteriall, and one that will be very angry with all that do not prefently fubmit to his dictates, And for advancing the reputation of his own skill, cares not what unworthy tiny reflexions he casts on others. It were not amisse, if he were made acquainted, that for all his slighting of the Universityes, there are here many men, who have been very well versed in those notions and Principles which he would be counted the inventer of, and that before his workes were published. And though he for his part may think it below him to acknowledge himselfe beholding to Mr *Warners* Manuscripts, yet those amongst us who haue seen and perused them must for many things give him the honour of precedency before Mr *Hobbs.*

The other (as farre as his character may be pickt out of his writings) is an angry fanatick man, who wanting himselfe such Academicall Learning as would become his relation, would needs perswade others against it, like the Ape in the Fable. But there is reason to hope that he may be shortly called to an account, and lay'd open by a person of eminent worth, whom he hath weakely provoked.

The last is this worthy Author, who by a smattering and superficiall knowledge hath raised himselfe a repute amongst his ignorant followers. In the strength of which he comes forth to teach the Universities. I should have used him with much more tendernesse and respect, it it had not been very evident to me that it was not so much an ingenuous affection to the advancement of learning, as a froward and malicious prejudice against the Universities, that put him on to this worke.

But by this time I have tired you as well as my selfe, let me crave your pardon for this tediousnesse, and that you would continue to esteeme me for

S I R

Your most *Affectionate*

Friend and Servant

N. S.

B

SIR,

IF I should gaine no other fruit beside the pleasure of my giving testimony to the service and respect I beare you, it were a reward exceedingly beyond the labour of the taske which you (by recommending) have imposed upon me. The advancement of Learning and the consideration of designes tending that way, are things exceedingly suitable to my desires, these things have beene the argument of much discourse, which I have had the hapinesse to have with you. I must needs say that I should not more desire (next to the matters of the highest concernement) to meet with a Booke of any other argument, then such an one as should propose *expedients for the perfecting and promoting of all kinds of Science.* And that is the undertaking of the Booke you are pleased to send me, (in the Title-Page of it) so that the pleasure you are pleased to give me in offering me under the notion of satisfying your desires that which is so suitable to my owne, takes off all consideration of labour in turning the times of my diversion to scribling, and yet leaves me the hopes of your Acceptance, as if I had taken paines, or done something in your service.

I can easily conceive, that upon the ground which I have laid (of my delight in writings tending to the advancement of Learning.) I may raise a suspicion that out of compleasance to you I would diminish the service which herein I offer you. Seeing the disappointment of our earnest expectations in things we seriously desire, doth use to be unpleasant to us, and such a disappointment you have sufficiently fore warned me of in your Epistle. But I must professe I am farre from any such reach in Complement. *Designes* that way, do allwayes please me however managed, prouided it be not in the way of a dull and nauseous mediocrity. You may perhaps Sir, impute this to some peculiary in my disposition. Yet I have observed in other men, that they have expressed as great a pleasure at the combate of *Clinias* and *Dametas,* as of *Amphialus* and *Musidorus,* and when *Pontens* was in towne, I saw the soberest of the spectatours as much affected at the imitations of the Zany, as at the Active, and (in their kind) admirable performances of the cheife Actor.

There is an excellécy in that which is uncouth, aswell as in what is

handsome

handſome; and it is enough for me if any thing be excellent in its
kind, and ſuch I found (upon my ſlight peruſall) to be the Booke
you ſent me, which to my Lord *Bacons* Advancement, and thoſe
which ſome others have deſigned, beares ſuch proportion as I have
intimated.

It remaines therefore that I humbly thanke you for ſo farre con-
ſidering my Genius, which all wayes inclining me to Idleneſſe,
you have found out a way to imploy my vacancyes with a juſt ſatisfaction, ſuch as doth ariſe rather from being ſlightly buſied
then not at all, rather from Trifling then perfect Idleneſſe.

In complyance therefore with your deſire, I mean to runne over
this reverend Authour, not ſtaying upon his expreſſions, or making
a toyle of a pleaſure but briefely touching upon the things he mentions, taking no care either of my paſſions or expreſſions, any farther then to reteine them within the compaſſe of civility .

Thoſe things which you have taken the paines to confute, I ſhall
not ſo much as once recite , the remainder I ſhall careleſly and
ſlightly (that is, in my apprehenſion moſt becomingly) ſpeake to.

'Tis true, you have given us a perfect character of him in your
Epiſtle; but becauſe ſome may conjecture that he knowes himſelfe, better then you know him (though in truth you are much a
better judge of him then he is of himſelfe:) I ſuppoſe it may not
be unuſefull to gather together that Character which he hath
given of himſelfe, that doing him no wrong, and forming a juſt
Idea of him in the beginning of my Diſcourſe, the Reader may be
prepared for a due reception of that which followes·

We may underſtand him by his ſtile (*oratio indicat virum*) and by
his paſſions, wherein its hard for a man to diſſemble.

H E enters in feare & proceedes in jelouſies. His firſt feare is (of   Epiſtle.
affrighting the tender Scholars) leaſt he ſhould be looked on
as ſome *Goth* or *Vandall*, *Hunne* or *Scythian* comming like a torrent from the
Boreall mountaines of cold ſtupidity &c. But for that his comfort is, that
others cannot more *Experimentally* and *Apodictically anatomize his Idiocracy* then himſelfe, wherein beſides the ᶹ+Θ of his elloquence,
there is likewiſe a βάθος of ſence not fathomable by common un-
derſtandings: as how others ſhould at all experimentaly, or he himſelfe
ſhould *Apodictically anatomize* his *Idiocracy.*

His next is a doubtfull pang, leaſt he ſhould be charged wi h o-
ver much confidence, & the propoſall of fame for his Guerdon but
here againe his boſome is his Sanctuary, I find him valiant (your pe-

full men are alwayes fo) the fanctuary of his breft and a fentence
of the *Accedence* are his retreat;&this is his comfort a *man is a man
though he have but an hole on his head,* and *homo is a common name for all
men.* 'Tis to be hoped his Examen may be favourable to the Gra-
mar,who is thus beholding to the Accedence; Yet fome men think
he could not want an high degree of confidence that fhould expect
fame from compiling fuch a worke as this.

His next encounter is againft the fufpition of Avarice, as if he
would ruine Univerfities to fhare in the fpoile. But this he doth
fufficiently confute by an Argument of fuch a weighty confequence, as I hope no man will be fo uncivill as to deny. For he
is *no Deane nor Mafter Prefident,nor Provoft,Fellow,nor Penfioner,*and leaft
any man fhould fufpect him to be of another order which he hath
omitted *viz.* a Scholler;he gives affurance to the contrary by that
new ellegance which he hath added to an old verfe,

    Qui cadit in terram non habet unde cadat.

Which he hath reformed it into nonfence: Indeed although we
hope that none could fufpect him of any fuch interft;Yet all thofe
Parties ought to thank him for his care in giving the world this
fatisfaction.

By this time he fuppofes the droufy world awakened by the
found of his thundering ftile(and by the Proclamation of his hero-
icall defignes) to enquire into the Origine and Education of him
that dares cenfure (and defy all the Univerfityes in the univerfe
Though he might chofe to anfwer; he won't be Cinicall but fay,
That Hercules is eafily known by his foot, and the Lyon by his paw, his
Treatife fhall fhew that he is a *free borne Englifhman* (of the houfe
of the *Webfters*) *and thats enough for modeft inquirers.*

And now one would think this Herculean Lyon fhould be no
more afraid,but againe behold he trembles,leaft fome fhould think
his Treatife to be like *Plato's Republick:* Sr *Thomas Mores Utopia,* or
the *Ld. Bacons new Atlantis.* But if they fhould do fo, they were
furely much to blame, and 'twere an unpardonable errour, I fhould
be very glad to rid him from this feare, but I confider it is the
deftiny of fuch *Heroes,*borne for reformers of the world,to be men
of working fancies,fubject to may feares & trances His predeceffor
in the Military way (the famous *Hero* of the *Mancha* miftooke
a windmill for an inchanted Caftle, and this man (man did I fay,
this *Hero*) lyes under the fame delufion, relieve him I cannot, lament him I muft,

    O Webfter Webfter quæ te dementia cepit.

                                               He

He hath a petty scruple yet remaining, least he may possibly be charged with an infirmity of pilfering or nimming: But *he can say with Macrobius, Omne meum, Nihil meum,* the Treatise is of his own invention (he found it in *Helmont, Verulam, Gassendus,* and some others) he hath indeed taken some *hints* to the mountenance of three quarters of the Treatise, but he *took them from strong men, fighting with the steely instruments of Demonstration &c.* and no man can accuse him of *singularity,* whilest Noble Heroes beare him *Company.*

Thus have you Sir, a character of this Noble Reformer, given us liberally by himselfe, he would not calumniate the Academies, (but censure the *corruptions* of the present *Generation*) he professes he hath *not done all he could,* so that if he faile, we must blame his *weaknesse* not his *Will;* where by the way, observe the consequence of his reformed Logick, he could have done more if he would, and yet we must blame his *weaknesse* not his *will.*

Hitherto you have had *his* Apologies, he will now put *us* to *ours,* for *Explicit Epistola, Incipit Examen Academiarum.*

CAP. 1.

Of the generall ends of erecting publique Schooles.

HE acknowledges, that *no Nation hath been so ferall as not to honour Literature, for the Indians had their Brachmans &c. and these had their publick Schooles.*
The man we see thinks it brutishnesse not to honour Learning, & the way for Learning to flourish, to be by instituting Academies. How infinitely are we beholden to him for this testimony.

Yet they had not so farre as he can gather (and thats as farre as some milder Author will furnish him, for its hard to name from whence he had his Catalogue of *Brachmans, Magi,* and *Druides,* there are so many who taken with the bombast of their names love to recite them) *any publick salaryes: But their merit was their maintenance &c.* Here first it will be worth the while to observe his course of reasoning, how it differs from ours in the Universities.

1. He cannot *gather they had publick Salaries.*
2. Therefore they had no Salaries at all (for *Their merit was their maintenance.*)
3. Yet *their excellence in arts procured them Advancement.*
I see the reason why he is offended at our Logick; But (to answere

B 3

(were serioufly) if he have any meaning in this touch, it muſt be of bad ſignification to the Revenues of the Univerſities.

But it would be ſad, if things ſhould be modelled by this mans reading, or Univerſities were to ſubſiſt upon his collections.

Tis true, we never read of *Æſculapius*, what fees he took, nor of the price of *Homers* Ballads, yet we know that *Homer* had a mouth, elſe how could he ſing? And by the Immortality of his Workes we know that his drink was not water.

---- *nec vivere carmina poſſunt*
Quæ ſcribuntur aquæ potoribus.

This mans predeceſſor in the way of Knight Errantry, had like to have runne into a grievous miſtake, becauſe he had never read in any Author, that they uſed to carry money; and if M. *Webſter* compoſe himſelfe to the model of what he reads concerning thoſe ancient Worthies, I confeſſe I ſhould feare to keepe him company; for not reading of any ſhirts or ſhooes that they made uſe of; I know not how ſweet & cleanly I might find him.

Well Sir, that which followes is very ſad, and you having anſwered the Theologicall part, I intend to skip it over.

The ends of erecting Academies, have been in his account, the ſame in generall to all people, though they have differed in particulars.

Viz.
- Politick, in reference to the Common-wealth
  - Military.
  - Civill.
- Religious, ſerving to
  - Idolatry amongſt the Heathen.
  - The Miniſtry amongſt Chriſtians.

The Politick uſe he approves of, to the great happineſſe of the Univerſities, rejoyce therefore O ye Academies, for ye may remaine notwithſtanding the *ſtrenuous endeavour of the Scythians, the Gothes, the Vandalls, and the Huns. Dicite, Io Pæan.*

But the Religious uſe of them he diſapproves, and here it is that you have ſufficiently contunded him, and ſaved us the labour of a Reply, I ſhall not therefore need to ſpeake a word to his Theologicall Arguments, the judicious Reader will excuſe this Chaſme, being ſo happily prevented by your Learned Strictures, I ſhall touch upon that which you took no notice of.

It fell within the compaſſe of his wit, being ſo vaſt and comprehenſive to diſcerne, that languages may be judged uſefull to
Theology

Theology, fee therefore how he will elevate their reputation.

It is not (he faies) *concluded which are the Originall Copies: and tongues teach but the Grammaticall fence.* It is indeed difputed which Copies are *Authenticall*, betwixt men of his Religion, and thofe of ours, but the want of Grammar, hath made a Proteftant of a Friar, for by tranflating the word Authenticall, into the word Originall, he hath (by meer chance) renounced the Tridentine Councell, tacitely acknowledging the vulgar *Latine* not to be Authenticall.

But hisLogick is as fortunate as hisGrammar, he arguesTongues to be unneceffary to *Theology* (for I am loth to offend his tender eares or head) becaufe they *teach but the Grammaticall fence, and a literall underftanding:* Sir, you may perhaps demand a reafon of the confequence, thinking the knowledge of the Grammaticall fence, to be neceffary to the attaining of the Spirituall meaning, but I fhall defire to be heard as to the Antecedent, and to be his remembrancer, that Tongues, nay Letters, have taught a way of Myfticall Theology, as myfticall as need to be, and not unworthy to be compared to his which followes; 'tis pitty he had not heard of the myfteries of the *Gnofticks*, nor the *Ziruph Gematry* and *Notariacon* of the *Cabaiifts*, that one might have gained his favour to the Greek, the other to the Hebrew Tongue, to the advancement of *Marcus* and *Colarbafus*, and the fparing of *Behemen* & *De Fluctibus*.

But the knowledge of Tongues is built upon no furer a foundation then traditionall Faith. Alaffe! who knowes there ever was fuch a language as Greeke or Hebrew or Latine, or that the words do fignify as we are told. Mr*Webfter* is a deepe thinking man, and will not be put off without a *demonftration* or *revelation* (you charge him wrongfully with Popery he hates traditions) and will not *I* warrant you upon tradition believe that *caput* fignifyes a *head*, or that this word *head*, can reprefent that noble part of his ftiled in the verfes before his Book his *bonny fconce*, where fo much wit & Learning is inskulled, in this point furely he may fay, if *he be not guilty of too much* Preface: *dubitation, with Pyrrho, he is not over confident with Ariftotle.*

But there are erroxrs in all tranflations, therefore toungs are unneceffary. how neceffary to renounce their reafon, is it for thofe who deale with them of theMyftery.Some would have thought becaufe there were errours therefore the ftudy of Languages are neceffary; that were indeed the Logicall confequence, but the other is the Mifticall.

His laft Argument of makingmen proud of their skill you have
answered

anſwered, and this for the firſt Chapter as to what you thought
worthy of your notice, the Second concerning Schoole-Theolo-
gy, hath felt likewiſe the weight of your hand: I paſſe on therefore to the Third, being earneſt to taſt of his Humanity.

CAP. III.

*Of the Diviſion of that which the Schooles call Humane Learning,
and firſt of Tongues or Languages.*

THAT which he Propoſes in the Third Chapter is to
ſpeake
1. Of the diviſion of humane Learning, made by
   - The Schooles.
   - Himſelfe.
2. Of Languages, where he propoſes,
   1. Their uſeleſſeneſſe.
   2. A Diſpute about the way of Attainement,
      Whether that by Grammar be the beſt.
   3. Errors of Grammar.
   4. Advancements, by
      Hieroglyphicks.
      Symboliſmes.
      Steganography.
      Univerſall Character.
      Language of Nature.

The firſt part of his undertaking, I ſhall not ſtand much upon,
becauſe the good man ha's hinted at ſome others worthy of more
conſideration, the good man (for I feare I offend when I call him
Maſter *Webſter*, becauſe of *pag.* 11.) is offended that knowledge
ſhould be divided into Speculative and Practicall: *Naturall Philoſophy hath for its object, Corpus Naturale mobile, and the end is not Speculation, and ſo its practicall. Mathematicks hath taught men to build houſes, &c.
therefore that is Practicall, and the Schooles would have them Speculative.*
A ſad thing, and worthy the Animadverſion of this great Reformer.

Now if the Schooles ſhould anſwer, that the end of theſe Sciences may be practiſed, and yet they may be ſpeculative, I know
not what he would reply. I am much given to obſerve the courſe
of his ratiocination, which alwaies ends in Myſtery. See then
how

how he proceeds for Naturall Philosophy: This cannot be Speculative, for the end of it is more sublime then to rest in Speculation. Well, whats the end? to behold *the eternall power and Godhead*, that's *speculation*: but farther, to be drawne to worship him, thats indeed practife; But lastly, to worship him, that we may come to the vision of him, that's Speculation; the end therefore of it may be Speculation, and fo the Schooles escape a whipping.

For what he saies concerning the Mathematicks, as you know Sr it cannot choose but move mee, they have bin foetime accounted my Miftreffe, and Jealousy muft work when I find another courting her, and that so paffionately that he falls into an Extafy: (*O fublime, transcendent, beautifull, and most Noble Mistreffe* (quoth he) *who would not be enamoured on thy Seraphick pulchritude &c.*) But making my approach to him, I find him at his diftance, praying (like fome moping Friar to the Lady of *Lauretto*, or like) the Nephew of the Queene of Faery, and uttering a fpeech to her, made by *John Dee* in his Preface, enough to fatisfy mee, that fhe is yet pure and untouched by him, and hath not entertained him into any familiarity.

Pag. 10

Seriously Sir, had he read the Book as well as the Preface, nay had he underftood but the two firft Propofitions, he would have perceived, how Theorems doe ferve in order to Problemes, and practife may be the end of contemplation, and fo againe the Schooles might have efcaped him.

Well! but fee him divide now the Arts and Sciences, behold him coming to it with his cleaver, or rather with his Herculean beetle endeavouring to fplit them in three peeces.

1. *The firft are thofe that though they feeme to conferre fome knowledge, yet they doe it in order to a farther end, and fo are inftrumentall.*

And this part, according to this Author, ought to comprehend all Arts and Sciences, and fo the block of Sciences, hath efcaped the wedge, though it hath felt the Beetle-head.

2. *Thofe which conferre knowledge of themfelves, and are not inftrumentall to others, as Naturall Philofophy, &c.*

Here the Beetle rebounds, and gives himfelfe a blow, for *can the fcience of Naturall things, whofe fubject is Corpus Naturale mobile,* p. 18. *chufe but be fubordinate and inftrumentall to the difcovery of God, and the prefervation of health?* p. 18. 19.

3. *The third fort are thofe, which though they conferre fome knowledge, and have fome peculiar ufes, fo they feeme neceffary as ornamentall.*

C   Wee

We see the blow the Beetle gave him, hath wholly bereft him of his sence, a sad example upon a man, that not contented with the old, would set himselfe to make amongst us new divisions.

Well may he loose his senses, but he will never loose his mettle, he no sooner awakes out of his trance, but biting his tongue by chance, upon that occasion he falls upon the thought of Tongues and Languages. Wherefore woe be to them.

1. *The Knowledge of tongues beareth a great noise in the world* (and is *it not strange that tongues should keep such a noise?*)*and yet there is not much profit by them.*

The profit that is by tongues is only $\left\{\begin{array}{l}\text{1. } \textit{To understand one another.} \\ \text{2. } \textit{To make forreigne negotiations and to traffick}\end{array}\right.$ *and therefore 'tis not worth the while to learne them.*

The Argument is somewhat mysticall, I shall endeavour a little to unfold the mystery; All good things relate only to the body or mind, and the lives of men are divided into these foure

kinds $\left\{\begin{array}{l}\text{Πολιτικὸν.} \\ \text{Ἀπολαυτικὸν.} \\ \text{Θεωρητικὸν.} \\ \text{Χρηματιστικὸν}\end{array}\right.$

Riches or pleasure carry the greatest sway, and those are carryed on in the world by Negotiations and Traffick, these administer to every Nation whatever is the peculiar advantage of any one, & furnishes them all with Gold & Silver, &c. which men have agreed to make the common measure of riches, and with all things conducing to health and pleasure. Now there is no *traffick* without the use of Languages, *therefore there is not much profit in them.* Well these are commonly counted good things, but our *Zetetique* or *Sceptick* may be in that a *Stoick*, these are *commoda* not *bona*, things that are good and profitable are the goods of the mind, and those are attained by making use of the Discourse and writings of men of all Ages and Nations, and that is not to be done without skill in Languages, *So that againe there is but little profit by them.*

'Tis true no sort of men can well be without thē, as they cannot be without the Sun, (his heat to nourish, his light to guide them) therefore the use of them is little, this is his Logick, but I am apt to forget my selfe as oft as I shall fall into his Mysteries.

2. *But if Languages were worth the while to learne, yet the way of teaching them (by Grammar &c.) is not the best.* Either the way must be by Grammar, or by Exercise in Colloquy, if the latter it must

be

be gained by côverſation either $\left\{\begin{array}{l}\text{at home} \\ \text{or} \\ \text{abroad.}\end{array}\right.$

Firſt for the Learned languages, Latin, Greeke, Hebrew and the reſt of that ranke, whether ſhall a man travell to converſe with ſuch as will ſpeake to him in thoſe tongues: as for other tongues, as French, Italian, Spaniſh &c. his advice will be to travell into thoſe Nations. But if any man make it his buſineſſe to comprehend them all, he muſt either hire men ot all ſorts to be with him as Converſers, or muſt apply himſelfe to all, (travelling till he meet with them) ſo that the reſult will be that inſtead of ſome daies in his ſtudy, a man ſpends many years in travell or converſation, and all for ſaving the expence of time and charge s.

The way of Converſation, makes men *ready* and *confident*, but that alone will never make them *accurate*, an inſtance whereof we have, in that none that have no skill in Grammar, can ever amongſt us (though they ſpeake excellently) attaine the true writing of our Engliſh Tongue, and though many have come to be knowing men, as to the ſubſtance, and vaſtly read, yet I never knew an accurate man, fit to write or ſpeake in any learned Language, who neglected the Grammar of it.

This I thought proper enough for an Academicall man to take notice of: as for his exceptions to the Grammar, as being void of *Evidentiall perſpicuity*, and not coapted to the tender capacities of young years &c. I leave them to the Schooles of the lower forme to anſwer. The man ſuppoſes that Univerſities, like to the *Scholæ Illuſtres* of the Jeſuites, teach the Latine Grammar, and to goe through even the *loweſt* elements of learning : but you know Sir, that it is neither uſuall nor lawfull to teach the Latine Grammar in the Univerſities. If this man have ever ſeene any Univerſities, *Stat. Cant.* they have been the Romiſh Schooles and Academies, to whoſe elevation, the Learning which he diſcovers, and the reformation he propoſes, are (to uſe his excellent phraſe) *coapted.*

But in truth I am extreamly raviſhed at the defects he finds in Grammar, and his propoſalls for its advancement, how ſweetly and congruouſly hath he drawn in to the reliefe and advancement of Grammar and Language, thoſe things which mortall men intended to ſet in oppoſition to them. It is reported of Friar *Bacon*, that *time was* when by ,the ſtrength of Alchymy, he made a Brazen head to ſpeake *Time is* &c. but how farre hath our Friar exceeded him, who taking of *Hieroglyphicks, Emblemes, Symbols*, and

Cryphography,

Cryptography, and according to his capacity, hath extracted out of silence, an advance of Eloquence, and from dumb signes a Grammar. Sir, I doe not deny that the consideration of these things may very well accompany the consideration of Grammar, and the defects in these kinds may be spoken of very methodically, together w th the defects of Grammar, they being all converfant (though in waies as absolutely different as the eare is from the ey) about signification, and generally referring to it: but to make them all one, or parts of each other, amounts to no lesse then a great want of confideration.

It is a thing to be acknowledged by all confidering men, that knowledge is conveighed by fignification of our notions to one another, that signes may be made (by inftitution of men) in any way which doth admit of a fufficient variety, and that knowledge may be communicated, as well by the eye as by the eare, but to fay that by introducing that way, either Grammar or Languages fhould be advanced, it were as myfticall as to affirme, that the day light is advanced by the coming of the night, or that he would kill a man for his prefervation.

To difcourfe concerning *Hieroglyphicall* (or *Emblematicall*) and *Cryptographicall* Learning, is as *needleffe,* to men that know any thing, as *ufeleffe* to M *Webster,* who out of the abundance of his ingenuity, confeffes the *Cryptographicall* Bookes of *Porta, Agrippa, Tritthemius,*&c. to be written to his *wonder* and *amazement;* what was the defigne of them, and to whether Pallas they referre, he troubles not himfelfe to know, it is enough for him, that *Orthography* and *Cryptography* have the fame end, and he hath heard that the firft is a part of Grammar: and why may not *Emblems* be a part of Grammar, as well as *Etymology,* they begin both with a letter, the word founds as well, and *Emblematicall* is a neater word, and fuits perhaps better with his mouth then *Etymologicall.* Befides.

Hierogliphicks and *Cryptography,* were invented for *concealement* of things, and ufed either in myfteries of Religion which were *infanda,* or in the exigences af Warre, or in occafions of the deepeft fecrefy, (fuch as thofe of Love, which is not to be owned, or of the great Elixar, and the like) and Grammar is one of thofe Arts and Language one of thofe helps, which ferve for *explication* of our minds and notions: How incongruous then is it, that the Art of *Concealement,* fhould not be made a part of the Art of *Illuftration;* furely it would make much to the advancement of Children while they are learning the Elements of Grammar, to be put upon the

fpecula-

ſpeculation of the *Menſa Iſiacæ*, the *Canopi*, and *Obeliskes*, the *Theſaurus Hieroglyphicus*, or *Groſſchedel's Magicall Calendar*; This would certainly effect, even in Children, what *Porta & Agrippa* have done to M. *Webſter*, bring them to *Wonder* and *Amazement*.

But he hath extreamely diſobliged whoſoever have been Authors of the Symbolicall way, either in Mathematicks, Philoſophy, or Oratory, to bring them under the *ferula*, and make thoſe who have exempted themſelves from the encombrances of words to be brought *poſt liminio*, into the Grammar Schoole, it was little thought by *Vieta*, M. *Oughtred*, or *Herrigon*, that their deſignation of quantities by Species, or of the ſeverall waies of managing them by *Symbols* (whereby we are enabled to behold, as it were, with our eyes, that long continued ſeries of mixt and intricate *Ratiocination*, which would confound the ſtrongeſt fancy to ſuſtaine it, and are with eaſe let in to the Abſtruſeſt, and moſt perplexed depths, wherein the contemplation of quantity is concerned)ſhould ever have met ſo ſlight a conſiderer of them, as ſhould bring them under Grammar. It is very well known to the youth of the Univerſity, that the avoiding of confuſion or perturbatiõ of the fancy made by words, or preventing the los of ſight of the generall reaſon of things, by the diſguiſe of particular nũbers, having paſſed through ſeverall formes of operation, was the end and motive of inventing Mathematicall Symbols; ſo that it was a deſigne perfectly intended againſt Language and its ſervant Grammar, and that carried on ſo farre, as to oppoſe the uſe of *numbers* themſelves, which by the Learned, are ſtiled *Lingua Mathematicorum*, with whom ἄῤῥητον and *numero inexplicabile* are equipollent: But Mr W. makes me wild to follow him in his myſteries.

The uſe of Symbols is not confined to the Mathematicks only, but hath been applied to the *nature of things*, by the Pythagorean Philoſophers, and diverſe of the Cabaliſts, and to the *Art of Speaking*, by diverſe both Jewes and others: and this Symbolicall art is that *Ars Combinatoria*, frõ which *Picus Mirandula* & others, make ſuch large undertakings. The Pythagoreans did make Symbols of numbers, deſigning (*ex Arbitrio*) the parts of nature (as the ſupreme mind, the firſt matter &c.) by them, an inſtance whereof is *Platos, Timeus*; the Combinatorian Jews (*viz.* the Author of *Jezirah* and others) and from them *J. Picus: Schalichius Lully*, and others, have made Symbols of the Letters of the Alphabet, ſo that א ſignifies with them *God:* ב the *Angelicall Nature* &c. The uſe of this way with all Symbolicall writers old or new, (*Numeralls, Li-*

teralls,

teralls, Algebraicalls (for there want not such as have designed things by the notes of *Cossic* powers) is to discourse (that is to compare *subjects* and *subjects*, *subjects* and *Predicates*, and to deduce conclusions) freely without the trouble of words, upon which while the mind of man is intended, it neither sees the consequence so cleerely, nor can so swiftly make comparison as when it is acquitted of those obstacles, an instance whereof every man hath in casting an account by *Sarracenicall Ziphers*, which is much more certaine and speedy, then if the numbers were designed either in words at length, or in the letters of any Alphabet; if ever there be a speedy way made to the attainement of Knowledge, it must be by making a shorter, and clearer cutt to the understanding (by the way of signification) then that which is travailed now by words; which advancement of Learning and Knowledge, will bring (not an advance, as this man innocently supposes, but) an elevation and uselessenesse upon Language and Grammar.

For this effect is that which is pretended to by the *Universall Character*, about which he smatters so deliciously *viz.* To take away from every Nation the necessity of Learning any other beside their mother tongue (which no Nation is taught by the rules of Grammar) by designing all *things* & *notions* by certaine common signes which may be intelligible by all alike though diversly expressible (as our numerall notes, the notes of the 12 Signes &c.) You see Sir how methodicall the man is by bringing this under Grammar, however, I shall take this hint to speake a little freely concerning this Argument.

Sir when I first fell from that verbose way of tradition of the *Mathematicks*, used by the Ancients, and of late by almost all (such as *Clavius* and the like) who have written huge Volumes of particular subjects; into the Symbolicall way, invented by *Vieta*, advanced by *Harriot*, perfected by Mr *Oughtred*, and *Des Cartes*. I was presently extreamly taken with it, finding by this meanes, that not only the substance of those vast Volumes might be brought into the compasse of a sheet or two, but that the things thus reduced were more comprehensible and mannageable; the labour of the braine much taken off, and a way layd open (by the various comparisons and applications of quantities)for invention and demonstration of infinite propositions with more ease then before we could vnderstand those which others had invented for us. And I was put upon an earnest desire, that the same course might be taken in other things(the affections of quantity, the object of universall

sall

fall *Mathematicks*, seeming to be an Argument too slender to engrosse this benefit.) My first proposall was to find whether other things might not as well be designed by Symbols, and herein I was presently resolved that Symboles might be found for every *thing* and *notion*, (I having found the variety of many millons of signes in a square of a quarter of an Inch.) So that an Universall Character might easily be made wherein all Nations might communicate together, just as they do in numbers and in species. And to effect this, is indeed the designe of such as hitherto have done any thing concerning an Universall Character. And the thing thus proposed is feasible, but the number of severall Characters will be almost infinite (at left as great as the number of primitive words in the most copious tongues and the learning of them either impossible or very difficult. Of this kind I have seen severall *Essayes*, one in Print, another in Manuscript shewed to K. *Charles* (containing the first Book of *Homers Iliads* done into Characters,) but in truth such as would never be received, or if they should, would give us no other benefit, besides a communication without language (which is that which is spoken of the *China* Characters.)

So that the tradition of Learning, or faciliation of it would be but little advanced by this meanes. But it did pesently occurre to me, that by the helpe of Logick and Mathematicks this might soone receive a mighty advantage, for all Discourses being resolved in sentences, those into words, words signifying either simple notions or being resolvible into simple notions, it is manifest, that if all the sorts of simple notions be found out, and have Symboles assigned to them, those will be extreamly few in respect of the other, (which are indeed Characters of words, such as *Tullius Tiro's*) the reason of their composition easily known, and the most compounded ones at once will be comprehended, and yet will represent to the very eye all the elements of their composition, & so deliver the natures of things: and exact discources may be made demonstratively without any other paines then is used in the operations of specious Analyties.

And to such a character as this, there is but one thing more desireable, which is to make it effable, because it is a dul thing to discours by pointing & indication: and as to this there is thus much obvious, that if the first & most simple things & notions are so few as is the nüber of consonants, & the modall variations so few as may be expressed by Vowels and Diphthongs, this also may be done with great

H

great eafe and cleareneffe, otherwife not without admitting Ho-
monymies and Synonimies into that language. And here alfo, a
fucceffe hath been found much beyond expectation, *viz.* that the
characters before defcribed may be utterable, and the names be
made up of the definitions of things, or a complexion of all thofe
notions, whereof a Complexe is compounded, every fimple notion being expreffed by one fyllable, and the moft complexe notion,
confifting of as many fyllables, as it doth of fimple elementall notions. This defigne if perfected, would be of very great concernement to the advancement of Learning, and I know one in this U-
niverfity, who hath attempted fome thing this way, & undertak's as
farre as the tradition of *reall Learning,* by which I underftand the
Mathematicks, and *Naturall Philofophy,* and the grounds of *Phyfick.*

However M· *Webfter* will be brought by this, to acknowledge
that thefe things are confidered in the Univerfities, and that they
only are not dry, whileft he and his friends are madid.

Such a Language as this (where every word were a definition
and contain'd the nature of the thing) might not unjuftly be
termed a naturall Language, and would afford that which the *Ca-
balifts* and *Rofycrucians* have vainely fought for in the Hebrew,
And in the names of things affigned by *Adam,* which M. *Webfter,*
paffing the bounds of fence and reafon, would bring under the
Laws and regulation of *Donatus,* although as he *concludes* moft
Grammatically, *C. ult.* it be not *Acquifitive* but *Dative.*

Sir, familiarity with M. *Webfter* makes me bold with him, and
that hath encouraged me, to deny that ever there was any fuch
Language of Nature, and to offer him this Demonftration.

TheParadificall Protoplaft, beingCharacteriftically bound to the
Ideal Matrix of Magicall contrition, by the Symphoniacall in-
fpeaking of *Aleph tenebrofum,* and limited by *Shem hamphorafh* to the
centrall Idees, in-blowne by the ten numerations of *Belimah,* which
are ten and not nine, ten and not eleaven ; and confequently
being altogether abforpt in decyphering the fignatures of *Enfoph,*
beyond the fagacity of either a Peritrochiall, or an Ifoperime-
trall expanfion. The Iynges of the fætiferous elocution, being
difpofed only to introverfion, was deftitute at that time of all
Periftalticall effluxion, which filenced the Otacoufticall tone of
of the outflying word, and fuppreffed it in fingultient irructations.
But where the formes are thus enveloped in a reluctancy to *Pam-
phoniscall* Symbols, and the *Phantafmaticall* effluviums checked by the
tergiverfation of the *Epiglottis,* from its due fubferviency to that
concord

concord and harmony which ought to have been betwixt lapfed man and his fellow ftrings, each diatefferon being failed of its diapente neceffary to make up a Diapafon no perfect tone could follow. And confequently this Language of nature muft needs be impoffible.

I am apt to fufpect that this demonftration may to fome feeme fomewhat obfcure, but I am very fure that if Mr *Webfter* doth underftand what he hath tranfcribed upon this fubject it muft have to him (to ufe his own phrafe) *an evidentiall perfpicuity.*

Thus having demonftrated what I undertooke, I make an end of this Chapter, and proceed to comment upon your text, concerning that which followes.

CAP. IV.

Of Logick.

HOw great a favourer of Sciences Mr *Webfter* is, will appeare in this, that in every chapter his Difcourfe (If I may be bold to call it fo without a Catachrefis) equally runnes againft the Schooles, and the arts themfelves. I am perfwaded he ufed to be forely *beaten* in the Schooles with ftripes, and that hath raifed up in him, this fatall indignation, wo worth the hand that gathred the twigs, that made the rod, that whipt the ------- for what if he were uncapable of Arts? *Ex quovis ligno non fitc̃c.* & whatthough frõ a child he were given to Pilfering, & to Plagiarifme, we know that every thing would live, & if he now can make a Book from whence he hopes that he fhall *volitare-----vivus per ora virum,* & yet take of that Booke, whole fheets together from other Authors, mentioning them only now and then in the margent, as if he quoted a line or two of them, if I fay by this trade he can live, yes. and rant amongft the Levellers, and be fuffered to fpend much paper, let them fay what they pleafe, the man is to be regarded both as a wit, and a great paines-taker.

That which followes & is confiderable in this whole Booke, except his raptures when he falls in contemplation of Magick, Aftrology, or *Behmens* workes is intirely taken from others, but they are *ftrong men,* theres his *valour,* and they are none of his *acquaintance,* theres his ingenuity this Chapter begins *pag.* 32. and reaches to the 40. *pag.* of thefe, his 33. *pag.* is taken from *Gaffendas* his *Exercitations pag.* 162. his 34th from L. *Bacon pag.* 33 (in 16⁰) his 36th from

D   *Gaffend.*

Gaffend. Exerc. pag. 100,101, 102, his 37. and 38. out of *Helmont.*
pag. 42,43,44. the reft of the Chapter out of *Verulam* and *Agrippa,*
and thus I could give an account of all the reft were it not to be
Jejune and troublefome.

But to come to our Examen his fcope being to fpeake againft
the Logick taught in our Univerfities, his Difcourfe runs upon
thefe heads.

  1. *Logick is a meere verball conteft.*

  2. *It is ill applyed for the finding forth of verity, Induction being laid a-*
fide and Syllogifme taken up.

  3. *It teaches no certane rules of* $\begin{cases} \textit{Abftracting notions.} \\ \textit{Fitting words to notion.} \end{cases}$

  4. *It is made a part of Phyficks, intricated with thorny queftions &c.*

  5. *Ariftotles Logick is defective &c. as followes in Gaffend. locis ut*
fupra.

  6. *There are errours in the parts, viz.*

    1. *In Definition.*

    2. *In Divifion.*

    3. *In Argumentation by Syllogifme.*

      1. *Their conclufion not neceffarily compels affent.*

      2. *Syllogizing doth not teach that which we are ignorant of before.*

      3. *Syllogifticall conclufions beget but bare opination.*

  7. *Lullyes Art (an Alphabeticall way for Syllogizing) better then the*
other, deferving wonderous great praife, yet leaves the mind vaft and
unfatisfied. So great is the difference betwixt putation and true know-
ledge.

If the man had intended to fpeak to our Capacityes, he fhould have
firft examined what Logick is ufually taught in Univerfities & difputed againft it; now he hath roved at all and fome interchangea-
bly, accordingly as the fortune of his Collectors hath enabled him,
fpeaking firft againft the Boyes, for hiffing, then againft Syllogifme, then againft Definition, then againft *Ariftotle,* then againft
Definition &c. And after that againft *Ariftotle* and Syllogizing: you
fee Sir the generofity of this man he will not make ufe of Logick a-
gainft it felfe, and you will think me ridiculous in anfwering to
his Allegation (the Univerfity being wholy inconcerned,) but ile be
exceeding briefe.

  1. A Syfteme of rules directing us to the knowledge of the
truth begets no inteftine warre no humming, hiffing, nor *obfufca-*
tion.

2

2. The ufe of Induction is taught in the Univerfity as well as the ufe of Syllogifme; Logick is univerfally fubfervient to the enquiry of all truths; Induction is ridiculoufly applyed to Mathematicall truths, and Syllogifme is to be applyed to Phyficks; it was a misfortune to the world, that my Lord *Bacon* was not skilled in Mathematicks, which made him jealous of their Affiftance in naturall Enquiries; when the operations of nature fhall be followed up to their Staticall (and Mechanicall) caufes, the ufe of Induction will ceafe, and Syllogifme fucceed in the place of it, in the interim we are to defire that men have patience not to lay afide Induction before they have reafon.

3. Logick doth teach certaine rules of Abftracting notions *viz* by examining the Agreements and difagreements (which they call the Genus and Difference) of things, and if our notions of things have been rafhly abftracted, the fault hath been either in the obfcurity of nature, or in the dullneffe or impatience of Phylofophers & not in the Logick of the Academies. The notions of things being rightly abftracted they are rightly affigned to words by Definition.

4. The queftions concerning the entity of Logicall notions, and other Phyficall and Metaphyficall things, are not (to my Knowledge) mingled with the tradition of Logick, (otherwife then to afford examples to the Rules of it) fo that this complaint may concerne others, but not our Univerfities.

5. *Ariftotles Organon* is not read to the youth of this Univerfity, (how juftly I contend not) neither was it ever underftood, or ever will be by M. *Webfter*, then why fhould we fall out about it?

6. 1. It is a prodigious Ignorance in *Helmont* (from whom M. *Webfter* without regard to common honefty , hath taken what enfues) to think there are no other, or fcarce any differences known, befide Rationall and Irrationall: This is frequently met withall in the vulgar Syftems of Logick as an example, and he thought no more was knowne: without regard to all demonftrative Mathematicall knowledge: but he could not fpeake of things he underftood not; why then fhould the blind lead the blind?

2. Something he would have fpoken againft Divifion , but he had it not about him; fo we can only thanke him for his good intentions in that particular.

3. His Exceptions againft *Syllogizing* (I meane his new fupply out of *Helmont* are thefe.)

1. Their Conclufions doe not neceffarily compell Affent. *viz.*

D 2   M,

M. *Webſter* is one who can grant the premiſes in a true Syllo-
giſme, and yet deny the concluſion. I Anſwere this is by a ſpe-
ciall gift.

2 His Second exception, I ſay, that the eduction of a third
Propoſition, or truth from two that were known before, is a
teaching of what we knew not, otherwiſe no man living need
to ſtudy for any Demonſtrative Knowledge: tis poſſible M. *Webſter* may know that *totum eſt majus ſua parte*, and the other Axioms in *Euclid*, yet I dare ſay, he underſtands not, that in a
Rectangled Triangle, the ſquare of the Hypothenuſe, is equall
to the conjoyned ſquares of the other ſides, much leſſe any of
the Propoſitions concerning the Regular Bodies, or Conic
Sections.

3. And whereas he ſajes, that Syllogiſticall concluſions beget *but bare opination*; we ought to pardon him, *Helmont* told him
ſo, and he knew not that there was ſuch a thing as *Syllogiſmus
Demonſtrativus*, and what would you have of a Cat ? &c.

7. But though he have deſpiſed theſe waies, he will give an excellent account of the Art of *Lully*, and indeed his deſcription argues him a man of profound ſearch into the things he deales with:
it is he ſaith, *An Alphabeticall way for Syllogizing*: a deſcription ſunke
many fathoms beyond the profundity of truth or ſence, and if
there be any ſence aſſigneable to this deſcription, it will amount
to ſuch a Definition of Geometry as this, *It is an Art of Knowing
ſomething by the helpe of Letters, Syllables, Words, and Figures*: a matter of grievous ſkil and judgement to diſcover. Sir I need not
own my converſation in that Art of *Lully* : yet I meet with few
that have conſidered much more of it then my ſelfe, and this I
undertake to be accountable for to M. *Webſter*, that neither that,
nor Logick are unuſefull; yet that Logick conduces more to the
invention, and ſearch, and ſtrict examination of Truth, and that
other more to the invention of Arguments for diſcourſe : the one
more appropriate to *Logicall*, (as 'tis called) the other to *Rhetori-
call*, or *Poeticall* invention ; the one is a very good way for begin-
ners, the other extreamely uſefull to men that have already attained to the knowledge of things, to fetch the notions of things
with eaſe and celerity in their view ; and fit men for ſecure and
ready ſpeaking. I have now done with his Chapter of *Logick* and
come to that concerning *Mathematicks*.

CAP.

C A P. V.

Of the Mathematicall Sciences.

THE Mathematicks are extreamely beholding to him for his Favours '(but sure without any speciall desert from him) He hath heard of their *perspicuity, veritude,* and *certitude ,* and complaines they are so slightly handled, without any solid pra-ctice, or true Demonstrations.

You know Sr ,how much this makes towards a bribeing of mee; My clamour is against the neglect of Mathematics in our method of study,& you would think I cannot chuse but receive a coplacen-cy from his concurrence;!yet such is the perverfenes of my nature, that I have not upon any occaſion,felt my spleen so high,ſtreining upon a downe-right indignation,as when I find him and Mr *Dell* praiſing the Mathematicks : for why ? what have the Mathema-ticks deſerved? that theſe men ſhould render them contemptible by their commendations: You know Sir , it was heretofore ac-counted an inſtance of Mathematicall skill , to give the dimenſi-ons of *Hercules* from the meaſure of his foot, what if I ſhould ad-venture to give you the meaſure of this Mathematicall *Hercules,* or *Herculean* Mathematian. Sir ile begin to rant the ſociety with theſe men having brought me to it, and I will give you the(Ma-thematicall) meaſure of two of them together Mr *Webſter* and Mr *Dell.*

The meaſure of their pous (for they tread both in the ſame ſteps and are Mathematitians both of a ciſe) I take meerely from their buzzing Diſcourſe about Mathematicks,and lay this for my Aſſer-tion as the reſult & ſumme that may be collected fiom what they have ſaid in that argument (where I put with the jejuner diſcourſe all the Rhetorick Poetry. All all the raptures, extaſyes and excla-mations,& bring them into this æquation)& that if A be a ſymboll of a known meaſure of skill to be expreſſed in the number 666.the skill of them both put together will be equall to $Aq---AgCCC$,(the miſchiefe is they do not underſtand me) and thence it followes as a corollary,that neither of them ever underſtood one demonſtra-tion or æquation, and for aſſurance of what I ſay, I undertake, that if either or both of them joyntly or ſeverally be able to re-ſolve a common adfected æquation, or give the Geometricall effection of it (that which many Boyes in the Univerſity are able

to

to do) I will procure them one of our Mathematick Professors places.

But he sayes *The Schooles have done little or nothing to advance learning, or promote Science, tis true that my L. Nepair, Mr Briggs, and Mr Oughtred, (private Spirits) have done something &c.*

Will he be allwayes so mysterious? Was not Mr *Oughtred* Fellow of K. Colledge in Cambridge, and Mr *Briggs* first Fellow of St *Johns*, afterwards Professour of *Geometry* at *Gresham* Colledge, and did he not lastly live and dye Professor of Geometry at Oxford, did not most or all of those he mentions afterwards, Professe and read the Mathematicks in severall Schooles and Academies, and is not *Gassendus* (from whom he takes whole sheets together of this *Rapsody*) Professour of Astronomy at *Paris*.

What then doth this man meane, to say the Schooles (as he termes them) have not advanced these sciences; dos he expect that the Colledge buildings, or Sr *Thomas Bodlyes* frame should do it? Indeed they will do it as soone as he. But I forget my selfe, the summe of his complaints is this.

1. *That Arithmetick and Geometry are neglected, the Schooles contenting themselves with verball disputes of magnitude, &c.*

2. *That Opticks have received no advance.*

3. *That the Theory of Musick is neglected.*

4. *That the Astronomy Schooles teach according to the Ptolemaick System, which they maintaine with Rigour.* And against this his spirit runs out in very many Arguments.

5. *They are ignorant of the other parts, as Geography, Hydrography, Chorography, &c.*

6. *They doe not professe the divine Art or Science of Astrology.*

7. Somewhat he would say of *Staticks, Architecture, Pneumatithmy, &c.* Commemorated by Dr *John Dee.*

Concerning these, I shall speake as briefely as is possible.

1. *Arithmetick* and *Geometry* are sincerely & profoundly taught, Analyticall Algebra, the Solution and Application of Æquations, containing the whole mystery of both those sciences, being faithfully expounded in the Schooles by the professor of Geometry, and in many severall Colledges by particular Tutors, and were he an Idoneous Auditor, I undertake he should receive full satisfaction here in that particular, however I will be bound he shall be wrought upon (as he expresses it else-where) even to *wonder* and *amazement.*

2. His next complaint is, that the *Opticks* are neglected, (I cannot

not

not fay what they are generally, but this I know, that there have been lately given by fome perfons here inftances of more folid knowledge of all forts of radiation or vifion, then ever were here, or indeed elfewhere before, and that fuch things are ordinary now amongft us (done by fome amongft our felves) as heretofore were counted Magicall.

3. The Theory of *Mufick* is not neglected, indeed the Mufick meeting, by the Statutes of this Univerfity, appointed to be once a weeke, hath not of late been obferved, our Inftruments having been lately out of tune, and our harpes hanged up, but if fuch men as he fhould pleafe to come among us, and put us to an examen, without doubt we fhould then have a fit of Mirth &c.

4. But of all things the *Aftronomy* Schooles he is moft offended at, as maintaining with Rigour the *Ptolemaick Syftem*: And againft this he difputes with Arguments able to turne a *Copernican* into a *Ptolemaick*: the thing, as to our Univerfity, you know to be moft falfe; I believe there is not one man here, who is fo farre Aftrono-micall, as to be able to calculate an Eclipfe, who hath not received the *Copernican Syftem*, (as it was left by him, or as improved by *Kepler, Bullialdus*, our own Profeffor, and others of the *Ellipticall* way) either as an opinion, or at leaftwife, as the moft intelligible, and moft convenient Hypothefis. For my felfe, you know well my principles of Phylofophy and Aftronomy, and how little this whole Pamphlet concernes me, yet in defence of *Ptolemy* this may be faid with juftice, that there is no Aftronomicall Book in the World, which may not be better fpared then his Μεγάλη Συνταξις: Sir *H. Savile* (then whom in his time, Europe had not a better judge of things of that nature,) faies of it, *nihil illi par aut æquale*: and I heard this lately difcourfed and demonftrated, by one (having relation to him) who himfelfe is yet a Copernican of the Ellipticall family; had this man ever feen the Almageft, or *Ptolo-mies Hypotypofis*, he would have known, that *Ptolomy* never medled with folid Orbes, he only falved the *Phenomena*, which were left him by *Excentricks* and *Epicycles*, and medled not with the Phyficall part at all: and indeed there is no Mathematick Book in the world more learned or ufefull in its kind, then *Ptolemies Almagift*, but it is above the capacity of M. *Webfters* cife to underftand either his folution of Triangles, his inveftigation of Apogees and Excen-tricities, his Demonftration of the Inequalities of the Planets, his concluding of them from the Phenomena of nature, and his exhi-bition of them by his hypothefis.

The

The Method here obfervèd in our Schooles is first to exhibit the *Phenomena,* and fhew the way of their obfervation, then to give an account of the various Hypothefes, how thofe Phenomena have been falved,or may be (where the Æquipollency or defects of the feverall Hyppothefes are fhewn.) And laftly to fhew how the Geometricall Hypothefes are refolvible into tables, ferving for calculation of Ephemerides,which are of quotidian ufe,and if Mr *Webfter* have any thing to amend in this method, and will afford it our Profeffor, I will undertake he will be thankfull for it.

The puerility of his Arguments your felfe have noted, they are facred I will not name them.

5. It is not faire to fay we are ignorant of *Cofmography*, unlefe he had tried us,indeed, if we be fo, I know fome muft anfwer for it, Sir *Henry Savile* hath laid it upon one of his Profeffors to Read publickly after the body of Aftronomy, thefe Arts he mentions, and if he be ignorant of them, let M. *Webfter* informe againft him, and take his Profeffion, winne it and weare it. You will give me leave Sir, to publifh in our vindication, what your felfe and I know to be true. Thefe Arts he mentions, are not only underftood, and taught here, but have lately received reall and confiderable advances (I meane fince the Univerfities came into thofe hands wherein now it is) particularly Arithmetick, and Geometry, in the promotion of the Doctrine of *Indivifibilia*, and the difcovery of the naturall rife and mannagement of Conic Sections and other folid places. Opticks and Perfpective, by various inventions and applications on Gnomonicks and picture Aftronomy in polifhing, and indeed perfecting the Ellipticall hypothefis, and rendring it Geometricall; and furely if we may ftill enjoy the encouragement of the Higher Powers,we may hope in a little time, to give a good account of our felves, as to thefe particulars.

6. But the mifchiefe is, we are not given to *Aftrology*, a fad thing, that men will not forfake the ftudy of Arts and Languages, and give themfelves up to this high and Noble Art or Science,he knowes not what to call it: Nay call it that ridiculous cheat, made up of nonfence and contradictions, founded only upon the difhonefty of Impoftors, and the frivolous curiofity of filly people, fo as none but one initiated in the Academy of *Bethlem*, would require of us, that we fhould be Philofophers and Mathematicians, and yet not to have outgrowne this gullery. I fpeake not to him (for he underftands as much of Aftrology as of other things) but to thofe he fo highly adores(for one of whom *viz.* Mr *Afhmole,*

I

I have a very good refpect) I make this proffer, that if they can affert either upon the g. ounds of reafon, or conftant experiment, any one rule of Judiciall Aftrology, nay if they can maintaine, that the very foundations of them, are not frivoloufly and ridiculoufly laid and retained, I fhall joyne with Mr. *W*. in defiring that the *Thundering Fulpit men*, may fubmit to the Blundering Hell-pitmen, and that *Divinity* (he will let me ufe that word rather then loofe a Conunrim) may give way to *Divination*. The pretence of Aftrology is to divine by the Syzyges of the Planets. The Planets are confidered, as they refpect either (1) the 12 houfes, or (2) the fignes of the Zodiac, or (3) one another, or (4) according to their fite and native powers,

Againft them I affert, that their Houfes have no foundation, for whereas there are three waies of affigning them, either by dividing the Ecliptick, the firft verticall or the Æquinoctiall into 12 equall parts, they have forfaken the two former, and called the laft the rationall way (as condemning the two former of irrationality) yet this rationall way ferves but for fome parts of the fphere, and thofe that live under a right or parallel fphere (if any doe) muft be deprived of the benefit of Aftrology, becaufe in a right fphere they are confounded, and in a parallel there are no houfes.

2. In relation to the fignes of the Zodiac, the Planets are conceived to have their Exaltations or Diminutions, and here they difcover a moft profound ftupidity: about the time when this folly took place, the Apogees and Perigees of the feverall Planets being by Aftronomers determined to be in certaine places of the Zodiac: this exaltation or depreffion, in refpect of diftance, they Coxcomically have underftood in refpect to their virtue, and though their Apogees be changed, they ftill retaine in thofe very places their Exaltations.

3. Their number of Afpects is Arbitrary, and there may as well be made 600 as 6. and granting there were any reafon or ground for their good or bad fignification, they muft fignify to one another, not to us.

4. Laftly, the vertues of the Planets themfelves, that they are hot and cold, male and female &c. is ridiculoufly founded ; who ever felt the heat of *Mars*, or cold of *Saturne?* The whole Theory is formed with refpect to the Peripateticall Syftem, the conceit of the foure Elements, and if they fhould be granted, conduce nothing to the fortune-telling which they profeffe.

E

I have but touched thefe things, yet fo as I have ftrook at the root of their whole impofture, and if they can fatisfy in thefe things, I will be their Profelite.

7. Seeing Mr *Webfter* had nothing to fay of *Staticks*, *Architecture*, *Pnemaththmy*, &c. I only fhall fay that all or moft, have received fome improvement in this place, as we fhall make appeare when he makes his vifitation.

CAP. VI.

Of Scholaftick Phylofophy.

THis Chapter of his confifts of two parts, an affirmative and a Negative; the firft concernes the way of Phylofophy, which he faith is profeffed in the Schooles *viz.* The Ariftotelicall way: in the other he would exhibit the *Defiderata*, thofe things whereof the Univerfities are ignorant.

He difputes againft the Ariftotelicall Philolophy in more then twenty whole pages of this Chapter, but his difpute is interrupted by the *Defiderata:* for from *pag.* 53. to 67. *inclufivè*, he is Ant-Ari-ftoticall; thence to the 78. p. come in his other exceptions, and from the 78 *page* to 83. *(viz.* to the end of the Chapter *)* he hath ano-ther bang at *Ariftotle.*

You know Sir, how little either I my felfe, or our Univerfities, are concerned to intereffe our felves in this quarrell, confidering the liberty that is here allowed and taken, this Difcourfe may per-haps concern *Collegium Conimbricenfe* or fome forraign Univerfities, and let them Anfwer it.

Yet I muft confeffe I wondered at this chap. both at the learning, the Inequality, and the method of it; I prefently found fome things in it to exceed the Genius of our Reformer, and fome things well becomming him both in refpect of his Learning, Method, and In-genuity.

Concerning his *Defiderata* I fhall fpeake briefely by themfelves, after I have given an account firft of his Antariftotelicall matter, then of his Method.

I have formerly intimated how good he is at taking hints, I for-got to give notice in the laft Chapter of that faculty of his; Now I will not fee him wronged; my Propofition is, That there is not one Argument againft *Ariftotle*, which he hath not taken entirely out of *Gaffendis*

Gaſſendis Exercitations *adverſus Ariſtoteleos*, beſide **a little out of**
Helmont, to ſpare words l have annexed this **Table.**

Webſter. Page	*Gaſſend.* Page	Here come in the *Deſiderata*, Afterwards	
53	53,54,55		
54	56		
55	58,59,60	*Webſter.* Page	*Gaſſend.* Page
56	60	78	141
57	62,63	79	146,167
58	64	80	167
59	78	81	170, 171,172
60	79	82	186
61	81,83	83	189,195
62	84		
63	90,92		
64	93		

Webſter.	*Helm.*
65	46
66	*& deinceps.*
67	

You may think Sir I love the man, otherwiſe *I* ſhould not take
this paines with him; this concernes his I earning, that which diſcovers his ingenuity is, that in the tranſcription of all theſe 18
whole Pages out of *Gaſſendus*, he never quotes him . only for a
line or two by the by, *pag.* 66. he names him.

ℤ. But you will wonder why this chaſme ſhould be betwixt
pag. 67. and *p.*78. and why he could not have given *Ariſtotle* his
lurry altogether?

Anſ. I anſwer becauſe his Tranſlator failed him, who ſhould
have brought it to him altogether.

Mr *Webſter* being above, or without all skill in Languages, and
deſtitute of revelation , was forced to get another to tranſlate (he
onely attempting at one ſmall parcell *pag.*64. *Accedebat ad hæc ingenium viri (Ariſtotelis) tectum & callidum &c.* which he conſtrues, *there
happened to theſe things the cloſe wit of the man &c.* though his tranſlator
ſtayes, yet (ſenſible in how great need the world ſtood of his la-

bour) he goes on, and when his Tranflator brings in his remnant,
he claps it into the reft crying firft come firft ferved, and that's the
juft account and reason of this Method.

The fumme of his complaints is this.

1. *Naturall Magick is abominated, and profecuted with fire and fword,
and not only fo, but the name of it execrable &c.*

2. *The fublime fcience of Pyrotechny, or Chymiftry neglected.*

3. *Medicine* 1. *Turned to flattery &c.* 2. *Ill bottomed upon falfe Phylofophy.* 3. *The Galenicall way not advanced.*

4. *Difcoveries in Anotomy* 1. *Ufeleffe (as Circulation)* 2. *Defective,
as to the difcovery of the Signatures of the invifible Archeus.*

5. *Chirurgery defective in curing the Lupus, Cancer, &c.*
Againe, that the Schooles are ignorant of

1. *Celeftiall Signatures, and Subceleftiall Phyfiognomy,* viz. *Meteoro-
logicall, Mineralogicall, Botanicall, Anthropologicall.*

2. *The three great Hypoftaticall foule-ravifhing Principles, Salt, fulphur,
and Mercury.*

3. *Magneticall Phylofophy.*

4. *Atomicall Learning.*

To all thefe I fhall make a very briefe reply.

Anf. 1. It is furely a wonderfull thing, that naturall Magick
fhould not only be *profecuted with fire and fword,* but that it fhould be
execrable alfo. Yet notwithftanding this lamentable perfecution, I
dare adventure my life, That M. *W* may paffe fafely with this Examen, carrying it either in his *pocket,* or in his hand, or in his mouth
through both the Univerfities of this Nation, the feverall Colleges of Eaton, Winchefter &c. the College of Phyfitians at London, and all the reft, (provided he have a care how he paffes by the
College at Bethlem) without any danger of Bell, Booke, or
Candle, Fire, Sword or Execration. As for thofe Authors who
have treated of that Argument fuch as *Agrippa, Porta, Wecker,* & the
reft, you know Sir how oft they have deluded us how very flender a
proportion of truth is conteined in their volumes, that they are
not refpected here becaufe of the name Magick, much leff for any
conjuring they teach, but for the cheat and impofture which they
put upon us, eluding credulous men with the pretence of fpecificall vertues, and occult celeftiall Signatures and taking them off
from obfervation & experiment (the only way to the knowledge
of nature) The difcoveries of the Symphonies of nature, and the
rules of applying agent and materiall caufes to produce effects, is
the true naturall Magick, and the generall humane ends of all
Phylofophicall

Pylofophycall enquiries; but M. *Webster* knew not this, 'tis plaine therefore he is no Witch, and is therefore free from perfecution.

2. Chymiſtry you know is not neglected here (there being a conjunction of both the Purſes and endeavours of ſeverall perſons towards diſcoveries of that kind, ſuch as may ſerve either to the diſcovery of light or profit, either to Naturall Philoſophy or Phyſick. But Mr *Webster* expects we ſhould tell him, that we have found the Elixar, (ſurely we are wiſer then to ſay ſo) yet we can recommend him to one of his faith, who hath been threeſcore years in the purſuance of it, and two years ſince believed he was very neare it.

3. By what Chymicall operation *Phyſick* ſhould be turned into *flattery*, in truth I cannot fancy. The practice of Phyſick hath been bottomed upon experience and obſervation.

4. And that is the reaſon, that the diſcoveries of the Circulation of the blood, of the *venæ lacteæ*, both Meſentericall and Thoracicall, of the *vas breve*, and ſeverall new *ductus, vaſa lymphatica* &c. have not made an alteration in the practiſe of Phyſick, anſwerable to the advantage they have given to the Theory ; and the ſecurity and confirmation they have brought to the former waies of practiſe.

As for his *Poſtulatum* of diſcovering the ſignatures of the Inviſible *Archeus* by Anatomy, it is one of his *Roſycrucian Rodomantados*; would he have us by diſſection ſurprize the *Anima mundi*, & ſhew him the impreſſions of a thing inviſible ? Yet the Schematiſmes of nature in matters of ſenſible bulke, have been obſerved amongſt us, and collections made of them in our inquiries, and when the microſcope ſhall be brought to the higheſt (whether it is apace arriving) we ſhall be able either to give the ſeminall figures of things, which regulates them in their production and growth, or evince them to lye in quantities inſenſible, and ſo to be in truth inviſible.

5. If neither Phyſick nor Surgery ſhould be defective, he ought to believe, that man ſhould be Immortall, or at leaſt, be as long lived as the *Roſycrucians* tell him. Yet Surgery as well as Phyſick, hath even in our time been extremely advanced, this place hath given late inſtances of both; (particularly in recovering the Wench after ſhe had been hanged at leaſt halfe an hower, and others which I could mention) And the Colledge of Phyſitians at London is

E 3   the

the glory of this Nation, and indeed of Europe, for their Learning and felicity, in the cures of desperate Ulcers and diseases, even of the Cancer, and those he (ignorantly) mentions, which have been diverse times performed, by D. *Harvey* and others.

As to the Ignorance he charges upon us, I Answer.

1. It is the destiny of proud and ignorant men, such as having nothing of science, have yet the unjust desire to be reputed Rabbies, and the Impudence to attempt to be Reformers, that being diverted from the reall and solid wayes of knowledge, they dwindle after the windy impostures of Magick and Astrology, of signatures and physiognomy, and the like, and if we follow them not madding in these pursuits, we pray that we may be excused.

2. I have formerly given some intimation of our Chymicall society, so that I hope it will be charitably concluded, that we are not ignorant of those hypostaticall principles: yet how they should come to ravish the soule of M. *Webster*, I cannot tell, unlesse it should be in contemplation of the benefits he hath received from them, *viz.* of Salt at Dinner, of Sulphur in the Mange, and of Mercury in Salivation.

3. Magneticall Philosophy is not neglected here, your selfe Sir, are conscious of some Instruments that are prepared for those experiments (as Loadstones rough and polished, armed and naked, a Terrella and diverse others) and how it is a reall designe amongst us, wanting only some assistance for execution, to erect a Magneticall, Mechanicall, and Optick Schoole, furnished with the best Instruments, and Adapted for the most usefull experiments in all those faculties.

4. How happy are you and I Sir, and our ingenious acquaintance, (whose studies are toward Physick or Philosophy) in this place, who are all employed to salve Mechanically, and statically the Phenomena of nature, and have in some parts advanced the Philosophy of those he mentions ? How will it comfort us that we do, and have done in many things, what he would have us?

Qui monet ut facias, quod jam facis ipse &c.

But least we should be lifted up, behold him in the next Chapter thundering against the remainder of Arts and Sciences.

CAP.

CAP. VII.

Of Metaphysicks, Ethicks, Politicks, Oeconomicks, Poesy and Oratory.

YOu see Sir, how thick they come together, and yet the Chap. consists but of three leaves, and part of them is taken up with the repetition of that learned Proverbe, *Hercules is knowne by his foot, and the Lyon by his pawe.* Do not you think Sir, that this man lookes like *Hercules* ? He thinks so, and he knowes how he lookes; even like *Hercules Furens,* and thence is the inequallity of his Ravings. You had him in the former Chap. in his combate with *strong men to take from them their steely armes of demonstration;* But no Mortall wight, no *Hero* is able to persist to perpetuity: we see here the great *Alcides* or *Goliah* fainting, not able to weild his Weavers beame, or *Fustilogge,* letting it fall at all adventures, himselfe forlorne of friends, his strength and reason fled away.

But though the storme be past therere may be danger from these after drops, *Alcides* may stuble, & oppresse the Sciences with his fall and a man may be wounded with the convulsive graspe of a dying Lyon. Let us observe, therefore and either decline or repell these last attempts against the Learning of the Academies.

Against *Metaphysicks* his exceptions are these

1. *It brings no better instrument for the discovery of truth, then the ope-ration of the Intellect.*

Why! hath Mr *W.* any better instrument then this ? Is it sense, or is it revelation ? What is his instrument or toole, that he pre-ferres before the Intellect of man ? The man is mad why doe I trouble him ?

2. *It containes no certaine principles, the principle of mens Cogitans, is more certaine, and undeniable then that of the Schooles, Impossibile est idem simul esse & non esse.*

It seemes he is in a case to swallow Contradictions, and can af-sert that a thing can *simul esse & non esse* (I warrant this man doth believe transubstantiation) how is his throat widened since he was so streight as not to admit the inference of a conclusion in a true Syllogisme? but then was then, and now is now, *omnium rerum est vicissitudo.* Yet *Des Cartes* will give him little thankes for acknow-ledging his Principle, *Cogito ergo sum,* if a thing may *simul esse & non esse.*

3.

3. The fumme of the remainder is this, (though by a fpeciall gift he hath multiplyed it into three arguments) *That Metaphyficks is of no Profit but to obfcure the truth, hath produced none but weake frivolous o-pinions concerning God &c. and the poifonous Cocatrice egs of Altercation.*

I anfwer Sir that I have no inclination to grapple with the wind, or deale with wild univerfalityes, I am of opinion, that there is much to be confidered of, & amended in the Metaphyficks; but that upon this occafion, he hath only difcovered an art he hath which might have faved'him the labour of all particulars, by faying at once both to the Schooles and Sciences that they are evill and not good, yea even wicked frivolous and abominable.

His next touch is at Ethicks, and his Exceptions are

1. Againft *Ariftotle, who was a Heathen, and did not acknowledge God.*

And you fay Sir, Mr *Webfter* is a Friar, yet *Ariftotle* acknowledged a Firft Mover & if that be not God what is it.

2. *He placed the fummum bonum in the exercife of virtue, but the fummum bonum is not attaineable in this life.*

But he was difputing what was the *fummum bonum* in this Life, and if vertue be the way to Life Eternall, it is certainely that *fummum bonum.*

3. *They have taught nothing practicable.*

We are forry that Mr *Webfter* finds Juftice, Prudence, Temperance, Modefty &c. unpracticable, but fo it feemes it is with him, and yet he will be our Reformer.

4. *Ariftotle takes the preheminence of that which is deduced from the Principles of Chriftianity, and is unjuftly preferred before Socrates, Plato, Zeno, Seneca, Epictetus, who containe more precious Treafure.*

But where is it O thou roaring Lyon, (feeking whom thou maift devour) or rather thou Effex-Lyon, that *Ariftotle* is preferred before Chrift ? Is it at Oxford or at Cambridge ? Are not the Chriftian Ethicks of *Daneus, Scultetus, Amefius, Aquinas,* others, befide all thofe Authors you have mentioned, read & ftudye,d and preferred before him in the Univerfities ? What fhall be done unto thee O thou leafing toungue ?

Politicks.

His exception againft the Politicks read in the Univerfities is very faint and thinne being only this, *That Plato, Bodin, Machavell, are as good as Ariftotle (though he have many things of fingular ufe, which is the firft good word he hath given him) and that our Country man, M. Holbs, is more profound, and yet we read Ariftotle in the Univerfities.*

Rhetorick.

Rhetorick.

And the same is his Exception against Rhetorick. *We read Ari-*
stotle, and spend too much time upon ornamentall Oratory and Poetry, which are
gifts of nature.

Ans. Had this man found any one that had written whole
Bookes against these Arts of *Aristotle,* so as *Gassendus, Helmont, &c.*
against his *Logick* and *Naturall Phylosophy,* and a Translator ready to
assist him these Arts and Sciences had not thus escaped him, now
he can only clatter at *Aristotle,* and clamour against the Schooles
for reading him. *Plato, Bodin, Macchiavel, are as good as Aristotle* : well,
and *Aristotle* as good as them; what then ? But Mr *Hobbs* is more
profound &c. 'Tis true our Theologues say he is bottomed in the
great Abysse. Againe, *Aristotle in his Rhetorick must give way to*
Plato ; I will not repeat what I have said, and you Sir before me,
concerning the Liberty and variety amongst us. But I affirme, that
supposing those *Morall* Authours which even now he mentioned,
Zeno, Seneca, Epictetus, or these *Politick* writers or *Rhetoritians*; did
conteine things better in their kind then *Aristotle,* yet they are not
so fit to be read in Univerfities by way of Institution, as he. They
have written diffusedly *stilo oratorio,* or use by way of Dialogues,
but have not given a briefe Methodicall body of the things they
handle. The businesse of such as have the institution of youth, is to
give them, first a briefe and generall comprehension of the kinds
and natures of those things, about which their studyes, and endeavours are to be employed, and so to excite & stirre them up to
a deeper & more thorough consideration of them, to set them into
a way of study and knowledge, but no man is made perfect
in any kind by the meere endeavours of a Tutor, but for
that they must have recourse to their industry, their ingenuity,
and their inclination. Now the chiefe reason as I conceive,
why *Aristotle* hath been universally received as *Magister Legitimus* in
Schooles hath been; The universallity of his Enquiries; the brevity
and Method of them; fitting them for Institutions, and not the
truth or infallibillity of his Workes : Ignorance or want of
consideration of that end, mixt with pride and Arrogance and an
Ambition to be a reformer, hath produced this glorious worke of
Mr *Webster.*

He hath now done with the Learning of the Univerfityes, indeed
he had done with it long agoe, and will have a fling at their
Customes and Method.

F

CAP.

CAP. VIII.

Of their Customes and Method.

WHat *Erasmus* said concerning the Popes Crowne, and Monkes bellyes, is more fit for a Fryar to speak, then for us who live upon College Commons. To come therefore briefely to his Exceptions.

1. His first is, *That all our severall Colleges are tyed to one Method, carried on in one way, bound to the same Authors.*

The charge is utterly untrue, yet were it so, it were no inconvenience (unlesse he could demonstrate an errour in our Institutions) that those who are to engage in the same Scholastick exercises, should be trained up in the same Authors and Method.

2. *But our Exercises are slothfully performed, our Publick Acts being kept but foure times in the yeare, that is in the Termes, which, if one should tell them in plaine termes, are but usually idle termes.*

Would not some man as knowing as himself imagine our Terms to last some four dayes or thereabouts? But you know Sir, they take up the greatest part of all the yeare, and that in the vacations our Schollars are not exempt from exercise, either in the College-Halls, or in their Tutors Chambers.

As for his quibling about termes, (it being the only wit that he hath offered at) I will upon no termes spoile his Conundrum, yet I must confesse some grudging I have, that he should set up in two trades at once, Quibling and Reforming.

3. *The custome is Injurious which ties men to a set time of yeares and Acts, before they can receive their laureation.*

Of all men living I know no reason why such as he should complaine of this: alas! why should such men be left behind their over nimble fellowes? Me thinks he should be comforted, in being suffered to Leird it in a crowd of better company. But seriously Sir, I use to admire in this the prudence of our Ancestors; to stay a while for a degree (which yet this mã would not have us so proud and arrogant as to conferre) it is no prejudice to mens worth or Learning; those Colledges have not been least renowned where the locall statures oblige them to stay the longest ; we are not destitute of other equivalent encouragements, in case of an egregious proficiency: and if upon such pretences, time and exercises should be dispensed with , the overweening of men, and the partialities

234

allities of friends, would prove very prejudiciall to the true and sincere interest of worth and Learning.

4. His next scandall is, *At the Humming and Hissing of Boyes, rather like Geese then Bees &c.*

Indeed Sir, the Boyes are to be chidden, yet I must needs tell M. *Webster*, that all are not Bees that buzze, and it appeares their hissing hath been his great vexation; but that he was never troubled with their humming.

5 He complaines, *That their Disputations are about Notions and paper-Idols.*

Was there ever, or can there be a Disputation about any thing else but Notions? Would he have them bring forth Bread and Cheese & Dispute *de gustibus?* Or would he have the Consecrated Host brought in, and paper-Idols converted into Wafer-Idols of more savour?

6. And in earnest, it is a heavy thing, that they make use still of the Latine Tongue in all their exercises.

Indeed Sir, this is a sad and grievous complaint, and hath not fallen from him without reason. His reason I discovered in his Chapter about *Philosophy:* let others admire his wit, I am for his judgement: you say Sir, he is a Friar (whether black or gray, of the Family of the Creepers, or the Skippers it matters not) now Sir, if he could reforme out of the Universities, our studied Arts and Languages, so farre as to banish from us the use of even the Latine Tongue, and put us into a course of studying Magicall signatures, Astrology, and *Jacob Behmen;* his modesty might admit of demanding a Canonization, and this great Mathematician, might justly conclude his account to his holinesse, with an ὅπερ ἔδει ποιῆσαι.

P. 8, 9, His next three complaints I shall make bold to put together, as containing our adhering to Antiquity, our being sweyed by plurality of voyce, and our adhering to *Aristotle.*

O *Aristotle*, are you there! I wondered where he was all this while, when M. *Webster* was in distresse for want of him: but he is a Peripatetick, and will never leave these courses, till M. *Webster* turne him out from among the Academies; however for us, let M. W. answer for our affectation of novelty and singularity, and we shall well enough evade the charges of these Paragraphs.

10. His last complaint is, that we doe not read the Mathematicks.

Indeed we doe not so much and earely as is fitting, yet this I

must

muſt needs ſay, that we read Ptolemy, *Apollonius*, and *Euclide*,&c. and he hath read nothing but *Iohn Dees* Engliſh Preface : make roome now for his Expedients.

CAP. IX.

Of ſome Expedients or Remedies in Theology, Grammar, Logick, and Mathematicks.

DID not I heretofore intimate, that I found M. *Webſter* to be a pittifull man, and now Sir you ſee it plainly proved by this Chapter, and thoſe which follow,

Una eademꝗ manus vulnus opemꝗ feret.

he that hath hurt the Univerſities will heale them. You know it is the cuſtome of thoſe generous ſoules, who for the health and ſafety of the generality of men, doe uſe to aſcend the banke or publick ſtage, to give poyſon to ſome that are about them, to wound or ſcald them, not that they delight in torturing the creature, (that were cruelty) but by the ſmart of ſome few, to convince the unbelieving multitude of the celeſtiall energy of their Balſames; they only wound, that they may cure the wounded. And now for Application in ſhort, that's the deſigne of this noble Gentleman: yet leaſt any man ſhould think the remedies worſe then the diſeaſes, I am reſolved here to joyne with him, and with ſteely arguments, to confound his gainſayers.

For Theology.

1. His firſt remedy is, that men ſhould lay aſide the *ſuffering of themſelves*, to be ſtiled by the *Blaſphemous* title of *Divines*, and that the people ſhould call them *Theologues, as they doe in Scotland.*

I am for Theologue, Divine is a thinne ſtingy word to it, this fills the mouth better, and is fitter to aſtoniſh, comes nearer too to a Magicall noiſe, (and Magick is almoſt Divine p.68.) I would have the people call them Theologues, and this is my reaſon; his reaſons are myſticall, *becauſe the other is blaſphemous* : yet nothing more frequent amongſt the Antients then Θεῖος ἀνὴρ ἔςι : and thoſe who have ſought Epithites for *Plato*, *Ariſtotle*, and Ptolemy, called the firſt of them Θεῖον, the ſecond δαιμόνιον, and the laſt θαυμάσιον, I am perſwaded without any intention to Blaſpheme. In the laſt place, I muſt pray you not to miſtake him, as a favourer of the

Scottiſh

Scottifh intereft, for it is well known he is a Leveller, and by confequence an adverfary to the High-lands.

  2. His next remedy is, that the Scriptures be wholly laid afide
in Scholaftick exercifes.

The truth is Sir, he hath fpoken fo excellently in his remedies,
that all the fervice I can doe him, is only to unfold his meaning.
I fay then that his meaning is not, that the Scripture fhould be laid
afide in morall exercifes, (for he would have *them* deduced from
the principles of Chriftianity *p.87.*) nor yet in Phyficall exercifes,
(for he would have *fome Phyficall Learning introduced into the Schooles,
which is grounded upon Scripture Principles p.* 105.) but his meaning is
only, that the Scriptures fhould be laid afide in Theologicall exercifes, and who does not fee what a remedy to Theology that
would prove?

  3. That the difcoveries of God by reafon, may be a part of
Naturall Philofophy.

For why? the fubject of Naturall Philofophy is *Corpus Naturale Mobile.*

Concerning Languages.

  1.2. His firft and fecond Remedies for Languages are, *that we
fhould advance our owne, and have a compendious way for teaching
forraigne Languages.*

Who ever thou art that denieft thefe to be fpeciall (or rather
indeed generall) remedies in this malady, I fay unto thee, thou
Lieft, and art ftiffnecked: moreover I fay, that they are excellent
remedies, as being part of the univerfall medicine.

3,4. *That* { Languages, Comenius } { *Janua Linguarum.*
in teaching { Grammar, M. Brinfleys { *way in his* { Grammar Schoole.
  may be followed.

Comenius I know, and that his way is ufefull, Mr *Brinfley* I have
not the happineffe to know, any otherwife then by M. *Webfters*
commendation, being one of his favorites I fhould be glad to ferve
him: I conceive by M. *W.* his defigne is, *that Children fhould be well
inftructed in the Accedence before they learne their Grammar.*

  5. In his fift remedy he difcovers a maine fecret, that *Irregulars*
fhould be learned *without rule*, and that the Irregulars being
learned, the rule alfo of the Regular *Nounes* and *Verbes*
would be facile and briefe, as being but one rule for all.

Indeed the Children ought to cry *gratias*, for if for one play-
day, and that a broken one, they ufe to doe it, how many play-
F 3 dayes

daies hath he procured them ? befides the prefent fport he makes
them.

After all this he feares it may be imagined, that he fhould proffer at advancing *Symbolicall* and *Cryptographicall* Learning, the
univerfall Character, and Language of Nature.

I teftify they doe him wrong that thus imagine, and never underftood well what formerly he delivered in that Argument: I had
him prefently in the wind, (fuch was my felicity) and durft then
have fworne (if need had been) that it was even juft as now I find
it : that concerning *Cryptography* , *Symbols* , the *Univerfall Character*,
he knew nothing; and that his difcourfe of the Language of Nature, did fignify only this, that wanting the ufe of other languages, even of the Latine, he had obtained a gift as ufefull , *viz.* a
Canting Language.

Next in order followeth Logick.

1. His firft remedy is, that we find out what reafon is in its in-
trinfeck nature and operation. And examine wherein mans
reafon exceeds the reafon of other Animants ; and here he
faith it will be found, there is no fpecificall but a gradual difference.

M. *Webfter* having difcovered that betwixt his reafon, and
his horfes, there is only a graduall difference , hath given
much light in the prefent enquiry; only he hath concealed from
us, which of them hath the advantage of degrees, and whether
thofe Degrees are divided by minutes, feconds, and thirds, and
whether in the fexagefimall or decimall way. When he fhall have
holpen us in thefe fcruples, I pray Sir, let us make the beft we can
of this remedy.

2. That the principles of Syllogifme be cleared and demonftrated.

Becaufe 'tis very hard for him to underftand, that *Quæ eidem funt
æqualia, vel inæqualia; funt inter fe æqualia vel inæqualia. Or Quæ conveniunt
in uno tertio vel non conveniunt; inter fe conveniunt etiam vel non conveniunt,*
his reafon differing but gradually from the reafon of other Animants.

3. That fome prevalent way be found out , for difcovering
and rectifying the fallacies of the fences, for Abftracting
adequate notions, and giving appofite denominations to
them.

Now Sir, what fay you to M. *Webfter* ? Had he had the luck
to have added the Quadrature of the Circle, with its Appendices

in

in *Geometry*, and the Phylosophers Stone in *Chymystry*, what could more judiciously and comprehensively have been required?

4. That induction may be improved, and to that end Experiments frugiferous and luciferous may be made.

The thing that is here proposed I do exceedingly like, and seeing it is an Amphibious argument, belonging to *Physick* and *Logick* both, I will not be so unreasonable as to quarrell with him about his Method or disposition.

The *Mathematicks*.

The Mathematicks should come to be spoken of, but they being what they are, (able to shift for themselves) and he being able to make a (scambling) shift without them, and it being terrible hard for one utterly unacquainted with them to speake any tollerable sence in this Argument, he being wisely-wary, wishing well to the Mathematicks and Mathematicians, (I meane the Copernican Astronomers) having spoken against *Ptolemy*, having had a twitch at *Aristotle*, and having no more to say, concludes the Chapter.

CAP. X.

Of some helps in Naturall Phylosophy.

HOw can it chose but be well help't up, when he shall set his hands to it who is so great a *Naturall-Phylosopher?* In this Chapter he first discusses that great Question, *what shall become of Aristotle?* And then proceeds to his Remedies.

The first in truth is decided (in my opinion) not without some judgement, how ever it comes to passe.

There are many things in him good (in truth very many excellent things, all his Historicall parts of nature are excellent, and so is his Rhetorick, and all his other workes) only his Physicks is to be eliminared, it being founded upon either false, or not intelligible Principles, referring all things to that System, and modell of the World, which time and observation have manifested to be untrue: the Astronomy depending thereon (upon that System of foure elements, and a Quintessentiall solid Heaven) falls necessarily upon the removall of his Physicks, or rather the Physicall part of that Astronomy.

You see Sir, how loath I am to vary from M *W.* my opinion concerning *Aristotle* being even coincident with his: yet I think

Aristotles

Ariſtotles Bookes, the beſt of any Philoſophick writings, & that when theſe things are laid aſide, that which remaines deſerves for him the honour that ought to be given to one of the greateſt wits, and moſt uſefull that ever the World enjoyed.

Farther, I muſt enforme M. *Webſter*, that the thing he doth deſire, is already performed in our Academies, there being no man, any thing deeply ſeene in Naturall Philoſophy, who goes about to ſalve things upon the principles, of matter, forme, and privation, or the firſt and ſecond qualities. So that I feare his *molimina* againſt *Ariſtotle*, will by ſome witts, be accounted disingenious, and his reflections upon our Univerſities, unworthy and impertinent.

But to come to his Remedies.

1. His firſt is, *that my L. Bacons way may be embraced. That Axioms be evidently proved by obſervations, and no other be admitted &c.*

I am wholly of his judgement, yet I have an itching deſire to know what *Lilly*, and *Booker, Behmen*, and all the families of Magicians, Soothſayers, Canters, and Roſycrucians, have done to vexe him, ſince he was writing of *Mathematicks*, and *Scholaſtick Philoſophy*, that having cheriſhed them then, and put them in hopes of his bleſſing, he ſhould now of a ſudden caſt them off, betaking himſelfe to their deadly enemy.

2. The ſecond Remedy is, *That ſome Phyſicall Learning may be brought into the Schooles, that is grounded upon ſenſible, Rationall, Experimentall, and Scripture Principles, and ſuch an Author is* Dr Fludd; *then which for all the particulars, the World never had a more perfect piece*

How little truſt there is in villainous man! he that even now was for the way of ſtrict and accurate induction, is fallen into the myſticall way of the *Cabala*, and numbers formall : there are not two waies in the whole World more oppoſite, then thoſe of the L. *Verulam* and D. *Fludd*, the one founded upon experiment, the other upon myſticall Ideal reaſons; even now he was for him, now he is for this, and all this in the twinkling of an eye, O the celerity of the change and motion of the Wind.

3. His third remedy is, That the Philoſophy of *Plato* and *Democritus*, of *Epicurus* and *Philolaus*, of *Hermes* and Dr *Gilbert*, be brought into Examination and practiſe.

He meanes that theſe be examined by thoſe that can underſtand them (himſelfe being unprovided in that kind,) that we chuſe the good, and refuſe the evill. You will ſay, if *De Fluctibus* be ſo perfect, what

what need we go any farther? I warrant you Sir, he knows both why and wherefore, though I can see no reason for it.

4. That youth may put their hands to labour, and their fingers to the Furnaces: that the Mysteries discovered by *Pyrotechny*; and the wonders brought to light by *Chymistry* may be familiar to them.

All that I can do here is to explaine his meaning, least the remedy should loose its operation [It is not his meaning, that the youth should put their fingers *into* the Furnaces, for that would make them dread the fire, nor yet *unto* the Furnaces, for that would smut them, but *to*, that is, towards the Furnace.] He hath likewise taken care that we should not confound in this Paragraph Chymistry and Pyrotechny, the *wonders* of that, and the *Mysteries* of this. Chymistry is well knowne, Pyrotechny is the Method of *fireworkes*, the Mystery of making *Squibs* and *Crackers*.

5. The last remedy is, That Galenicall Physick may not be the prison that all men must be enchained in.

See Sir how one may live and learne! I ever thought that Galenicall Physick had served to make men loose, and not to be a prison to them. I can but thank Mr *Webster* for this discovery, *Ingratum si dixeris, omnia dixeris.*

Metaphysicks.
His remedy for Metaphysicks is to read *Des Cartes.* Yet had he read him till he had understood him, the world had been deprived of this Herculean labour.

Ethicks.
Ethicks is better taught by President. Which made him shew his manners in dealing with the Universities.

Rhetorick and Poetry.
Rhetorick and Poetry are gifts, and he hath nought to do with them, for why? Kings and Emperours cannot make an Orator or Poet, Much lesse can he make either of them. A sows eare will never make a silken Saile.

CAP. XI

Some Expedients concerning their Custome and Method.

Whosoever shall consider the Errours charged upon the Universities in his eight Chapter, and the Expedients here proposed, if he do not acknowledge the Remedies here applyed

G   to

to be the very genuine & naturall ones hinted by the Indication of the Diseases: I say he labours in his Judgment, and is a *Dis-Idoneous* Auditor of Mr *Webster*.

For If the Disease be, that the body of the University is bound, (bound to one Method) can there be a surer remedy, then to use a solutive Medicine, to give them a purge and set them loose? If it labour of Idlenesse or a consumption of time, can any remedy be more naturall, then that time should not hence forth be trifled away? These are his *Recipes*, carried on thus to the last, against which the tongue of envy, cannot say but they are proper to their Maladyes.

Yet I must speake to them in severall.

1. That there be a liberty in the way and Method of Study.

I have formerly hinted to him, that our Universities are pretty well furnished with this medicine, so that he shall doe well to vent it upon those forraigne ones from whence he is come.

2. That time be not mispent in the Universities.

Some captious ones have asked, why then he would not take care, to keep his Workes from coming hither to be read? to whom I answer, that he never did intend they should come hither, he meant them to a party in the City, and takes no pleasure I dare say, that I should spend this time about him; well this is not the only thing wherein it is my happinesse to agree with M. *Webster*.

3. That there be not a set time for degrees, but that merit, not years should take place, and be rewarded.

How fitting this is, I have endeavoured to shew p. 4 0.

4. That in their Exercises, it be tried what they can doe, that (nature having given them two hands) they may learne to worke &c.

The reasons of this may be many, I shall name only two. First, because he hath been used to weed the Garden, and to other labour in his Covent: then why should not we? Secondly, because if his reformation shall take place, we must be put shortly to work for our livings, therefore tis good before hand, for each man to be provided of a Trade.

5. That Exercises may be in English.

His reason is, *least we* forget the English Tongue, which would be very sad if it should fall out: *Mine* is, that M. *Webster* and others of his measure, be not deprived of the benefit of them.

6. That neither Antiquity nor Novelty take place of Verity, nor the Authority of *Aristotle*, or any other, should enchaine us.

What?

What ? againe at *Aristotle* ! nay verily now he is to blame : This remedy had been a pure one , if he could have let *Aristotle* alone: the fetching him in here , I feare, may give occasion to some,to think he does it out of spight.

7. Lastly, the order he prescribes is this , that they be taught, 1. *Mathematicks*. 2. *Tongues*. 3. *Physicks*. 4. *Logick* 5. *Metaphysicks. &c.*

Not that all men should be bound to the same Method, (as is above expressed) beside M. *Webster* studied all these together, which hath made him so equally skilled in all, that there is not any thing to chuse betwixt his skill in every one of them, no man being able to speake, whether he be a greater Mathematician, a Linguist, or a Philosopher. .

And now Sir, you judge that I have faithfully performed what I undertook, at the opening of his Remedies : I having stuck to him as close as needed to be, and to speake truth , as close as his sent would suffer mee.

Sir, I have ran through this Pamphlet, and I think I have in some measure , made good the character you gave me of him in your Epistle; you know Sir, I am not of those who hate to be reformed; it hath been my earnest desire, that men of Parts and Experience would meet together , and consult about the Advancement of study, by the most convenient method, That would produce something worthy of our age of light ; the raw and crude attempts of such men as these, are slight and very Ridiculous , no waies considerable, unlesse it shall be in their excitations of us, to reforme such Errours as we find , to assert and vindicate the honour of these places. A thing which would speedily and plentifully be performed, if our designe of Printing Bookes, and setting up a forreigne correspondency were once accomplished. There is one thing which this sort of Pamphleteers insist on , which as it is pursued by my L.*Verulam*, so it carries weight with it , but is very impertinently applied , either as an exception against us , or as a generall rule to be imposed upon us in our Academicall institution. It is,that instead of verball Exercises, we should set upon experiments and observations, that we should lay aside our Disputations, Declamations,and Publick Lectures, and betake our selves, to Agriculture, Mechanicks, Chymistry, and the like.

It cannot be denied but this is the way , and the only way to perfect Naturall Philosophy and Medicine : so that whosoever intend to professe the one or the other, are to take that course,

and

and I have not neglected occasionally to tell the World, that this way is pursued amongst us. But our Academies are of a more generall and comprehensive institution, and as there is a provision here made, that whosoever will be excellent in any kind, in any Art, Science, or Language, may here receive assistance, and be led by the hand, till he come to be excellent; so is there a provision likewise, that men be not forced into particular waies, but may receive an institution, variously answerable to their genius and designe.

Of those very great numbers of youth, which come to our Universities, how few are there, whose designe is to be absolute in Naturall Philosophy? Which of the Nobility or Gentry, desire when they send their Sonnes hither, that they should be set to Chymistry, or Agriculture, or Mechanicks? Their removall is from hence commonly in two or three years, to the Innes of Court, and the desire of their friends is not, that they be engaged in those experimentall things, but that their reason, and fancy, and carriage, be improved by lghter Institutions and Exercises, that they may become Rationall and Gracefull speakers, and be of an acceptable behaviour in their Countries.

I am perswaded, that of all those, who come hither for Institution, there is not one of many hundreds, who if they may have their option, will give themselves to be accomplished Naturall Philosophers, (such as will, ought certainly to follow this course) the paines is great, the reward but slender, unlesse we reckon in the pleasure of contemplation; that indeed is great and high, but therefore to draw all men that way, by reason of the pleasure, were to present a Feast all of Custard or Tart, and not to consult the variety of Tasts, and tempers of our Guests: But I have been too much and long extravagant and idle: if out of all this you shall be pleased to raise a Contemplation of your power over mee, and shall from thence receive a complacence, it is the only aims and interest of, S I R,

Your Most &c.

H·D.

An Appendix Concerning what Mr *Hobbs* and Mr *Dell* have written touching the Univerſities.

SIR, when I conſider how I have ſpent that little time, which I have hitherto beſtowed upon Mr *Webſters Examen*, and into what a temper of mind I have fallen upon that oc-caſion, the ſatisfaction I receive from what I have done, is ſo ſmall, that were I not held on by the power you have over mee, in truth I would excuſe my ſelfe from any farther trouble. Now it ſeemes I muſt goe on, and being tired with idle play, I muſt ad-dreſſe my ſelfe for a much more conſiderable encounter. You know Sir, and have obſerved in your Letter to mee, how vaſt a difference there is, betwixt the Learning and Reputation of Mr *Hobbs*, and theſe two Gentlemen, and how ſcornefully he will take it to be ranked with a Friar and an Enthuſiaſt: The Anſwer to this, if he complaine, will be, we found him *inter Grues*, and could not without prejudice let him eſcape: However I ſhall deale with him as reſpectfully as I can, giving him leave to heare him-ſelfe ſpeake at large, (a thing he is infinitely taken with) and ma-king ſuch replies, as Truth and Reaſon ſhall ſuggeſt in our con-cernements. I intend only to conſider what he hath ſpoken of the Univerſities in his *Leviathan*, or rather what I have therein obſer-ved to that purpoſe, laying together ſuch paſſages as may make him to be underſtood.

That men may be able fully to comprehend the meaning of this Author, we muſt carefully by way of preparation, ſearch for

his ⎧ 1. End and Deſigne.
⎨ 2. Judgement, concerning the meanes of attaining it.
⎩ 3. Expectation as to ſucceſſe in his Deſigne, and the conſequences of it.

1. It appeares that the end he propoſes to himſelfe (in his *Le-viathan*) is, that the World ſhould be regulated exactly, by that

modell

245

modell which he there exhibits, and that his reason should be the governing Reason of Mankind.

This is (I conceive) so evident, that he will not denie it, and so frequently insinuated, that it's needlesse to be particular. The close of his second part, and 31 Chapter, is with an intimation of a desire, that *by the exercise of entire Soveraignty, his truth of speculation may be converted into the utility of practise.*

2. The meanes he proposes to accomplish this end, is the *publicke Teaching of his Leviathan:* which he would *have protected by the exercise of entire Soveraignty.* ibid.

Now this publick teaching may be either in the $\begin{cases} \text{Pulpits.} \\ \text{Universities.} \end{cases}$

The Divines and others who make shew of Learning, derive their know-ledge from the Universities, and from the Schooles of Law, or from the Books which by men eminent in those Schooles and Universities have been published. It is therefore manifest, that the instruction of the People, dependeth wholly upon the right teaching of Youth in the Universities. p.179,180.
So that the way he proposes to accomplish his great designe, is, the Publicke reading of his *Leviathan* in the Universities, (especially of England) and in order to this, he hath declared himselfe concerning his Booke, the Universities, and himselfe. 1. Concerning his Booke in the review. p.395. " That it may be profitably Prin-ted, *and more profitably taught in the Universities.* 2, and 3 Concerning the other two. p.180. In answer to these two Questions.

1. *Are not the Universities of England learned enoug) already (to teach the People their duty ?*
2. *Is it you (Mr Hobbs) will undertake to teach the Universities ?*
Where the answer to the first, is, *That the Universities have not been able to plant the true Doctrine* (which is his.)
And to the other, that any man which sees what he is doing, may easily per-ceive what he thinkes.

His immediate desire and judgment is therefore, that his *Leviathan* be *by entire soveragnity imposed upon the Universities,* there to be read, and publickly taught.

3. It will now concerne us to consider his expectation and hope, concerning the accomplishment of this (sober and modest) designe. Upon the prevailing or failing of which hope in his mind, the destiny of the Universities (as to his endeavours) shall depend. If he have hope that he shall be publickly taught in the U-niversities, it will be convenient for him only to endeavour this

Peice

peice of Reformation, and to assert their usefulnesse being so ordered. If there be little hopes of obtaining this publick Authority for this great *Leviathan*; To what end then serve the Universities ? Shall other things be taught there publickly, and this be looked upon as the writing of a private Author ? It will then concerne him to fall downe right upon them on every occasion to endeavour to blast them, and to proclaime them uselesse to the world.

And here indeed we find him fluctuating betwixt despaire and hope, p. 193. sometimes, "*At the point of believing this his labour as* "*uselesse as the Commonwealth of Plato. At other times recovering hopes, that* "*one time or other this writing of his may fall into the hands of a Soveraigne,* "*who by the Exercise of entire Soveraignty, in protecting the publick teaching* "*of it, will convert this truth of Speculation into the Utility of practise.*

How happy Sir had it been, if his hopes might have reigned perpetually in his mind, that so the Universities might have obtained a Patron of this great man, but he is well in yeares, and Jelousy and Spleen have prevailed over him, and in conclusion, he deales with us accordingly; indeed Sir, somewhat *Puerilely*, in insulting over us without cause, *Tetrically* striking at us without any occasion, *Unreasonably*, in charging us with some things we are not guilty of, and condemning us for other, without convincing us of any fault. This is that we shall demonstrate in our just defence, There are two passages by the by, and one entire Chapter which will concerne us to confider.

His first passage is in the 1. *Chapter* p. 4. Where having determined *Sence to be nothing else but a perception of a motion made upon the Organ*, He adds, *But the Phylosophy Schooles through all the Universities of Christendome grounded upon certaine texts of Aristotle, teach another Doctrine (viz. that sence is made by a Species &c.)*

1. As for the thing here charged upon all the Schooles of Christendome, you know it Sir to be untrue.

The other Theory of explaining sence upon the grounds of motion, was almost generally received here before his Booke came forth. Being sufficiently taught by *Des Cartes, Gassendus*, S. *K.Digby*, and others, before he had Published any thing in that kind.

2. That which he so much glories in, is not his owne invention, but is contained for substance (as I am certainely informed by one who hath seen it) in Mr *Warners* Papers, which Mr *Hobbs* had long since in his hands, and is delivered in the very beginning of that tract of vision, which treats *de penicillo optico.*

3

I

3. If Mr *Hobbs* had invented this, who hath not (so farre as I can learne) added any thing considerable to the inventions of other men: It might have been needlesse, upon so slight an occasion, to insult over all the Schooles of Christendome ; but his mind was intent upon his designe, and at this time his *hope* had possession there; *He sayes not* (therefore) *that, as disapproving* (yet) *the use of Universities, but to let men see what would be amended in them.* page 4.

But that which followes after is indeed of worse consequence, and is (to speake the best and mildest of it) an evidence of a fuming spleene, and an instance of despondency in his designe.

A touch he is thought to give us in his Kingdome of Darkenesse, where he makes a comparison of the Papacy with the Kingdome of Fayries. The words are (p.386.) *In what shop or operatory the Fayries make their Enchantments, the old Wives have not determined; but the Operatories of the Clergy, are well enough known to be the Universities, that received their Discipline, from Authority Pontificiall.*

In truth Sir, I hardly know how to behave my selfe upon this occasion. First, I know not whether he intended this to concerne our Universities or not; if not, he might have done us the Justice, to have separated our case from that of Popish *Universities*; if he did intend to cast a contumely upon us, I am yet at a losse how to answer him. This whole discourse is freakish and unbecoming the Archipoliticall gravity of a Master of the world. our Universities have bin Modelled by commission from the Civill Power. Seeing the old Women have found no operatory for the Fairyes; it was a needlesse Sollicitude in this Reverend old man, to seeke one for the Clergy. Well Sir, seeing he will have his frollick, I am resolved to answer this passage with a Crotchet of a Friend of mine, whose observation, is that however the *Fayries* are sayd to be harmelesse in their dancings, he is sure the Hobbe-goblins are spightfull and mischeivous in their Friskings.

But hitherto we have been but girded at; his maine forces he hath gathered into the Chapter preceding this, *viz.* the 46. whose title is of *Darkenesse from vaine Philosophy, &c.* but its designe is against Universities. And this Chapter containes,

1. A discourse concerning, the beginning and progresse of Philosophy.
2. Concerning the originall, & Progresse of Schooles.
3. The unprofitablenesse of Schooles.
4. Of Universities, and a generall charge against them.

5.

5. Their particular errours.

The two firſt parts of this Chapter, ſeeme not to be of any ſpe-ciall concernement to us, and I ſhall have that regard to him, and to my ſelfe, not to oppoſe him without neceſſity: were it requiſite ſo to doe, it were eaſy to manifeſt, that his ſentence concerning the beginnings and progreſſe of knowledge, is neither ſuitable to Reaſon nor Hiſtory: the ſuppoſition laid as a lemma to that ſentence is, that *hearding of men like beaſts* together, their *feeding upon Akornes*, and drinking water, *their wanting for ſome time the uſe of ſpeech*, &c. things neither ſuitable to thoſe Authentick Hiſtories which ought to have authority amongſt us, nor yet to the con-luſions of Reaſon, running back from the preſent ſtate of the world, to the temper and ſtate of earlier times. But to drive this home were to unravell the whole body of his Politicks, and to diſſolve this goodly work, which is not to be done occaſionally in ſuch an Appendix; the time may be, when after Mr *Hobbs* ſhall have pub-liſhed his other Philoſophicall Workes, from whence the riſe of this Great one is fetched, ſome friend or other of ours may ſet a-part ſome time, to weigh and examine all his Labours, and then to render him what ſhall be due to the Truth and Demonſtration of his Aſſertions.

You know how much may be ſaid for that *Origine & derivation of knowledge*, which the Bookes of *Moſes* deliver to us; And for the *Origine* of Schooles, which is the ſecond part of this diſcourſe: as we cannot deny them to have been the productions of *Peace* and *leaſure*, ſo I conceive it is an exceſſive inſtance of Spleen and Melan-choly, prejudiciall even to the whole courſe of Life and Profeſſi-on of M. *H.* to call the Diſcourſes and Contemplations of the An-tient Philoſophers, by the name of *Talke* and *Idleneſſe*, and to com-pare the Exerciſes of *Plato, Ariſtotle, Zeno,* and the Antient Worthies, (without ſome of whoſe endeavours, there had ſcarce at this time been either oportunity of knowing much, nor had the World per-haps ſet ſo high a price on knowledge,) to the *prating and loitering uſually exerciſed in Pauls Church, and More-fields.* The world had then another eſteeme of thoſe Exerciſes, *who publickly upon this occaſion erected Schooles for Lectures, and Diſputations, almoſt in every Common-wealth.* And it is in the ſtrength of the reputation of Philoſophy gained that way, that M. *Hobbs* findes a regard amongſt men, de-ſirous of knowledge, and not for the eminence of what he hath publiſhed, in any kind exceeding the productions of thoſe men whom he deſpiſes. Thus much in generall concerning the two

H

ſirſt

firſt parts of this Chapter. The Third is, *the Inutility of the Antient Schooles.*

The diſtaſt he hath conceived againſt our Univerſities, hath not ſuffered him to containe his Rage within any bounds. *What hath been the utility of thoſe (Antient) Schooles? What Science is there at this day acquired by their Readings and Diſputings.* p 369.

The meaning is, there never was any profit by Publick Schooles. This concernes us, and we will examine it particularly.

The ſubſtance of his reaſoning is this, (ib.) *Naturall Philoſophy cannot be had, without having firſt attained great knowledge in Geometry.*

That we have of Geometry (which is the Mother of all naturall Science) we are not indebted for it to the Schooles.

Plato forbad entrance to all that were not in ſome meaſure Geometricians, &c.

Sir, here it is that I cannot but complaine of miſguided Rage in M. *Hobbs*; againſt this paſſage I aſſert, that not onely Geometry was taught in the Antient Schooles, but that to thoſe Schooles, we owe the Geometry which we have.

Much we owe to the Schoole of *Athens*, and even to *Plato's* Schoole (the *Academy*) much more to that famous Schoole of *Alexandria*. *Plato* was He, who when the Oracle required the duplication of the Cubicall Altar, expounded it of the recommendation of the ſtudy of Geometry to them, ſhewed them that the particular ſolution of the Problem, muſt be by the invention of two meane proportionalls betwixt two lines given, propounded the Problem to his Scholers, who wrote ſeverall things concerning it.

Proclus doth often referre the invention of Propoſitions in *Euclides* Collection, to the Schoole of *Pythagoras*. *Theudius Magnes, Cyzicinus* the Athenian, and others, are delivered to us by *Proclus*, in the Second Book of Commentaries upon the firſt Element of *Euclide, in Academia ſimul vacaſſe quæſtionibus Geometricis enucleandis.*

But the Schoole of *Alexandria*, hath been ſo renouned for delivering of the Mathematicks, that in truth I cannot but wonder at the aſſertion of M. *Hobbs.*

It was begun by *Euclide* there, not long after the building of that City, in the time of *Ptolemæus Lagi.*

It was continued by the Diſciples of *Euclide*, who left many behind him, as *Pappus* acknowledges in his Collections.

To it we owe all the great Mathematicians, which ever were amongſt the Antients, ſuch as *Eratoſthenes* (who ſet up the Inſtruments

ments at *Alexandria*, by which men made the observations of *Hipparchus*, and *Ptolemy* the foundation of all Astronomy) *Archimedes*, *Apollonius* (the great Geometrician) *Ptolemy*, *Theon*, *Diophantus*, and very many others.

Nay, Sir *H. Savile* hath asserted, that from the time of *Euclide* to the *Saracenicall* times, there never was a great Mathematician, who was not borne at *Alexandria*, or had not studied some yeares there.

I would gladly know, what is there in Geometry, or all Mathematicks, which we are not indebted for to some of these, I speak not of Propositions, but of the way and method of mastering all kinds of Problemes. The Analyticks was their Art, the Exegeticall part hath indeed been found out by *Vieta*, and the Geometricall effection of solid and lineary Problemes, by the immortall wit of *Des Cartes*, but had it not been for those, we never had enjoyed the benefit of these.

I have heard that M. *Hobbs* hath given out, that he hath found the solution of some Problemes, amounting to no lesse then the Quadrature of the Circle, when we shall be made happy with the sight of those his labours, I shall fall in with those that speake loudest in his praise, in the meane time I cannot dissemble my feare, that his Geometricall designe (as to those high pieces) may prove answerable to a late Opticall designe of his, of casting Conicall glasses in a mould, then which there could not be any thing attempted, lesse becoming such a man, as he doth apprehend himselfe to be.

Brietely as to the case in hand, either M. *Hobbs* did know of these Schooles, or not; if he knew not of them, I dare undertake him not to be so great a Geometrician as he pretends to be, and that he is defective at his chiefe weapon.

If he did know of them, where is his ingenuity in asserting the inutility of Schooles? and that we are not beholden to them for our Geometry?

It is not in vaine Sir, that I have charged these things upon his spleene, which yet will more appeare by that which followes. *Pag.* 370.

4. That which he there asserts concerning Universities is, that whereas an University is an Incorporation of many publick Schooles in one Towne.

1. *The Principall Schooles were ordained for*
The Romane Religion.

The

The Romane Law.
The Art of Medicine.

To this it is eafily anfwered, that however the Ordination of them hath formerly been, the two Univerfities have fince the cafting off the Papall Yoke, been regulated by the Civill power, and been conformed to it, fo that the Difcourfe of the Romifh Religion or Law, with reflexion upon us, is disingenious , and nothing to this purpofe.

2. *For the ftudy of Philofophy, it hath no otherwife place, then as a Handmaid to the Romifh Religion.*

This is in truth fo Barbarous an Affertion, as nothing befide the Reverence to his Grey Haires, reftraines me from fpeaking bluntly of him: what friends to the Romifh Religion our Univerfities have brought forth, that party have felt. And it is faid that Mr *Hobbs* is no otherwife an enemy to it, fave only, as it hath the name of a Religion.

3. *And fince the Authority of Ariftotle is only current there, that ftudy is not properly Phylofophy but Ariftotelity.*

How farre the Authority of *Ariftotle* is current amongft us, Sir both you and I have fpoken.

What his defigne is concerning the publick reading of his *Leviathan* Himfelfe hath told us.

From whence it is manifeft, that the only thing which paines him is the defire that Ariftotelity may be changed into Hobbeity, & infteed of the Stagyrite, the world may adore the great Malmesburian Phylofopher.

4. *For Geometry till of very late times it had no place at all. And if any man by the ingenuity of his nature had atteined to any degree of perfection in it, he was commonly thought a Magician, and his Art Diabolicall.*

Geometry hath now fo much place in the Univerfities, that when Mr *Hobbs* fhall have publifhed his Philofophicall and Geometricall Peices, I affure my felfe, I am able to find a great number in the Univerfity, who will underftand as much or more of them then he defires they fhould, indeed too much to keep up in them that Admiration of him which only will content him.

And if in our times thefe ftudies have been advanced, we might have expected from a temperate man, rather the commendation for our Advance, then an exprobration with the ignorance of our Anceftors.

The truth is Sir, about that time when Mr *Hobbs* was converfant in Magdalen-Hall, the conftitution and way of the Univerfity might

might (likely) be enclining to ...

courſe ſeemes like that of the ſeaven ſleepers, who after many
yeares awaking, in vaine addreſſed themſelves to act according to
the ſtate of things when they lay downe.

I ſhall ſpeake no more to this fourth head. And to the fift, containing an enumeration of particular errours: They all or moſt are
reſolved into that Ariſtotelity he Charges us with, and require
no Anſwer, ſave that we enjoy a liberty of Philoſophizing, and
that if he ſhould do us the honour to come amongſt us, I am perſwaded he would hardly find any other fault with us, except that
great unpardonable one, that the publick reading of his *Leviathan*, is not by a Sanction of the *Magiſtrate* impoſed upon us.

5. The particular errors which he would charge us with, are
neere twenty in number, amongſt which there is not one, either in
Philoſophy, Politicks, or Divinity, which he hath proved, or can
prove, both to be an Error, and to be maintained by our Univerſities. I ſhall give a briefe account of them all.

1. His firſt Error charged upon us, is the Doctrine of *Abſtracted
Eſſences*, and *Immateriall Subſtances*.

Concerning which, as I cannot but acknowledge his Ratiocination to be good, as to the former part, *viz.* of *Univerſalls*, and
formall *Entities*: ſo I am willing to make good upon a juſt occaſion, that Being is a ſuperiour notion to Body, that Immateriall ſubſtance, or ſeparated Subſtances, is no contradiction, and that the
Truths of Philoſophy, are better ſalved upon that ground, then
upon his imagination.

2. His next quarrell is at *Nunc ſtans*, the common definition of
Eternity: This I affirme to be more intelligible then a ſucceſſive
Eternity, or a progreſſe *in infinitum*, which is the contrary poſi-
tion.

Of all that which followes, I doe not know one thing which
is held by any of us.

3. As *That one Body may be in many places, many in one.*
4. *That Gravity is the cauſe of heavineſſe.*
5. *That Quantity is put into Body already made.*
6. *That the Soule of man is Poured into the body, meaning it literally and
groſſely.*
7. *That the power of willing is the (totall) cauſe of Actuall willing.*
8. *That Fortune or Ignorance, is an occult cauſe of things, although we
may not profeſſe to know the cauſes of all things.*

Theſe

These are the Errors in *Naturall Philosophy* charged on us, and yet not one of those positions generally maintained by us.

Morall Errours are these.

1. *That one makes things Incongruent, another the Incongruity.*
2. *That private appetite is the rule of publick good.*
3. *Lawfull Marriage is unchastity.*
4. *That all Government but Popular is Tyranny.*
5. *That not Men but Law Governes.*
6. *That humane Lawes ought to extend to the inquisition of mens Thoughts and Consciences, notwithstanding the conformity of their Speeches and Actions.*
7. *That private men may interpret the Law, and restraine where the Soveraigne hath left a liberty*

Concerning all which Positions, I am perswaded he cannot instance in one University man, who hath published such an opinion, as he would put upon the whole Universities: it is true, that in the first of these, when the question is, Whether there be Free will in man, or God be the Author of sinne, men fall frequently into very great difficulties: but either Mr *Hobbes* ought to have cleared one part of these two; or not to have charged upon us, either the obscurity of Truth, or the imbecillity of humane Nature.

As for the rest of them, he may better assert, that there are Universities in the *Moone*, and that they maintaine all those Positions, then impose them upon us. There it will be hard to prove the contrary, We *now* challenge him to make proofe of what he hath delivered, and Promise to give him satisfaction.

There remaines three other Charges, *viz.*

1. *The Insignificant Language of the Schoolemen (the Commenters upon Peter Lombard.)*
2. *Errors from Tradition (as the Histories of Apparitions and Ghosts, &c.)*
3. *The suppression of Reason and true Philosophy.*

But these with the other charges, are so extravagant, and so much forced to appeare against us, that had he not been in great necessity, and much constrained to it by his passion, I am perswaded, he never would have produced them, as Arguments of our disgrace. What is the language of *Peter Lombard*, or the Writers upon the Sentences, to the Universities of *Oxford* or *Cambridge* ? When were we troubled or frighted with Ghosts or Apparitions ? Whose Reason or Philosophy have we supprest ? Or is it such a

Crime

Crime to Affert the Attributes of God, and the Naturall Immortality of the Soules of Men, that it fhall exempt our Adverfaries
from the Common Lawes, Honefty, and Ingenuity, and excufe
the moft groffe and palpable Calumniations of us? Nay, the de-
lation of us to the Civill Magiftrate, and the Endeavours for our
Extirpation? But he hath done what becomes a man of his judgment and Principles, let us be anfwerable to ours, not returning
railing for railing, or fcorne for fcorne, but making an end of this
contention, let us releafe the Reader from farther trouble.

Concerning

Concerning Mr *DELL*.

IT remaines now, that I fhould take into confideration what Mr *Dell* hath written in our concernements, but that which he hath done, is fo little either in Magnitude or Vertue, that I can hardly perfwade my felfe to make a bufineffe of it.

The caufe of *Learning*, its neceffity and ufefullneffe to the Minifters of the Gofpell, though it be of generall importance to all men, whofe intereft it is, that the Blind be not leaders of the Blind, yet feeing the defence of it is taken up, by one fo able and ready to maintaine the Truth, (Mr *Sydrach Sympfon*) I look upon it as forreigne to our prefent engagement, and fhall therefore wholly decline it.

Our view is only of a Poft-fcript to his Book, called the *Triall of Spirits*, where he delivers his judgement concerning the Reformation of Univerfities. The piece is fhort, it containes many things wherein we agree with him, and fome few wherein we differ.

1. He would not have Children *have nothing to doe, but to doe nothing.* Very witty, No more would we.

2. He thinkes it meet, *the Magiftrate take great care for the education of youth* We alfo think it meet.

3. That Schooles be erected in greater Townes and Villages, *that none but Godly men, and fober and Grave Women have charge of of them.* Very good.

4. That they firft teach them to read their Native Tongue, [very neceffary] and prefently to read the Scriptures. Very convenient.

5. *That in Great Townes they teach them Latine, Greeke, and Hebrew, and the Latine and Greeke efpecially from Chriftian Authors.* (not from Heathen Poets &c.) This alfo is very Honeft.

6. *It may be convenient, that there may be fome Univerfities or Colledges, for the teaching Liberall Arts, as Logick, of good ufe in Humane things, though in Divinity gladius Diaboli, and Mathematicks, which*

which as they carry no wickednesse in them, so are they besides very usefull. This sentence, though as it concernes the use of Logick in Divinity, it be of an occult and not investigable sence, yet as it concernes the Mathematicks, it carries in it neither non-sence nor dishonesty, and is besides very allowable.

Thus farre then we are agreed, in that which followes, Reason will that we should differ from him.

1. He complaines that our Universities should only be at *Cambridge* and *Oxford*, and here he

1. *Charges them of Encroachment against the Law of Love, for Monopolizing humane Learning.*

2. *He charges them to have been places of great Licentiousnesse and profanenesse.*

3. *He asserts it to be more suitable to a Common-wealth, (if we become so indeed, and not in word only) and more advantagious to the People to have Universities in every Great Towne.*

To answer first to his criminall charges.

1. If Mr *Dell* be a graduate in the the University, he hath sworne to defend the priviledges of it, to do it all the Honour and right he can, If so how doth he encroach upon the Law of nature, Sacred amongst all not given over to Barbarisme. Unlesse he can prove the matter of that Oath to be unlawfull which is yet retained in every Corporatiô) I do not know any thing which can here excuse him from unrighteousnesse. If he himselfe be no Graduate, he doth indeed discover no more, but a disingenuous envy and (considering his relations) an unworthy ingratitude.

2. But particularly, first, that which he calls the Monopolizing of Learning by those two places, it is not to be charged upon them (neither is it farther chargeable then upon any corporation of men whatsoever) but it reflects upon the Soveraigne Magistracy of our Nation by whose ordination, the priviledges & statutes of both the Universityes have been alwayes regulated.

2. His second charge is generall, unproved, and no wayes concernes us; I am sure that this University cannot now be Justly taxed with any such Licentiousnesse or profanenesse: indeed the care and prudence and successe of our Immediate Governors, as to the Advancement of Religion and Learning is such as Mr *Dell* may envy but he will never equall it, I should be very loath to injure him, yet common fame hath brought his name hither with a Character upon it of one whose studyed designe is (by letting fall

I   all

all Difcipline) to let in Licence with all its ufuall traine, both into *Cays Colledge*, and that other Univerfity: and that the confequence of what he hath done hitherto, hath been fuch as tends manifeftly rather to the ruine then Reformation of that place.

3. His third affertion containes in the Parenthefis an unworthy reflexion upon thofe who have the mannage of the fupream power, and is in it felfe fuch as he cannot prove; were his defigne put in execution, it would tend undoubtedly to the difadvantage of Learning; there is nothing in the world more conducing to the enlarging of the minds of men and the compleating of their Knowledge, then the cōverfation with men eminent in all the feverall parts of Learning, and the honeft emulation of thofe that doe excell. This is to be had only where there are great numbers of Students and *Profeſſors*, and the caufe of the advance, in Learning encreafes alwayes with the variety and eminency of mens wits and learning who converfe together. To fpare more words in a Theoreticall difcourfe of this nature, we may cōpare together the Learning of the Univerfities, and Religious Houfes of foreigne parts, where it is evident, the difference in Learning is vaft; thofe are difperfed according to great townes, and remaine pittifully ignorant, thefe are one or two in a Nation, flourifhing with the profeſſion of all ingenious Learning.

Now that which he alleadges as a convenience in his way, *That People may maintaine their Children at home while they learne in the Schooles,* hath not been obferved to tend to an advance in learning but to the contrary.

We have not *Generally* obferved that Townf-mens Children prove the greateft Schollars; and thofe who would have their Children excellently learned rather choofe to fend them abroad to Schoole, or to travell, then keepe them at home. Having briefely examined this propofall, I fhall need only to mention his fecond; which is

2. *That youth may be fo trained up that they may fpend fome part of the day in Learning, and another part in fome lawfull Calling* (fuppofe of Weaving or making Shooes) *or one day in ftudy, and another in bufineſſe.*

How much he hath in him either of Learning or Judgement, he hath manifefted by this propofall; I am much affured, there is not a Learned man in all the world who hath not found by experience, that skill in any Faculty (fo as to exceed the fmatterings of fuch trifles as Mr *Dell*) is not to be attained, without a timely beginning

(65)

ginning, a conftancy and affiduity in ftudy, efpecially while they
are young: Had not Mr *Dell* abftained from reading of the Poets(rather becaufe they are too hard for him, then for any wickednefle
which is in them) he had long fince been perfwaded of this truth,

    Multa tulit fecitq̃, puer, fudavit & alfit.

    Udum & molle lutum es, nunc, nunc properandus, & acri*

    Fingendus fine fine rotâ -----

It is very probable that   Mr *Dell* may have given as much of his
time to fome other trade,   as he hath done to Learning or ftudy:
Indeed his Learning and Judgement fhewes it, (notwithftanding
which he may be (for ought I know) an excellent Artificer, his
wit perhaps lying that way) but if this courfe fhall be fet up, as
the only Authorized way of Inftitution, we may by this meanes
have ignorance enough to think highly of our felves, but we fhall
become the fcorne of all the Gallant Men in the Nations about us,
and Mr *Dell* fhall not need to torment himfelfe about Tithes, and
maintainance of Minifters, *the Romans will come and take away their*
Place and Nation.

Sir, I have now done what I intended, (as flightly as I could
runne over what you recommended,) and am ambitious only to
continue in the acceptance wherein I ftand with you,

As being your moft

Humble and Affectionate

Servant

H. D.

FINIS

259

HISTRIO-MASTIX.

A whip for WEBSTER (as 'tis conceived) the Quondam PLAYER;

OR,

An examination of one *John Websters* delusive Examen of Academies; where the Sophistry, Vanity, and insufficiency of his New-found-light (tending to the subversion of Universities, Philosophers, Physitians, Magistrates, Ministers) is briefly discovered, & the contrary truth asserted.

In the end there is annexed an elaborate defence of Logick, by a very Learned Pen.

Phil. 3. 2. *Beware of Dogs, beware of evill workers : who hatch the Cockatrice eggs, and weave the Spiders Web ; hee that eateth of their eggs dyeth, and that which is crusht, breaketh out into a Viper,* Isaiah 59 5.

Τιμὴ πέφυκε παιδεία βϱοτοῖς.

Mortalibus omnibus doctrina est honori.

Qui veritati contradicunt, & in sua vanitate decepti decipiunt, ranæ sunt, tædium quidem afferrates auribus, nullos autem præbentes cibos mentibus. August. *de convenient Decalogi.*

London, Printed in the Year, 1654.

❖❖❖❖❖❖❖❖❖❖❖❖❖❖❖❖❖❖❖❖❖

The Preface to the Reader.

Courteous Reader,

Fter I had finisht my Vindiciæ Literarū, or Schools Guarded, my Stationer sent me downe one Webster, an enemy to Arts and Artists, desiring me to send some briefe Answer to it ; upon this I fell to examine Websters Examen, and found him so foul false & bitter against Humane Learning, and Vniversities (both which I defended in my Vindiciæ) that I thought it convenient to vindicate what I had asserted, and to leave the Logicall

O 2   and

To the Reader.

and *Philosophicall part to be examined by these whom it more
especially concerned: which since
I penned my discourse, I find to
be done so elaborately and accu-*
Dr Wilkins,
and Dr Ward. *ratly, by* ✱ *two very learned pens
(in their* Vindiciæ Academi-
arum)*that I was resolved to lay
my own Answer by, and had done
so, but that I received a very
learned defence, of Aristotelian
Logick, which I judged worthy
of the publick view. If thou reap
any benefit by this Tract, let God
have the praise, and the Reverend acute Logician thy thanks,
whose elaborate Animadversions, have drawn this, from thy*

Kingsnorton
Spemb.4.
1654.

Friend and Servant
in the Lord, THO-
MAS HALL.

Examen Examinis:
OR,

A word to Mr *Webſter,*
concerning his examina-
tion of A C A D E M I E S.

SIR Hercules, (for in that
Title I perceiue you
glory)in your Epiſtle to
the Univerſities, you
tell us, that you never
feared any Adverſary,
for his ſuppoſed ſtrength, and if any one
inquire *Who,* or *What* you are, you tell
him, that you are neither Prelaticall,
Presbyterian. nor Independent. But
what ſhall we then call you ? if any one
O 3 aske,

aske, tell him (fay you) that *Hercules is eafily known by his foot, and the Lyon by his paw,* &c. We fee then who you are, *viz.* an Herculean Leveller, a Fa-

Jefuita eft omnis homo. Our *webfter* is fome kin to them, for he can change with every time, &c.

mafifticall Lion a diffembling Fryar, a Profane Stage-Player, and profeffed friend to Judicial Aftrology and Aftrologers, fuch as lying *Ly-ly, Booker, Culpepper,* &c. A great ftickler for the fire and Furnace of Chymeftry, for Magick and Phyfiognomy, *&o.* I muft confefs; I never yet faw your perfon; but let me tell you, I have feen your *Lious paw, and Levelling club,* wherewith you think to beat down Univerfities, Humane Learning, *&c.* and in their ftead, to fet up your owne *Idle and Addle conceits.* What fpirit leads you, appeares [*page 8 of your book*] where you tell us, *Arrius* is called a Heretick, but you queftion how juftly [a tender confcienced man indeed] but as for the Orthodox, Wo to them! for you tell us they all wreft the *Scriptures* to make good their Fenents [a heavy charge, could you make it good]

The Proverb faies, *Ne Hercules contra duos fod ta contra ducentos, imo fis-pugiss.* If *Hercules* may not fight againft two,

two, what an *Hercules* are yon, that dare oppose more then two thousand, and *Goliath*-like, bid defiance to all the Academies and Armies of the living *God*:you tel us plainly, that in your high flowne conceit, *Homo* is a common name to all men. All those *viri Dei*, those holy-learned men of God, which are in the Land, if they be not of your Familisticall-Levelling-Magicall temper; they are all in your eye, but *homines, plebeian,* low and common men, *&c.* How much better had it become you, like *Hercules,* to have endeavoured the cleansing of that *Augean* stable of errours, Heresies and blasphemies, which like a Morphew, have over-spread the face of the Church; to have cut off those *Hydra's* heads, and helpt our *Atlasses* to hold up the Heaven of the Church. It had been more for your credit and comfort to have imployed your time and Talent in defence of Languages, Arts and Sciences, (especially in such a season as this, when so many decry them) then thus to weave the Spiders Web, which may peradventure catch some feeble flies, when stronger ones break thorough.

O 4 'Tis

Bibitur auro venenum.

'Tis true, sometimes you gild over your errors with golden words, and set a gloffe upon your falfe wares : but poyfon is never the better for being drunke out of a golden cup, the whore of *Baby-lon* deales fo with her guefts, *Rev.* 17.4. and the Apoftle tels us, that falfe Teachers, with faire words and fine fpeeches, do deceive the fimple, with plaiftred words, they parget over the mat-

*Alludit ad Mercatores qui verbis fictis & arte compofitis, fupra veritatem laudant & extollunt fuas merces, ut facil ius eas extrudant, & carius vendant. Sic Hæretici ut fuam hærefim divendant, & fpargant, eam blandis & elegantibus verbis adornant, & quafi mereticem fermonis lenoci-nic fucant, ut videatur pul-chra & elegans inftar Helinæ. à Lapide in locum.

ter. *Rom.* 16. 18. 2 *Pet.* 2.3. * πλαςοῖς λόγοις, fictitiis verbis quia more plaftis ac figuli multa confingunt, ut hærefis fua idolum velent, veftiant & ornent.

But that you may fee your folly the better. 1. I fhall begin with your contradictions. Sometimes you plead for Academicall learning and anon you cry it downe ; like a Thiefe, we fometimes find you in the way, and prefently you are croffing it againe. Thus [*page* 3.] you cry up Humane Learning as good, excellent, and of manifold tranfcendent ufe; whileft moving in its owne Orbe, it enables men for all kind of undertakings, Military and Civill, without which, men doe not differ much from beafts, &c. [So *page* 8, 9] yet as if you had forgot what you had faid, said, in the same *page* you tell us (how truly let the world judge) that this humane learning, difables men for the Miniftry, is a vaine Tradition, and makes men uncapable of Gofpell myfteries, &c.

Quo teneam vultus mutantem protea nodo?

So, one while you plead for teaching children without the Grammar Rules | *page 22*] yet *page 24.* you cry up Mr *Brinflyes* way of teaching, which every one knowes (who knowes the Method of that Godly man) hath reference to Rules.

2. Your fophiftry, and fallacious arguing is very frequent, to give you a tafte onely, (for as you defire to ftirre up fome to plead your caufe, fo I doubt not but fome of the Lords Worthies, who have more time and Talents for fuch worke, will arife and plead his caufe more fully.) _{I find it done already, very acurately, by Dr *Ward* in his *Vindiciæ Academiarum.*}

1. You tell us, that humane learning puffs men up, makes men felfe-confident and proud; that it is but a carnall thing, a flefhly power, (juft fo fay your brethren, the Familifts, and Anabaptifts) that the * Apoftles never taught

I find it done already, very acurately, by Dr Ward in his Vindiciæ Academiarum.

1 He's againft Learning.

* I have proved the contrary in my Vindiciæ Literarum

or practiced any such matter, but bad us
beware of Philofophy, *Col,*2 8.for it is
a fleshly weapon, earthly, sensuall, divelish, an Idoll of mans inventing, spirituall sorcery or inchantment, yea Reason is a Monster, and the very root and
ground of all Infidelity, *&c.*

Answ. Behold here that *Damask-
Web,* (as his verifying friend cals it)
which Mr *Webster* weaves. 1. He Argues from the abuse of a thing, to the
taking away its use ; because some men
abuse humane learning to pride, and
selfe-conceitednesse, therefore away
with humane learning, *Non sequitur* ;
for then, because some men abuse, meat,
drinke, cloaths and riches ; wee must
throw away meat, drinke, cloaths and
riches.

2. It is not Philofophy simply, that
the Apostle condemnes, *Cel.*2. 8. but
vaine, spoyling, abusive Philofophy ; as
you may see more fully in my vindication of that place.

3. Neither is humane learning a carnall, fleshly, sensuall Idoll of mans inventing; but the good gift of God, comming from the Father of lights, who is
purity it selfe. As I have proved at large,
in

*V. Vindiciæ
Literarum. c,2.
page* 30.

in my *Vindicia Literarum.*

4. Neither is Reason a Monster (as you Monster-like affirme) but being rightly improved, is a great helpe in Religion ; as is excellently proved, by the learned *Culverwell* in his profound difcourfe, of the light of Nature : fit it is fit we fhould give unto Reafon, the things which are Reafons, and to Faith, the things which are Faiths.

Ob. But 'tis the fpirit (faies Mafter *Webfter*) that muft teach us, and the fpirit that muft unlock the Scriptures, and the fpirit that muft inlighten us, *&c.*

Anfw. True, but yet the fpirit of God works by meanes (as I have proved before in my *Vindicia.*) Who ever expects helpe from God muft not fit ftill and dreame the fpirit will help him ; but he muft arife, and ferve Providence in the ufe of meanes ; for the fpirits Teaching doth not exclude, but include the ufe of all good meanes, *&c.*

V. Vindicia Literarum, Prefa.

Yet that you fee Mr *Webfter's* Herculean ftrength, he comes now to grapple even with *Ariftotle* himfelfe [*c.* 2 6.] this Chapter he fpends wholly, in combating with him ; no leffe Adverfary then the Prince of Philofophers can

He's againft Ariftotle.

can try his ſtrength. 1. He tels us, that
Ariſtotle was but a man, and ſo might
erre; and is not Mr *Webſter* a man? and
doth he not erre with a witneſſe? 2. He
tels us, that what *Ariſtotle* hath written, was rather by a Diabolicall, then
a Divine inſtinct [I rather ſuſpect tha
he is led by a Diabolicall inſtinct, that
ſpeaks it.] 3 His Principles are falſe,
his Manners corrupt, many of his books
ſpurious; beſides, hee is ambiguous,
briefe, lame, intricate, erroneous &c. In
a word, a blind Pagan, the proud Stagyrite. [I wiſh he were not more blind,
corrupt and proud that ſpeaks it]

Qu. But ſince Ariſtoteliſcall Philoſophy wil not downe with Mr *Webſter,*
what new-light ſhorter cut, and eaſier
way hath this *Hercules* found out: for
like another *Cæſar, Viam aut inveniet,
aut faciet.*   He'll either find a way, or
frame you one out of his empty ſconce?

Anſ. Why, his Magick [*page 68,
&c.*] that noble, and almoſt divine ſcience (as he cals it) of naturall Magick.
This key (if you will believe him) will
better unlock natures Cabinet, then ſyl-
logiſmes; yet he complaines, that this
is neglected by the Schools, yea hated
and

*Note, 'tis Dia-
bolicall Ma-
gick, which
Webſter pleads
for, as appears
by his com-
mending Lilly
the Wizard.*

272

and abhorred, and the very name seems nauseous and execrable to them. [and that very justly considering whether your Magick leads men] But O Magick, Magick, where hast thou laine hid so long, that Mr *Webster* is faine to conjure thee up againe, and none but he and his associates, could find out this short cut before? 'Tis true, there is Astronomy, which is an Art that considers the divers aspects, and naturall properties of the Starres, and this is lawfull. But then there is * *Magia Diabolica*, a Divelish Magick, when men take upon them, to foretell things contingent, by the Stars, those are called judicial Astrologers, and in Scripture they are oft joyned with Witches, wizards, and Sorcerers, *Deu.*18 10,11. *Dan.*2.2, &c. yet this Devilish Art, doth Mr *Webster* plead for [*page* 51] and spends welnigh a *page*, in the commendation of Astrology and Astrologers, such as *Lilly, Booker, Culpepper*, &c. 1. He cals it a Science or Art. The learned * *Weemse* hath proved the contrary; yea, the Lord *Verulam* (whom he cites so oft) is here against him. Astrology (faith he) is corrupted with so much superstition,
that

* See *Perkins* 1 Vol.*p.*39. *and* 43,44.

* *Weemse* 4. Tom. on the Magitian. page 62.

Lord *Verulam's* Advancement of Learning *p*. 147.

that there is hardly to bee found, an
found part in it. S. *Auſtin* that had ſtu-
died this way, yet concludes, *Aſtrologia eſt magnus error, & magna demen-
tia* &c. 'tis a great errour, a great mad
neſſe, and ſuperſtition eaſily refelled.

*Aug. de doct.
Chriſtian, l.2.
chap.21.*

2. Yet he cals this a high, a noble, a
excellent * Science, and uſefull to a
mankinde; a ſtudy, not unbeſeemin
the beſt wits, and greateſt Schollars, n
way offenſive to God or true Religi
on &c.

* *Aſtrologia ju-
diciaria non
eſt Scientia.*
Theſ. Cantab.
1654.

A dangerous and falſe aſſertion, the
contrary whereof, is moſt true in the
judgement and experience, of all godly
learned men ſuch as *Calv n Beza, Perkins, Weemes, Gataker, Geree Vicars* &c.
they all condemne it, as a moſt ignoble,
dangerous ſtudy, unbeſee ing choice
wits, offenſive both to God, and all good
men. Hence theſe judiciall Aſtrologers
were formerly excommunicated, and
caſt out of the Church; and by the De-
crees of Emperours, baniſht out of the
Common-wealth. Never more need of
puniſhing ſuch offenders, when they are
grown ſo bold, and brazen-faced, as to
publiſh their lies and abominations in
Print to the world, and ſo provoke God
to

See *Mendelius
Phyſ. c.27,28.
page 630. 630.
and* Weems
*Magitian.
ſect.7.*

to forfake us, *Ifaiah 2.6. Therefore thou haft forfaken thy people, becaufe they be replenifhea from the Eaft,and are South-fayers, like the Philiftines.* 'Tis an Art that leads men to the Devil, I have con-ferred with fome, and read as much of others, who have gone about to ftudy this Art (as *Webfter* cals it) they have been faine to throw away their books, for feare of Satans appearing ; fo readie is he to ftep in, when once he finds us out of Gods way Ufuallie,fuch are Wi-fards, and therefore I cannot but won-der how Mr *Webfter* durft be fo impu-dent,as to commend the worth, vertue, and learning,not onely of thefe lying de-luding Prognofticators,*Booker* and *Cul-pepper,* but he alfo extols that lying,ray-ling, ignorant Wizard, *Ly-ly,*who hath not onely reviled the moft learned and Reverend Mr *Gataker,*with the Ortho-dox Miniftry of the Land ; but with his lies, hath abufed both Church and State, to the great difhonour of the Nation: as appeares by the pious and judicious Mr *Gataker's* Vindication of his Anno-tations,on *Jer.* 10.2.

And fince Mr *Webfter* talks fo much of this noble Science, and what sufficient

ent Reasons he could give in defence of
Mr *Lillie's* Astrology, he may doe well
in his next Pamphlet, to prove it a science, and to bring forth his strong Reasons. In the meane time I shall love
humane learning the better, whilest I
live, because 'tis opposed by Star-gazers,
and judiciall Astrologers: as *David* loved Gods Law the more, because wicked men sought to destroy it, *Psal.* 119.
126, 127. the Father tels us, *Nil nisi*
grande aliquod bonum quod à Nerone
damnatum, It must needs bee good,
which wicked *Nero* hates. So humane
learning must needs bee good, which
Astrologers and Wizards hate and oppose. And that you may see the same
spirit which breaths in *Lilly,* dwels in
Webster, he useth the lying, railing language of *Lilly.* Shall the thundring Pul-
pit-men (saies *Lillian Webster*) who
would have all mens faith pinned upon
their sleeves [this is as true as all the
rest] and usually condemne all things
they understand not [it seems Mr *Web-*
ster knowes more in this Art, then ho-
nester men doe,] make mee silent in so
just a cause? [Oh no, 'tis a time of liberty, and you think you may be bold,
but

but such as you must know, that though you may for a time, escape the punishment of men, yet you cannot escape the revenging hand of the Almighty, but as you have sinned against the Lord, so be sure first or last, your sinne will finde you out. And yet that all the world may see what spirit leads this man, tis worth observing, whom he commends, not only *Lilly* and *Booker*, but also Fryar *Bacon* [*sic mulus mulum*, it becomes one Fryar to claw another] and *Paracelfus*, a Libertine, a Drunkard, a man of little learning, and lesse Latine; he was not only skilled in naturall Magick, (the utmost bounds whereof, border'd on the suburbs of Hell) but is charged to converse constantly with Familiars, and to have the Devill for his Purse-bearer; yet this is one of Mr *Websters* society. *Nofcitur ex comite*, &c. Like Lettice, like Lips; such as his company is, such is he.

See more, *Fuls ters* Holy state. *lib. 2. cap. 3.*

Add to this, his praising the study of Physiognomy, as an excellent, laudable, and profitable Science; [which yet the Learned judge vaine and foolish] also his extolling of Chymistry, and preferring it before *Aristotelian Philosophy*,

P and

and advising schollars to leave their Libraries, and fall to Laboratories, putting their hands to the coales and Furnace. [So they may quickly find *pro thesauro carbones*, beggary instead of Learning, and walking thus in the sparks of their owne fire, he down in sorrow, *Isaiah* 50. 11.] this is Mr *Webster's* short cut, a quick way to bring men to the Devill or the Devill to them.

2. Mr *Webster* having sufficiently railed on *Aristotle*, the Prince of Philosophers, next he fals foule on *Galen*, the Father of Physitians, onely for building on *Aristotles* Principles; out of his ignorance, hee cals him an ignorant Pagan, an Idoll, a blinde guide, *&c.* and at last fals fouily on the Physitians themselves *page* 107.]

3. He's against Galen, and Physitians.

3. He comes now to Ministers, and railes on them, for suffering themselves to be stiled by that blasphemous title of Divines; this the Priests (that Title to shew his contempt of the Ministry, hee puts on the Ministers of the Gospell, though that Title be never given them, *quà* Ministers in al the New Testament) blasphemously assume to themselves.

4 He's against Ministers.

Ans. 1. Tis false, the Title is not blasphemous,

blafphemous, for 'tis given to S. *John*, who is called by way of eminency, and diftinction ὁ θεόλογος,, The Divine. As Theology and Divinity are termes convertible in our language, fo is a Theologue and a Divine, the fame in fenfe, though it differ in found: and therefore if the Scots do well (as you fay they do) in calling their Minifters Theologues; then ours do not ill, in fpeaking plaine Englifh, and calling them onely for diftinction fake, Divines (i) men fet apart for the ftudy of Theology or Divinity. Now fee the wit, or if you will the malice of this Magus, this Magitian (for hee pleads for the lawfulneffe of fuch Titles.) The Scots (faith he) may call their Minifters Theologues; but our people, may not call their Minifters Divines. This diftinction is like the mans, that faid, Pepper was hot in operation, but cold in working.

2. 'Tis falfe that we affume it, much more that we blafphemouflie affume it to our felves: if people will give us that Tule, onely for diftinction fake, who can hinder him?

3. The ground hee builds on, is rotten. *viz.* 1. Becaufe holineffe is effen-

P 2   tiallie

ti allie proper to God.   2. Be cause wee
are Holy and Divine by participation
onely, therefore wee may not be called
Holy and Divine.

Anf. The anſwer is eaſie. Though
to be holy and Divine, be eſſentially
proper unto God, yet by way of Ana-
logie and reſemblance, it is alſo given
to Angels and men. Hence the godly in
this life, are called Saints, holy, and in
the very letter, partakers of the *'Divine
Nature,* [2 *Pet.* 1. 4.] not eſſentiallie,
but Analogicallie, partaking of thoſe
graces whereby we reſemble God.

5 He's againſt   4. He fals foule on Magiſtrates, and
Magiftrates   teks them plainlie [*page* 98.] that they
muſt not at all intermeddle with the
things of God, leſt miſerie and deſtru-
ction follow them to the grave, &c.

Anf. What is this but to deſtroy the
Magiſtracie ? to rob them of their coer-
cive power, and make them like Saint
George, that ſits with a drawn ſword,
but never ſtrikes (a fit emblem of Mr
Webſters Magiſtrates.)

Ob. But Mr *Webſter* would have
them puniſh Theeves, Murtherers, A-
dulterers and Drunkards, onely they
muſt not puniſh the Saints, leſt God require

quire the blood of his Saints at their hands. [*page* 98.]

Anf. 1. If the Magiftrate muft punifh Theeves, Murtherers, *&c.* then *a forti-ori,* he muft much more punifh fpirituall Murtherers, Theeves, *&c.* for as 'tis a greater finne to kill the foule, then to kil the body, fo they deferve feverer punifh-ment. 'Tis no Policy, but cruelty, to fuf-fer Woolves and Foxes to deftroy the flock : neither is the coercive power of the Magiftracy, under the Law, aboli-fhed by the Gofpell, as is excellently cleared by Mr *Prin,* in a Treatife called the Sword of the Magiftrate ; and fince by Mr *Cobbet* on the fame fubject.

2. The Saints muft bee confidered under a double notion. 1. As Saints walking up to their principles and li-ving in the feare of God, and hee that abufeth and kils fuch Saints fimply on this account, muft look to anfwer for their blood.

But 2. Confider the Saints, as erring and wandring from their Principles, by Adultery, Murther, Drunkenneffe, Here-fie, *&c.* and fo they may and muft be punifhed, though not as Saints, yet as finning and tranfgreffing Saints : yea

P 3 though

though they should plead conscience for what they doe, and say, as Mr *Burroughs* in his *Irenicum c.6.p.34* proves.

Thus you see, how Mr *Webster* is against learning, against *Aristotle*, against Magistracie, against Ministrie, against Physitians, and against all that is truly good : like *Ismael*, his hand is against every man, and therefore It's just that every mans hand should be against him.

Q. But what is the summe of Mr *Websters* desires, and what would hee have us to studie?

A. Hee tels you. 1. That you must lay aside al your paper Idols, and sleight *Aristotle*, who hath in him, many things frivolous, vaine, false and needlesse.

2. He tels you, that you give up your selfe to Mathematicks, Opticks, Geometry, Geography, Astrology, Arithmetick, Physiognomie, Magick, Protechny, Chymistry, Pneumatithmy, Stratarithmetry, Dactylogy, Stenography, Architecture; and to the soule ravishing study of Salt, Sulphure & Mercury [a medicine for a Horse] These, these, if you will beleeve Mr *Webster*, are the onely excellent studies for Academians.

But

But Sir, if thefe inferiour Arts (the alwfulneffe of fome of them being juft-lie queftionable)be fo ufefull and excellent as you affirme, then *à fortiori Logique* (which you fleight as prejudiciall to Theology) and Phyficks, Ethicks, *&c.* with the fuperiour Arts and Sciences, muft needs be much more excellent, and therefore *Mr Webfter* is much to be blamed, for crying up thofe low, inferiour, emptie things; and crying downe thofe choice, ingenious, ufefull Arts and Sciences. which doe fo much fit and further men in their preparation to Divine ftudies.

To conclude, the world may here fee, what ftuffe ftill comes from Lame *Giles Calvers* fhop, that forge of the Devil, from whence fo many blafphemous, lying, fcandalous Pamphlets, for many yeers paft, have fpread over the Land, to the great difhonour of the Nation, in the fight of the Nations round about us, and to the provocation of Gods wrath againft us, which will certainly breake forth, both upon the actors & tolerators of fuch intollerable errours, without fpeedy reformation and amendment.

P 4   Since

Since I framed this difcourfe, there came to my hands, a very accurate and learned *Examen*, of Mr *Webfters* illogicall Logick, which now followes in it's order.

Examen

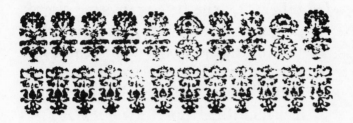

Examen Examinis.

An Examination of Mr
WEBSTERS Illogicall
Logick, and Reasoning even
againft Reafon.

HIS Mr *Webfter* (as I
suppofe) is that Poet,
whofe Glory was
once to be the Author
of * Stage-plaies, but
now the Tutor of U
niverfities. But be-   * As the Devils
caufe his Stage-Players have been dif-   Law-Cafe.
countenanced by one of the late Par-
liaments ; does hee therefore addreffe
himfelfe to the Army, for the like force,
and as little favour in behalfe of all Humane

mane Learning ? for advancement whereof, the best way being already found, he that seeks for another, desires worse (and so none at all) though he pretend to a Reformation. For my own part, I could wish that his Poetry still had flourished upon Mr *Johnson's* account, in his Epistle before one of his Playes (the Fox) to the two most equal Sisters; the Uuniversities (a far better address, then this here) but it is odious to be like the Fox in the Fable, who having lost his owne Ornament, envied his fellows theirs, by pretending burthen or inconvenience. I have neither leisure nor lust, to examine all his Examen; but yet to know *Hercules* by his foot, I cannot but observe, how in his Chapter of Logick, he Reasons against Reason: and as *Diogenes* accused *Plato*, with a worse pride of his owne ; so he prosecutes *Aristotle*, under the name of Arch-Sophister, indeed with his owne sophisms; which what may we call but envy and pride, those two Mothers (saith *Aquinas*) of discord: whil'st one through envy, recedes from the way and will of another, through pride, to prefer his owne As *Quintilian* (if that Dialogue

de

de Oratoribus be his) condemnes the Oratory of his time, as abused to incense the people in *Principes viros, ut est natura invidiæ:* not sparing (not onely *Sylla* and *Pompey,* but) even *Scipio* himselfe; or as *Livy: Et ante alios in Camillum.*

But what if Oratory be thus abused to calumniating, should there be therefore no Oratory at all? or if Logick to cavilling, no right reason at all? as indeed there is none such without the orderly use of it, for *rationis est ordinare* (saith *Aquinas*) and that is best done, not by the *Web* which is here woven, to unravell all Humane Sciences, but by the Art of Logick. Such a Master whereof, was *Aristotle* that of him we may say for knowledge, as for vertue, *Valerius Maximus* of the said *Scipio, Quem Deus immortalis nasci voluit, ut esset in quo se virtus per omnes numeros hominibus efficaciter ostenderet.*

But let us see, what against so gloria light, and to falsifie the sight or sense of all ages hitherto, is here produced by him, who *hoc tantùm rectum quod sapit ipse putat.*

Chap. 4. §. 1. What here he saith, is

no

no more then may be objected againſt any Science or Art (though never ſo much by himſelfe approved) e. g. his owne late Poetry, and now beloved Aſtrology (yea the Goſpell of Peace it ſelfe may bee abuſed for war and diſcord:) but whatſoever * the aim of the Logitian is, the * end of the Art is truth.

As to that of *Ariſtotle*, for which ſo vehemently he inveighs againſt, or rather proudly inſults over him; the more ſtrongly the opponent maintaines his part (for which purpoſe in his Topicks, he ſupplies him with ſtore of Arguments) the reſpondent his, the more effectuall is their diſputation, for the end thereof, *viz*. the diſcovery of truth; as *Scaliger* ſaith, *ut ex ſilice & ferro elicitur ignis, ita conflictu ingeniorum veritas.* And beſides, in his Politicks alſo, he obſerves the rules to be kept for upholding Tyranny: but will Mr *Webſter* therefore conclude, that he allows of that way of Government?

Sect. 2. Or is truth his owne end, in accuſing whole Univerſities of moſt rationall men, and even Logick it ſelfe, as proceeding very prepoſterouſly, whereas, Logick is indeed the Miſtriſs of

of all due method to all Sciences, and to himselfe if methodicall. As if the Prince in whom as supream consists the Order of the whole community, should be accused himselfe for breaking it, which as such, whether good or evil, he keeps, though if evill, not so well as he might; and by keeping his subjects in it, preserves them by it : for all things consist in order, which confounded, they come to naught. Logick, as such, proceeds orderly, directing the minde in the knowledge of truth, as first in the apprehension of simple Termes, and then in the composition and division of the same, and last of all in Discourse, without confusion, falshood or fallacy. In which last, it proceeds as well *à posteriori*, by induction, to find out the truth, or to know that such an affection is the true property of such a subject : as *à priori*, by demonstration, to perfect the knowledge of it : for then is the knowledge distinct and perfect, when the thing is known as it is, as the effect by the cause, as it is by its cause, which is the order of Nature : and not the cause by its effect, which is our Method, through the imperfection of our Intellect, deriving
its

its notions from sense, and so beginning
à posteriori, but *à parte rei*, indeed pre-
posterous. First, then doth Logick proceed preposterously, because to advance
our Reason as neer as may bee, to the
Angelicall manner of understanding,
by knowing things (as they are di-
stinctly and perfectly) it reacheth us to
proceed in the order of Nature, or
to begin *à priori*? 2. As to say that
induction hath altogether been layed a-
side, is most false, and against sense: So
Reason requires that syllogismes
(wherein we prove and demonstrate
the effect by the cause) be preferred before it. So that whilest he extols (and
for a new method of his own, against
all established and approved order) so
highly cries up induction before syllogismes; his owne is the errour which he
condemnes, and therein hee proceeds
preposteroasly.

Sect. 3. Here also the defect pretended, is his owne ; in not acknowledging, both how fit are the denominations of Genus, Species, &c. to the Notions thereby exprest, and these Notions
adequate to the things we conceive by
them. For gathering of which Notions,
the

the certaine Rules which he feems to
defire,but indeed rejects them,are thefe
two. Comparifon of things,as to that
wherein all agree, for the community,
and abftraction thereof, from differences, whether effentiall or accidentall,
for the unity of the fimple effence,
which hath thus the generall denomi-
nation of an univerfall, and is either of
one kind comprehending infinite fin-
gulars, accidentally onely different,
as *Homo*, and fo is fitly expreft by the
word fpecies: or generally comprehen-
five of divers kinds, both conftituted in
themfelves, and diftinct one from another, by their proper effentiall differences,as *Animal, Animatum, Compofitum,Corpus,Subftantia*, and fo as fitly is
called Genus;which is either *fummum*,
and fo is not at all; as a fpecies it felfe
fubordinate, as *fubftantia*, or *fubalter-
num*, which in refpect of a fuperiour,
Genus it felfe is a Species, and fo *alter-
no refpectu* both, as *Corpus, compofitum,
Animatum, Animal.*

The Genus then is divided into feverall fpecies, which are either *fubal-
terna*,as having under them other Species, in refpect whereof they are alfo
Genera;

Genera : or *infime*, as superiour to no species at all, but onely to its owne singulars; in which the division rests, as in so many Individuals.

Now, have we not here, both notions adequate to the things, and words as fit to expresse these Notions? or in all this excellent order, can Mr *Webster* invent confusion?

But he would shew, that bee hath read, and seems to understand the Lord *Bacon*, in his *Novum Organon*, though his testimony be nothing for him, * as Hypotheticall, and so not * Positively true, till the condition be first proved: but without any proofe thereof Mr *Websters* Thesis is absolute, and so false.

Sect. 4. The said Notions, and determinations, concerning which, there are given a few, plaine, easie, necessary and usefull Precepts, are some of the hardest passages wherein are exercised the unskilfull and tender wits of young men : and so far are the Questions and Disputes, which are agitated by riper judgements, from derogating from their Art, that rather they add to it, *&c.*

Ans. Whereas here he objects that they do not see that they act as foolishly

(even

(even thofe of the beſt judgements)
while they difpute of the very Art of
Difputing, as he that endeavours to fee
the proper vifion of his owne eye : his
owne is indeed the blindneſſe, in not
feeing the difference of Underſtanding
and fenfe.

Turpe eſt doctori, cum culpa redar-
guit ipfum.

For the eye, or the outward fenfe,
apprehends not its own Act, being neither colour, nor light, nor the difference
of its owne, from the proper objects of
other fenfes. e.g. that which pronoun-
ceth White to differ from fweet, is neither the fight nor taſt, whereof each
apprehend but one of them, and fo cannot judge of both ; but the inward or
common fenfe, as judge of the Acts
and Objects of all the outward: whereas the Underſtanding, whofe object is
univerfall, or all things knowable, is re-
flexive to know it felfe, its owne Acts
and Objects; and then as the foule of
man is both the Object, Subject, and
Author of its owne difputes, while by
reflexion, it knows it felfe. So the Logician reflecting upon his owne faculty, may difpute of what fort it is, whe-

Q   ther

ther Science or Art, which, as directing the mind by its denominations, propositions, syllogismes, where the end is to act accordingly, is an Art; and yet as reflecting upon it selfe, its owne Acts and Oojects, where the end is knowledge may be called a Science too.

Sect. 5. How can hee blame the Stagirite, for not defining or disputing, what Logick is, what a Category is, what substance or quantity is; if herein hee should act as foolishly, as he that endeavours to see the proper vision of his owne eye. But *ad rem.* Neither is he indeed, nor his Interpreters, guilty of such defects, as here he fancies, and fastens on him, whose end is contention, to make the contention endlesse. But for the proposition and distribution, two of his subjects.

Magnus Aristoteles *trutinando cacumina rerum*

In duo divisit quicquid in orbe fuit.

The members of which two heads, he handles in their order: Nor is therefore his Organon, so organized, a confused headlesse piece.

But such is his owne objection against his booke *de Interpretatione,* where

where the Moods of Propofitions, are
made neither more nor fewer then four,
viz. neceffary, impoffible, poffible, and
contingent. For what is fo plaine, as
that the matter of all difcourfe, is either
neceffary, or impoffible, or poffible, or
contingent ; and fo may well be reduced to thefe foure Manners or Moods,
fo called, becaufe they fpecifie, how the
predicate belongs, or not, to the fubject
of the propofition ; For all that we can
conceive or expreffe, is either neceffary,
if it cannot but bee, or impoffible if it
cannot bee, or poffible, if it may be,
though it be not yet, nor ever fhall bee ;
or contingent, if it be or fhall be, though
it might not have been, or may never
be.

But fee here, how Mr *Webfter*, fo fub-
tle and quick-fighted in feeing the Defects of *Arifotle*, is blind in his owne.
See it in his owne inftances. Having
premifed the definition of a Mood, that
it doth modificate the propofition (i) in-
dicate how the predicate is in the fubject, he infers, and infults, may not all
Adjectives by the like right be Moods?
No, becaufe they are all reduced to
thofe foure before mentioned : but hee

faith, if this be a Modall propofition, it
is a neceffary thing, that man is a living
Creature,thefe alfo are Modall ; it is an
honeft thing, that a man fhould be ftudious of virtue; it's a juft thing, a fonne
fhould obey his Father ; it's a gallant
thing to dye for ones Country. Where,
if his propofitions be thefe, man is ftudious of virtue, the fonne obedient to
his Father, one dyes for his Country,
their matter is all contingent.   Or if
thefe;man to be ftudious of virtue, is an
honeft thing, a fonne to obey his Father, a juft thing, one to dye for his
Country,   a gallant thing; fo his Adjectives are no Moods at all (to fhew
how the Predicate is in the fubject)
but themfelves the Predicates, and in
all his propofitions, the matter is onely
neceffary.

So that his errour is, as if *Ariftotle*
had defigned to affigne the Modall as a
diftinct fpecies of propofition, and not
onely to give one generall Rule, for all
the fpecies before enumerated, as that
their matter is either neceffary, or im-
poffible.or poffible,or contingent.

Sect. 6. Nor is he more Orthodox
or bufie,to better purpofe, in the matter
of

of definition, where the office of Logick is, onely to give the Precept or Rule, how it ought to be made, which to explaine by example, it takes the instance from other Sciences: Nor is Logick to define what *Homo* or *Animal* is, this being the part of Naturall Philosophy, as to treat of it's proper subject. Now the precept which Logick gives for the definition of things in *actu signato*, as that it ought to consist of the next Genus, and a constitutive difference, is n ost true, exact, and infallible: and therefore if in *actu exercito*, *animal rationale*, be not indeed the true definition of man, the errour is the Philosophers, who must find out for his owne subject, the next Genus, and constitutive difference (as *religiosum*, or the like, if not *rationale*) according to the Rules and Precepts, which in Logick he hath for both; to make (by the Rules for that too) the definition exact and perfect: So that the same which Mr *Webster* before objected against Logicians, as that they seem to make Logick a part of Physicks, hee is guilty of here himselfe.

But because as an open enemy to

Q 3   our

our Phyficks, as well as our Logick, he would equally glory in the defects and errours of both; the truth is that the errour is all his owne: for that bruit beafts are irrationall creatures, and fo rationall the proper difference of man, it appeares. 1. By comparing, as man with Angels, fo the faid bruits with man: For Angels are intuitive, meere or fimple intelligences,as feeing both in the fight of the fubject, what is attribu- ted or denyed to it without compofiti- on or divifion: and in the fight of the Principle,what flowes from it without difcourfe: and fo we men alfo are intel- ligent creatures, but not as Angels,the operation of whofe Intellect, is onely the apprehenfion of fimple termes, and not lyable to falfhood; for befides that we have two other, to compound or divide, and to difcourfe, and fo are ra- tionall too; which being thus our eflen- tiall difference, little lower then the Angels, is yet common to us with bruit beafts.

2. That *Rationle* is not a graduall onely, but our eflentiall difference, it is evident at leaft by this, that whereas *Gradus non variat fpeciem,* in us fpecifi-
cally

cally diſtinct, is the principle of reaſon, from any in bruit beaſts, as appeares ⭑ *à poſteriori*, by the properties of it, as aptitude to ſpeak, &c. which we have as rationall.

⭑As Mr *webſter* ſaith, that wee know nothing in nature, but *à poſteriore*, and from the affections and properties of things muſt ſeek for their cauſes.

And whereas further he ſaith, that irrationall is negative, and ſo can poſitively prove nothing. This his ſequell were true, if it were negative *ſecundum rem* and not onely *ſecundum vocem*. e.g. immortall is alſo negative, and yet if St *Pauls* Argument from the word mortall, be of force, when he ſaith, *let not ſinne raigne in your mortall bodies*; how much more is that of St *Peter*, *abſtaine from fleſhly luſts, which warre againſt your* [*immortall*] *ſoules*.

Now as immortall (applyed to God, Angels, and the reaſonable ſouls of men) implyes more then a meere negation of dying, for otherwiſe, all things but living creatures, ſhould be imortall. So irrationall, ſpeaks the poſitive and ſpecificall nature of a bruit beaſt, as rationall, that of man, though in ſo great a ſcarcity and inequality of words to things we bee deſtitute of a better way to expreſſe the ſame : for why doe wee ſay, that the Oxe is irrationall, and not

Q 4 as

as well that the ſtone is ſo, ſince the
negative of reaſon in both is alike, and
the habit undue to both; but that irrationall, implyes that poſitive Nature,
whereof the one is partaker, and not
the other.

2. I ſhould wonder that one who is
ſo contentious, ſeeking all occaſions to
cavill, ſhould omit diviſion; were it
not hereby evident, that hee hath nothing to ſay againſt it.

But why doth hee make ſuch haſt in
his wrath againſt Reaſon, to come to
Argumentation? or what can be made
more abſolute (without addition or
alteration by ſome curious wits, in ſo
many ages of men) or ſo exact as our
Are of ſyllogizing. But Noveliſts moved
with the ſpirit of pride and envy, are
out of love as with all that others have
invented, and not themſelves, ſo even
n oſt with the beſt, for the greater glory of reformation. Yea whereas other
inventions are concerning ſuch outward things, as we uſe more ſeldome,
wee have continuali uſe of our owne
Reaſon: and yet ſtill is our Art of ſyllogizing, ſo imperfect a thing, that now
one ſhould preſume to abrogate it? He
miſlikes,

miflikes, that fo many forts of our fyllogifmes conclude negatively, fince it is
fufficiently known, that *ae negativis
non datur fcientia:* but doth he not know
as well, that *per negativa datur?* yea,
himfelfe faith, and alledgeth his Author for it, that humane Science doth
confift in a certaine negation of falfity,
rather then in the affirmation of verity.

It is undenyably true (faith he) that
the knowledge of the premifes is more
certaine, then the knowledge of the
conclufion, and therefore undoubtedly
certaine, that the knowledge of the
conformity, betwixt the premifes and
the conclufion, doth præexift in us;
where both the confequent may bee
true, and the antecedent; but how doe
they hang together? Grammatically
indeed in the Copulative words, *and
therefore :* but hee defies all Logicall
wayes of Arguing. Or how is it that
the faid knowledge before, and without
the fyllogifme, may bee faid to be, or
præexift in us? not in Act, but onely
in aptitude (as * one faith, that *aptitudo
ad rem eft aliquid ipfius rei;*) which
aptitude is reduced to Act (without
*Alex. Alenf.
Metaphyf.*

which

which it fhould bee in vaine) or the
knowledge (faith Mr *Webfter* himfelfe)
excited by fyllogizing; and yet is fyllogizing alfo in vaine? or in procuring
that act, ufeleffe? elfe why doth he
fay, and therefore why doft thou
torment and macerate thy felfe in that
queftion, which is more fubtile to
defpife then to diffolve? which
(fince nothing can bee inferred from a
thing wherein it is not contained) is
another *therefore* without inference,
fubtilty beyond fenfe, and a fleighting
or defpifing (not of fome vaine queftion, but) of fo ufeful a thing, as the beft of
Logick it felfe, againft reafon.

Ob. And fo is that which here hee
objects, faying, that fometimes from
falfe premifes, there doth follow a true
conclufion, as in this fyllogifme,

Nullum adorabile eft Creator,
Omne fimulacrum eft adorabile, Ergo,
Nullum fimulacrum eft Creator.

Nor can it therefore be judged, that
the conclufion of fyllogifmes, doth of
neceffity compell Affens, or that the
con-

conclufion doth neceffarily depend upon the premifes, as the truth is not contained in a lye, nor the knowledge of
it.

Anf. 1. We fay not that that in fyllo-
gifms, which of neceffity compels, affent
is the conclufion it felfe, but the premifes, when out of them it is rightly proved (i) when the premifes both are
true and well ordered in Mood and figure, Affent to the conclufion is made
neceffary ; for *ex veris nil nifi verum,*
and that by vertue of the right order
and difpofition in Mood and Figure,
for otherwife out of true premifes, there
may follow a falfe conclufion : as

> *Omnis afinus eft animal,*
> *Omnis homo eft animal,* Ergò,
> *Omnis homo eft afinus.*

So then we are taught in the firft and
fecond part of our Logick, to make the
premifes true, and in the third, fo to dif-
pofe and order them, as to neceffitate
Affent to that, which we make our conclufion from; and yet is all this fo defpi-
cable, that Mr *Webfter* extolling his
owne fubtlety, and the force of his Underftanding,

derstanding, should not onely, not seek, but reject it's true helpes?

2. The conclusion indeed doth necessarily depend upon the premises, in respect of the forme at least, as the conclusion of a true syllogisme, and so doth that of his syllogisme before mentioned: or in respect of the matter too, as a true conclusion and so not.

3. Whereas it is objected, that as the truth is not contained in a lye, so no more is that true conclusion in the false premises.

The premises both are true (i) they are true propositions for the substance, categoricall, for the quantity universall, for the quality, *vocis*; the one Negative, the other Affirmative; and *rei*, both false; yea even because false, they are therefore true propositions. For in simple termes, and in speeches not enuntiative, there is neither falshood nor Truth; but if you make *Homo*, or *homo albus*, either true or false, you make a true proposition of it; and if to one such, you add another in Mood, and Figure, there is true disposition too, for a true syllogisme. So that even the true conclusion of false premises is con-

contained in and deduced out of them, in respect of the forme, for so are they also true; though not in respect of the matter, since that is false.

Lastly, To all that in the residue of the Chapter, he objects or cavils against Logick, may that serve, which before was answered? as that by direction thereof wee doe defend the truth, as the true definitions of things, and infer out of true premises, rightly ordered, undeniable conclusions, whereby wee have not onely bare Opinations, Putations, or probable Conjectures; but infallible Science, and Apodicticall to informe and satisfie the Intellect, by evidentiall demonstration.

Whereas Mr *Webster* cavilling against all reason, contradicts and confounds his owne. As first, when he saith [*Numb.*4.] a Chymist when he shews me the preparation of the Sulphur of Acrimony, the Salt of Tartar, the Spirit of Vitrioll and the uses of them, he teacheth me that knowledge, which I was ignorant of before, the like of which no Logick ever performed: having said immediately before, that demonstration, and the knowledge of it, is in the
Teacher

Teacher, in whom it serves to demonstrate and to shew it others, who learn
it of him. Againe [*Num.* 5.] he condemnes all Logick, as conducing to no
other knowledge, then such as is duely
probable and conjecturall; as if that
were not more then such, which is acquired by demonstration.

Besides, he most highly extols Astrology, and the now Professors thereof,
his friends, as common enemies with
him, as well even to Divinity it selfe, as
to Logick and humane learning; who
As the fall of presume by their Art, to foretell * such
Law and Di- future contingencies, as depending on
vinity. mans free will, are not known to An-
Durand and gels themselves, unlesse by * conjecture
others. onely, or revelation. And have any the
best Astrologers, to cleare a Light, as to
see by the Heavens more, then these
Heavenly lights themselves, or as Mr
Webster, then all wise men? Yea how
grossely have they failed in things even
As Mr San- meerly naturall, conjecturing at * raine
ders, one of the and showers, during all the late winter
most learned drought; but not at all of the later rain,
of them. as if God had provided both to discover their grand Imposturage and pre-
sumption, if not impiety, in taking men

off from himſelfe the firſt, to aſcribe all or too much to Nature, and ſecond cauſes.

All which is to me, a ſufficient evidence, that this great Examiner, notwithſtanding his faire pretences of Reformation and truth, might, if thoroughly examined himſelf, be found not ſteering his courſe indeed by right zeale to theſe, but by that which he alſo ſeems to diſclaime, even ſelfe-intereſt. In his Epiſtle Dedic.

However, certaine it is, that truth or reformation, cannot be truly ſought in a way againſt Nature as is here Mr *Webſters* in preferring himſelfe, before all the wiſeſt and beſt in all Ages to inform and Reforme his Mothers, the Univerſities; for

Nunquam aliud Natura, aliud ſapientia dicit.

Nature Gods owne true wiſedome is, and then,

Is never tharted by the truth of men.

uth and truth can never jarre. πᾶν Τὸ ἀληθὲς ſωκκαληθεύει. *Ariſtot.*

Quicquid exprimitur in natura, imprimitur ab intelligentia, ſcil. explicante, mediante naturâ. Alex. Alenſ. &c:
Opus natura eſt opus intelligentie.

FINIS.

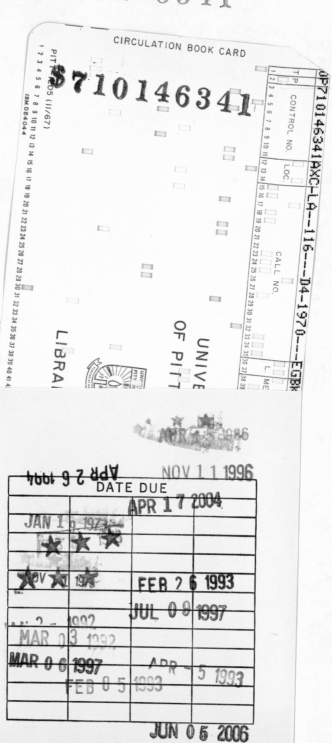